$PEND LE$$ ☑ NOW!

A Checklist Program for the Decidedly Unfrugal

A. Noonan Moose
Blogging at www.FrugalFringe.com

This reference book is designed to help you make informed decisions about your household spending, but is not intended to provide personalized legal, accounting, or financial advice.

Readers are encouraged to seek the counsel of competent professionals with regard to such matters as interpretation of the law, proper accounting procedures, and financial planning. The author and publisher specifically disclaim any liability, loss, or risk which is incurred, directly or indirectly, from the use and application of any of the contents of this book.

Whenever this book mentions specific companies, products, services, or authorities (including websites), the author and publisher are not making an endorsement; nor are any of those companies, products, services, or authorities (including websites) endorsing this book.

While the author has made every effort to provide accurate internet addresses at the time of publication, neither he nor the publisher assumes any responsibility for errors or for changes that occur after publication.

ISBN: 1482563002

ISBN-13: 978-1482563009

Printed in the United States of America

To Cathy

TABLE OF CONTENTS

A joyful verse for the frugal course . . .

> *Row, row, row your boat,*
> *Gently down the stream.*
> *Merrily, merrily, merrily, merrily,*
> *Life is but a dream.*

. . . repeat as necessary

PREFACE

I believe in the power of frugality. Its power derives from what it delivers: freedom from debt, low stress about money, and, ultimately, financial independence. I've witnessed all this firsthand. When I retired at age 48 and my wife at age 46, it wasn't because we were smarter or luckier than most. We weren't. We were able to retire because our frugality had become a deeply ingrained habit. We were set in our ways and our ways were modest.

As I define it, frugality is the habit of living well below your means by spending less. Few chart this course. Too many workers live paycheck to paycheck (68 percent of those surveyed). Too many households carry credit card debt (55.1 percent of card holders). And too many shoppers support far too many stores (46.6 square feet of retail space per American). By habit, most consumers race powerboats for gilded shores. Also by habit, a frugal fringe rows merrily in the opposite direction — gently down the stream, and well clear of hazards that sink many overspenders.

Many consumers hear about frugality, and some give it a close look. But it's hard to change boats in the middle of the stream. A switch to frugality produces great upheaval in anyone's life. It requires an almost obsessive commitment to new ways. Over time, of course, these new ways ripen into ingrained habits and life gets much easier. Most people, however, lose interest long before then. They return to their old familiar routines, leaving frugality to its small crew of obsessed oarsmen. Sooner or later, even devoted frugal fringers have got to wonder: with so few onboard for the ride, could the rowboat be ready for an overhaul?

When it comes to frugality, I'm evangelical. After retiring, I had time on my hands and fervor to spare. I brooded for hours over how to win converts, and kept returning to a central idea. Somehow, the transition from unfrugal to frugal needed to be streamlined. There had to be a way to make this lifestyle easier for newcomers to adopt;

a way to bottle up its obsessions so that anyone could pour out a small dose, return the container to the shelf, and get right back to the task of living. Something, perhaps, that looked like this:

> Passionate. Powerful. Sexy. OBSESSION CALVIN KLEIN is an intoxicating blend of florals and spices with an earthy warm base. A compelling fragrance that is intensely feminine and long-lasting.

Could frugality be repackaged into something this convenient—and this enticing, even? I figured that if model ships could fit into bottles, then rowboats had to be a cinch. So I sniffed around. Eventually, I found what I was looking for: a reliable vessel that would convey frugality's benefits to newcomers, but do it faster and with far less upheaval. This fresh approach to spending less—*passionate, powerful, and sexy*—appears within.

INTRODUCTION

We're all creatures of habit—especially when we spend. We have no other choice. Every year, hundreds of spending decisions confront us. We can't possibly reinvent the wheel for each new transaction. So to cope with the sheer volume of it all, we create expedient shortcuts that eventually turn into ingrained habits. These habits rule our choices. And they also provide a measure of comfort: whenever we pay for anything, we think we know what we're doing because we've done it the same way dozens of times before.

Like anyone else, you have your own spending routines. But here's the deal. These little habits shape financial futures. When you're set in your ways and your ways are modest, you likely face a lifetime of prosperity. However, when you're set in your ways and your ways are *immodest*, you likely face a lifetime of debt or, at best, a lifetime of meager savings. If you find yourself stuck in the wrong kind of spending ruts, you need to get unstuck—and the sooner the better.

This program—*Spend Less ☒ Now! (SL☒N!)*—jars you out of unfrugal spending habits fast. Into each and every transaction, *SL☒N!* introduces a new and disruptive element. Within weeks, frugal routines replace expensive practices. In the process, you save thousands and set yourself on a new course for financial success.

Since our purpose here is to destroy ingrained habits, let's begin with a quick look at one of the most familiar routines ever conceived: the much-maligned knock-knock joke. You may have heard this upcoming one before, but that's not important. The key is that you experience—or at least re-experience—what happens in the short time the joke takes to run its course.

"Knock-knock."

"Who's There?"

"Interrupting Cow."

"Inter—"

"MOOOOOO!!!"

Did you get it? Of course you did, but maybe not right away; and that's part of what makes this such a great gag—at least when you hear it the first time. The main pleasure, though, is that the interrupting cow takes one of the most rote pieces of shtick ever and shatters its mold completely. Now, why should you bother at all with a detour into grade school humor? As it turns out, this brash bovine has much in common with a mold–shattering method to slash household expenses.

THE NOT SO HUMBLE CHECKLIST

Imagine you're at home relaxed in your favorite easy chair. Depending on the season, a cool or warm drink sits within easy reach. All is right with the world. Suddenly, you hear two sharp raps at your front door. At first, you think you're about to endure another knock–knock joke. So you ask, quite tentatively, "Who's there?" You then hear an alluring voice from your porch stoop. But instead of joking around, the voice intones the name of some highly desirable purchase—perhaps it's a new HDTV, a trip to Cleveland, or the latest iWhatever. Before you can say "iWhatever who," a checklist—much like our impetuous cow—springs into action and plants itself squarely between you and the door beyond which waits your latest object of desire. It interrupts forcibly. It gets in your face. It disrupts your normal spending routine, because there's no way to reach what's beyond the door without first getting past the checklist.

As you no doubt suspect, all this disturbance is quite deliberate.

With SL☑N!, checklists become your own fiscal versions of interrupting cows. They intrude to save you money when your object of desire is new and alluring. They also butt in to help you save on more familiar visitors to your porch stoop such as cable companies, insurance agents, or trash haulers. In the past, whenever an opportunity to spend came knocking, by habit you may have answered immediately and surrendered your cash, with no questions asked, not even so much as a simple "who's there?" Until something new entered the picture, your costly routines continued uninterrupted. When you use *SL☑N!*, something new finally appears and sparks a change. Checklists disrupt your normal patterns, prompting you—MOOOOOO!!!—to take key actions to spend less. Within weeks, you see a welcome difference: a growing pile of cash in front of the door where so many dollars once exited your life.

Like grade school humor, *SL☑N!* is elementary. You make a single commitment. Whenever you're about to pay for anything—a product, service, or monthly bill—you commit to review a checklist tailored to that specific expense. Through this repeated ritual, a checklist always reaches you just as you're about to spend. That's the precise moment when you're most motivated to save and most apt to follow frugal advice. As you finish each transaction, you return *SL☑N!* to the shelf and get right back to your life—no obsession is necessary, and no radical financial changes are required.

Checklists form the basis of this program for good reason: *they're the best tools ever devised for delivering real time guidance on any task at hand.* Checklists embed themselves into common routines, condense complex advice into easy–to–follow bullet points, serve as memory aids, deliver help precisely when needed, prevent costly missteps, and, most important for our purposes here, they modify behaviors efficiently. *SL☑N!* brews up enough of this sweet ambrosia so that you'll find a checklist for almost anything on which you spend.

The checklists assume many forms. A few serve as quick references when you venture into the vast commercial wasteland and confront the likes of box stores, malls, and restaurants. Most are more detailed because you don't use them when you're mobile, but rather when you're planted safe at home with the monthly bills. Some checklists are like recipes because they provide step–buy–step instructions on how to spend less. More of them, however, are like smorgasbords because they let you choose whichever strategies work best for you. Whatever form any checklist takes, its mission remains the same: to get you into the habit of living well within your means and to get you there with the least amount of time, effort, and obsession.

HOW MUCH WILL *SL☒N!* SAVE YOU?

This is, of course, the burning question. Let's first look at how much mainstream households save, and then look at how well you can do.

When it comes to room for improvement, mainstream households enjoy rooms with very high ceilings. I envy their potential. They buy products and hire services without coherent systems for finding the best values. They pay for things they never consume (unread magazines, plastic from China, and premium TV channels). They misuse furnaces, air conditioners, and appliances, blissfully unaware of the heavy costs. They buy insurance, and pay high premiums without ever shopping their business elsewhere. They let trashcans eat their groceries and don't give it a second thought (this nation wastes 25 percent of its food). They borrow to purchase new cars and replace them every few years. Most expensively, they live in oversized houses, and spend decades paying off the extra square footage. In short, mainstream households are decidedly unfrugal.

Mainstreamers take on so much excess that it's easy to find them new riches. How much in new riches? Many frugal fringers know the answer to this question firsthand, because they once ran mainstream households themselves. They report that a conversion to frugality typically saves about 20 percent each year, and that these savings can be generated painlessly. Of course, if a little pain enters the picture, you can boost your savings to 50 percent or more. But for now, let's stick with the 20 percent figure as a reasonable target that's relatively easy to reach.

I don't expect you or anyone else to convert to frugality on the basis of mere abstractions, so these projected savings of 20 percent need to be placed into some context. To do this, I'll make an example of the decidedly unfrugal Jane Dough. Jane earns $50,000 annually, which is right around the national average. She wants to improve her finances, so let's compare two surefire moneymakers: (1) working 50 more hours at her job; versus (2) investing 50 hours on the checklists. Which approach produces better results? This chart shows the fruits of Jane's labors at her workplace:

1. Jane Dough Works 50 More Hours at her Job

Incremental Earnings ($25 per hour x 50 hours)	$1,250
Minus Social Security Withholding ($1,250 x 6.2%)	($ 77)
Minus Medicare Withholding ($1,250 x 1.45%)	($ 18)
Minus Federal Tax Withholding (at 25% rate)	($ 312)
Minus State Tax Withholding (at 5.04% average rate)	($ 63)
Net After–Tax Earnings:	**$ 780**

Not bad, but now let's see what happens with the checklists. Jane spends at the national average, which is about $44,600 after taxes. Since she's decidedly unfrugal, she can expect to save about 20 percent without torment. Let's run the numbers:

2. Jane Dough Works 50 Hours on the Checklists

Incremental Savings ($44,600 x 20%)	$8,920
Minus Social Security Withholding	($ 0)
Minus Medicare Withholding	($ 0)
Minus Federal Tax Withholding	($ 0)
Minus State Tax Withholding	($ 0)
Net After–Tax Savings:	**$8,920**

Moral of story: if you work 50 extra hours to improve your finances, it's much better to make $8,920 than $780. It's the difference between merely working harder and actually working smarter—*in Jane's case, more than ten times smarter.*

If you're not decidedly unfrugal, there's no way to tell upfront how much *SL☑N!* will save you. The answer depends, in large part, upon how much you've dabbled in frugality before and how many checklist strategies you adopt. Even if you're not a huge overspender, you probably have several discrete expenses on which you could save 20 percent or more. Your cell phone is one such possibility. If you switch from a monthly plan to a pay–as–you–go (PAYG) phone, that's a decision you make just once, but it echoes in savings for years to come. You might be skeptical about ditching your current cell plan. Fair enough. But hidden among your expenses lurk other opportunities to save that you *are* likely to find acceptable. Once adopted, these turn into "savings annuities" that grow your nest egg year after year without you ever lifting another finger (again, you work smarter, not harder).

Here's a list of savings annuities that I've found among my own expenses. Some I discovered long ago. Others, I discovered more recently. Spend some time looking the list over. Note the percentage I saved on each line item—usually, it exceeds 20 percent. More importantly, notice how many dollars were preserved for future use.

Moose's Savings Annuities

Line Item	Savings Tactic(s) [Year First Adopted]	Cost Before	Cost After	% Saved	Decade Savings
Pro baseball	Drop season's pass [2003]	$ 2,600	$ 60	98%	$25,400
Health policy	Increase deductible [2004]	$ 5,040	$ 3,333	39%	$17,068
Cell phones	PAYG, not monthly [2008]	$ 1,800	$ 200	89%	$16,000
Skiing	Nordic, not downhill [1990]	$ 1,620	$ 180	89%	$14,400
Dining out	Adopt various changes [2007]	$ 3,200	$ 2,000	37%	$12,000
Gasoline	Switch to a hybrid [2009]	$ 2,625	$ 1,470	44%	$11,550
Parking	Use pre–tax dollars [2003]	$ 1,800	$ 1,080	40%	$ 7,200
Health club	Workouts at home [2002]	$ 540	$ 0	100%	$ 5,400
Gas/electric	Adopt various changes [2009]	$ 1,930	$ 1,470	24%	$ 4,600
Books	Buy most used [1999]	$ 450	$ 35	92%	$ 4,150
Golf	Buy discount pass [2008]	$ 800	$ 400	50%	$ 4,000
Bank fees	Cancel cards with fees [2005]	$ 302	$ 0	100%	$ 3,020
Trash pickup	Switch to PAYG [2009]	$ 250	$ 34	86%	$ 2,160
Alcohol	Switch to box wine [2010]	$ 618	$ 407	34%	$ 2,110
Property tax	Challenge assessor [2005]	$ 2,200	$ 2,000	9%	$ 2,000
Long distance	Use calling cards [2002]	$ 200	$ 20	90%	$ 1,800
Auto policy	Pay annually [2009]	$ 1,429	$ 1,290	9.7%	$ 1,390
Newspaper	Subscribe on web [2005]	$ 164	$ 45	73%	$ 1,190
Movies	Use Redbox.com [2007]	$ 125	$ 25	80%	$ 1,000
Dry cleaning	Use home kits [1999]	$ 90	$ 5	94%	$ 850
Eye care	Visit Costco doctor [2008]	$ 150	$ 100	33%	$ 500
Landline	Negotiate lower rate [2011]	$ 327	$ 293	10%	$ 340
Totals		$28,260	$14,407	49%	$138,083

As the list shows, a few savings annuities can produce a huge nest egg in a single decade. This gives plenty of breathing room to combat the financial stresses that hit most mainstream households. But there's more good news. If you double the years involved and throw in compounded gains on investments, the nest egg grows large enough to fund major goals like college educations, mortgage payoffs, and retirements. And there's even more good news: while I scrounged *for years* to find my own annuities, the checklists help you find all of yours *right now*.

THE *REALLY* NOT SO HUMBLE CHECKLIST

Checklists have modest enough uses—laundry lists, to–do lists, grocery lists—but they can also perform vital roles. NASA uses them for rocket launches, pilots for takeoffs, and doctors for surgeries. In each case, checklists keep smart people from failing to perform basic and even obvious steps, which, if overlooked, could trigger disaster. These unassuming tools also get the job done when it comes to spending less. As proof, here's a checklist that brags nonstop about how well this format eases you into a frugal lifestyle.

☐ *Checklists Skip the Sermons.* Most frugality programs begin with ample doses of fire and brimstone. The purpose is to change your attitudes about the evils of overspending. With *SL☑N!*, however, you don't focus on changing your attitudes, you focus on changing your behaviors. You jump right in, you see the fast results, and sooner or later your attitudes change all on their own. In other words, you convert to frugality by doing frugality. So whatever the state of your current finances, *SL☑N!* doesn't waste time scolding you about them. As the late great Johnny Cochran might have said: "even if you're feckless, you can still grab a checklist!"

☐ *Checklists Are Habit Forming.* *SL☑N!*'s main premise is that our habits control the way we spend. According to experts, habits involve three basic steps. First, you experience a triggering event that signals your brain to take action (for example, each morning, the "trigger" might be finishing breakfast). Second, prompted by the trigger, you perform a routine behavior (you go to the bathroom, reach for the toothpaste, and brush your teeth). Third, you receive rewards that make you repeat the same loop next time around (in the short run, you enjoy clean teeth; in the long run, you avoid dentures). *SL☑N!* employs these same three steps—trigger, routine, and rewards—to transform you from a mainstream consumer to a frugal fringer. Anytime you're about to spend (the trigger), you work through a checklist (the routine). In return, you receive instant savings and, over the long haul, a massive nest egg (the rewards). Bottom line: if you brush your teeth every day, you can easily pick up the habit of spending less.

☐ *Checklists Have Impeccable Timing.* The world resounds with savings tips, but the advice rarely arrives at the precise moment you need it. You see something on TV six weeks *before* you shop for new tires, but by the time you reach the store the details are more than hazy. You run across a great website six weeks *after* you rent a car, and, of course, that help arrives much too late. With *SL☑N!,* however, you develop a routine of accessing tightfisted strategies precisely when you're most likely to use them: *at the point of purchase.* No matter what the transaction, a checklist's timing is perfect. All you have to do is to train yourself to reach for one whenever you spend—and that's as easy to remember as a great knock–knock joke (consider that cow a mne*moo*nic device).

☐ *Checklists Stop Impulse Purchases.* At times, we've all spent first and regretted it later. *SL☑N!* prompts you to think through each expenditure beforehand. This increases the time that passes between first deciding to spend and finally letting the dollars drift out your door—a slight delay that makes impulsive purchases impossible. When you slow down the spending process, you make better decisions, fewer mistakes, and, best of all, your savings increase dramatically.

☐ *Checklists Are Portable.* Copy the ones you need and take them along in your purse or on your person. If you're at a restaurant, take a peek at tactics that cut dining costs (Appendix 3). If you're at a gas station, look over strategies that save you at the pump (Appendix 6). There's even a good checklist that covers drinks out

(Chapter 14). Just make sure to work through it *before* you start slamming shots.

☐ *Checklists Are Customizable.* Treat the checklists as frameworks. They're like new homes in Levittown, Pennsylvania. Built in a hurry to meet the post–WWII housing crunch, these affordable houses all looked the same. But as decades passed, owners added garages, porches, and landscaping. Like a Levittown tract house, the checklists are something you own. Renovate. Cross out what doesn't work for you and add in whatever does. In a few weeks— not years—the checklists will fit better, and you'll get better results.

☐ *Checklists Work With Your Programming.* People prefer instant fixes to drawn–out solutions. Sellers know this, so they design stores and websites that exploit everyone's trigger–happy tendencies to the fullest extent possible. *SL☑N!* works with your programming—and not against it—by embedding checklists into every transaction you make. As you embark upon your latest opportunity to spend, a checklist infuses your decision with a healthy dose of frugality. Buying a small office copier and don't want to get duped in the process? For quick advice, consult the products buying checklist (Appendix 1)—it's all very gratifying in an instant sort of way.

☐ *Checklists Combat Forgetfulness.* You could plod through a book of 5,001 savings tips, but come next fall, how would you possibly remember the fine idea on page 197 that saves $65 on contact lenses? With *SL☑N!*, the only thing you need to remember is to pull out the appropriate checklist whenever you're about to spend. It does the heavy lifting while your memory stays free for other uses. Now, if only someone could build a checklist that shows where the car keys are . . . .

☐ *Checklists Sidestep Obsessions.* Like many on the frugal fringe, I invest untold hours to achieve small financial victories—in other words, I obsess. But you don't have to fuss with this as much as I have. Each checklist condenses what I spent years figuring out and delivers it to you in the most efficient form possible. In the end, you enjoy Moose-like savings without ever becoming much like Moose.

☐ *Checklists Bring Joy.* By necessity, you spend on things that don't provide much excitement: taxes, insurance, and utilities, for instance. These are essential expenses, of course, but only the dullest of the dull would claim they impart much zest. Other expenses deliver far greater bliss: pets, recreation, charities—and you could name many more. You would love to increase your spending on euphoria, but where can you find the dollars? Checklists provide an answer. They not only grow your nest egg, they provide extra breathing room to fund whatever matters most to you. And when you do spend on bliss, you spend smarter—the $100 it once took to buy happiness now costs much less, and this itself generates joy (as well as savings).

☐ *Checklists Are Systematic.* Vast forces are arrayed to make us cough up as much cash as possible. Every day, they carpet bomb our brains with temptations to spend: clever ads, bright stores, tasty restaurants, handy websites, and, even in these tough times, relatively easy credit. The media celebrates lifestyles of free–spending celebrities and reality stars. Even our government treats us more like consumers than citizens. As Burgess Meredith once rasped to Sylvester Stallone, "Whatcha need Rock . . . is a manager." Checklists are in your corner. They help you spot savings opportunities you might otherwise miss. They erase unfrugal habits. They cut through all the noise and provide a reliable, coherent system for a saner financial life.

☐ *Checklists Postpone Bean Counting.* Most approaches to spending less demand that you track every dollar made and spent. That's sensible advice, but let's get real. Few of us are born bean counters. Were it otherwise, this world would be filled with CPAs and there would be no poets whatsoever. With *SL☒N!*, you choose the Homeric over the numeric by reaching for checklists instead of ledgers or spreadsheets. As savings mount, you might be inspired to count your gains—at least on a trial basis. But you get to convince yourself of this gradually and without making any big commitment upfront.

ONE LAST THING

Savings await, but don't rush headlong into this just yet. Before you begin to tackle checklists, it's important first to review some mechanics about how *SL☑N!* works. That's covered next.

HOW TO USE THIS BOOK

If you've read this far, you're probably onboard with the idea of frugality—or at least willing to give it a try. If so, congratulations. With *SL☒N!*, you're about to embark upon a great financial voyage that will fundamentally change the way in which you spend, and do so quickly and easily. Before you cast off, let's take a tour of your new and improved rowboat.

OVERVIEW

SL☒N! deals with household spending and nothing else. It doesn't show you how to increase wages, invest savings, or plan retirements. Why not? Because these other personal finance issues are largely irrelevant unless you first acquire the habit of spending less than what you make. Your wages can increase exponentially, but if your expenses always outpace your income, you never get anywhere. And, of course, you can't ever invest or retire until you first create a surplus of cash. Without question, frugal routines form the starting point and eventual key to financial success. *SL☒N!* launches you from the dock, and not from somewhere out in the middle of the stream.

SL☒N! consists of three parts: (1) a checklist with training wheels that covers a single topic—the purchase of products; (2) dozens of workaday checklists that cover a wide variety of household expenses; and (3) tools that make the checklists easier to use and, in the end, more profitable. Let's consider each in detail.

In Part I, which consists of Chapters 1 through 7, the spotlight focuses solely on the purchase of products—transactions that you complete dozens of times each year. *SL☒N!* uses these routine dealings to introduce you to checklists and the basic themes of frugality. At this point you're still a newbie, so *SL☒N!* takes it slow and peppers you with dozens of examples.

At Part I's conclusion, the entire system for buying products gets reduced into a concise checklist that you can copy and take with you whenever you're about to spend (see Appendix 1). (Of course, when you read *SL☑N!* as an e–book, you don't need to make copies, you can simply power up your portable device.)

In Part II, which consists of Chapters 8 through 46, the focus shifts to the line items found in most American households. You may not think about your spending in terms of line items, but the federal government does. Since 1980, the Bureau of Labor Statistics has conducted an annual Consumer Expenditure Survey (CES), which canvasses the habits of 7,000 households in hundreds of distinct expense categories. Like the CES, *SL☑N!* follows the principle that household expenses get easier to analyze when you break them down into smaller pieces. Chapters 8 through 19 cover line items which are commonly regarded as *discretionary*. These include miscellaneous services (barbers, tutors, carpet cleaners, etc.), recreation, restaurants, travel, and charitable giving. Next, Chapters 20 through 46 cover line items commonly regarded as *nondiscretionary*. These include taxes, telecommunications, utilities, insurance, healthcare, groceries, autos, and housing.

By design, Part II works as a guidebook. Don't read it straight through—that's both overwhelming and boring. Instead, use Part II like you use road atlases, almanacs, or dictionaries. These references are exhaustive on the subjects they cover. But they're never exhausting because you use them only to fetch the information you need. Part II works the same way. Reach for it every time you pay for common costs such as phones, utilities, or insurance. Simply open the table of contents, locate your expense of the moment, and turn to the relevant chapter—the other checklists can wait for later.

Since you make most decisions about line items when you're safe at home, the Part II checklists generally aren't condensed. There are exceptions, of course. These appear in Appendixes 2–6, which, like the products buying checklist, you're free to copy.

In Part III, which consists of Chapters 47 through 50, *SL☑N!* presents an ever ready toolbox that helps you make better use of this program. Chapter 47 discusses techniques for active use of the checklists (such as savings logs, debriefings, and goals). Chapter 48 shows you how to build checklists for any line item these pages don't cover. (You won't build many. Based on CES figures, *SL☑N!* addresses about 95 percent of household outlays.) Chapter 49 provides credit card strategies that will add hundreds of dollars to your household coffers each year. Finally, Chapter 50 outlines automated bean–counting shortcuts that will save you hours of drudgery if and when you decide to crunch the numbers.

In the back of the book, endnotes appear. So whenever you see any statistics—survey results, CES figures, percentages—you can look them up for yourself.

THE POWER OF REPETITIVE REPETITION

Acts of deliberate repetition (row, row, row) provide a powerful way to reprogram unfrugal habits (spend, spend, spend). *SL☑N!* exploits the power of repetitive repetition over and over again. Here's a short checklist (and please forgive me if I repeat myself).

☐ *Repetitive Structures.* You get comfortable with *SL☑N!* fast because all the checklists are organized the same way—by chapter, strategy, and tactic. In Part II, where *SL☑N!* functions as a field manual for household spending, each tactic is coded. So when you see " 45.4.3," you know you're in chapter 45, strategy no. 4, and tactic no. 3—a helpful feature if you read the e–book or discuss the checklists with others. Sometimes you'll see additional entries below a listed tactic. If you see bullet points (•), those signify *examples* that explain the tactic in further detail. If you see additional boxes (☐), those spell out *sub–tactics* that might require your further action. Finally, if you see short discussions labeled "CODA," those describe moneysaving ideas that are worthy of mention, but unsuitable in most circumstances.

☐ *Repetitive Advice.* As you use *SL☑N!*, you'll notice that several different checklists suggest the same or similar tactics. This is by design. For instance, each time a checklist addresses insurance (Chapters 29–32), you'll see recurring advice to increase your deductibles. And in checklists about healthcare (Chapters 33–36), you're reminded several times to fund medical savings accounts that deliver huge tax advantages. And just about everywhere, you're advised to pay for expenses with reward cards instead of cash or checks (but *only* if you pay the cards off every month). If, as in these cases, the same tactics pop up repeatedly, it's an unmistakable sign that you should pop them into your own spending routines.

☐ *Repetitive Readings.* Some checklists, you consult only rarely, such as when you shop for used cars (Chapter 43) or suffer through home remodels (Chapter 46). Most checklists, however, you revisit often, such as when you buy products (Appendix 1), dine out (Appendix 3), shop for groceries (Chapter 37), or stop at gas stations (Appendix 6). Practice eventually makes perfect. With each checklist–assisted repetition, you adopt a few more tightfisted tactics and a few more unfrugal habits bite the dust.

☐ *Repetitive Chores.* Household routines often devolve into overspending. Edible groceries find the landfill, refrigerators eat up kilowatt hours, and appliances run half–full loads. To combat such waste, *SL☑N!* includes checklists that you can post wherever you incur losses: at trashcans, fridges, and clothes dryers (Chapters 22 and 37, Appendix 4). That way, whenever you're poised to squander, a checklist will be there to nag you into submission (or to at least inspire deep feelings of submissive guilt).

☐ *Repetitive Themes.* With checklists, you expose yourself to a steady diet of frugality's core themes. You research products, sellers, and services. You think about incidentals such as shipping costs, sales taxes, and return policies. You procrastinate on your purchases (as you'll see, that's a good thing). As these themes ripen into ingrained habits, you develop a mindset that's definitely outside the mainstream. But don't worry about becoming a stranger in a strange land—you aren't alone. As discussed below, there's a place to hang out with others who feel the same way about overspending as you do (and no, it's not Costco).

SAVINGS SUPPLEMENTAL: FRUGALFRINGE.COM

Any fringe needs a clubhouse. Nowadays, groups can dispense with bricks and mortar (expensive) and build their gathering places out of code and content (much cheaper). What does FrugalFringe.com offer? Feedback from your fellow checklisters, for one thing. And feedback from you, if you're willing to share, and I hope you do—especially when it comes to your ideas about how to improve *SL☑N!* for future readers. There's also lots about frugality that couldn't possibly fit into this book: case studies, cost friendly recipes, unbiased product reviews, checklists for unusual line items, a motivational blog, clickable links to websites (including those cited in this book), and more. The site is FREE, so visit whenever you're free as well.

ARE YOU READY TO SPEND LESS NOW?

You meet your first *SL☑N!* checklist in the next section. It gives you an effective system for product purchases—everything from aardvark cages to zydeco music. So if you plan to shop later today, read on. After the next few chapters, when it comes to saving on merchandise you'll be loaded for bear, or maybe even for some overly abrupt cow, but never, let us hope, for any well–intentioned Moose.

PART I

PRODUCTS BUYING CHECKLIST

PART I OVERVIEW

With Part I of the *SL⊠N!* program, you start out slow. Here you consider a single topic only: the purchase of products. Now, in order to spend less on products, you could invite some fringers along on your next shopping expedition. As you roamed the aisles, your entourage would bombard you with countless suggestions for savings. This would get annoying fast. So *SL⊠N!* lets you skip the posse of parsimony and bring along a checklist instead. This checklist presents everything you need to know in a convenient system. At this point, you're new to all this, so *SL⊠N!* devotes a full chapter to each of seven separate strategies.

Chapter 1: Don't Buy Anything

Chapter 2: Buy Something Else

Chapter 3: Research the Product

Chapter 4: Find Low Prices

Chapter 5: Pick a Low Price Seller

Chapter 6: Avoid Pitfalls

Chapter 7: Follow Up

When Part I ends, all the strategies for buying products are condensed into the portable checklist that appears in Appendix 1.

1

STRATEGY NO. 1:
DON'T BUY ANYTHING

Frugal fringers don't get the urge to buy very often, but when they do, crucial habits kick in. They consider all kinds of alternatives that involve no purchase whatsoever. Fringers know these alternatives by heart, *and by ingrained habit, they act on them regularly*. This chapter converts their routines into a smorgasbord of tightfisted tactics. Choose any of them and you'll satisfy your hunger for something new—and do it without a purchase.

☐ Avoid the Purchase Altogether

As any frugalist will let you know, you can, in many instances, "do without." To profit from this advice, however, you don't need to adopt some overly Spartan lifestyle. The fact is, doing without often involves no real sacrifice at all. The small trick is to find some way other than a purchase to erase your need or want. Review these examples to spark your own creative ideas:

- *Storage Sheds.* If you're about to buy a shed, then maybe you've crossed the threshold of having too much stuff. A purge might be in order. If you own items you haven't used for years, show them the door. Sell on eBay, host garage sales, or donate to local thrift stores. When you erase the need for extra space, you sidestep the cost of outbuildings.

- *Filing Cabinets, Photo Albums, and Bookcases.* Scan tax returns and bills to reduce files. Scan photographs to save on albums. Download e-books. A Kindle holds 3,500 of them, and at an inch per book that works out to 300 linear feet—the equivalent of 20 IKEA Billy model bookcases (you save $1,200).

- *Wine Refrigerators.* These keep bottles cool, but a corner of the basement does the job for FREE (and without electricity).

- *Paper Shredders.* To remove the need for this gadget, sign up to receive bills and statements via email. Any other confidential paper can be torn asunder by hand.

☐ Wait Until Later

Procrastination, for lack of a better word, is good. When you expand the time that passes between your first impulse to buy and the moment the dollars slip away, many wonders occur. Prices drop. Sales happen. Products improve. Rebates appear. Coupons turn up. You decide to do without. In short, if we procrastinated on our purchases half as well as we do on our chores, we'd all be much richer. Some examples:

- *Annuals.* Buy them a couple years after publication and save big. Little information changes. Do this for anything with a year on its cover, including atlases, almanacs, restaurant ratings, and travel guides.

- *Movies.* The average delay between theater and DVD release has narrowed to about four months. If you and a date watch 25 first run movies at the multiplex, you pay $500. If you wait awhile and rent from Redbox.com, the cost tumbles to $30—and you also save on snacks and sodas.

- *Holiday Stuff.* Frugal fringers mark their calendars this way: Valentine's Day items go on sale February 15, Easter supplies on the Monday after, Fourth of July stuff on July 5, Halloween gear on November 1, and Christmas goodies on December 26. Buy a day late and leave the seller a dollar or more short.

- *Championship Memorabilia.* When my beloved Red Sox won it all in 2004, my heart ruled my head as I paid retail prices for commemorative baubles (it had been 86 years since the last championship). After a few months, I watched in horror as my keepsakes began selling at steep discounts. When the Sox won again in 2007, I waited to buy. This time around I saved nicely.

- *Seasonal Stuff.* Buy at season's end and stow away for next year: garden tools, shovels, bikinis, snow parkas, etc.

- *Fine Art Prints (and Everything Else).* Let's say you want to buy a framed print. Before you rush into a purchase, test the level of your desire. Search Google Images for a high resolution image, right click your mouse, and set the picture as your computer screen's wallpaper. If after several weeks you're sick of it, you've erased your urge to spend without expense. Actually, this post–a–picture–and–wait technique works for any discretionary purchase. And instead of downloading the image, you can always rip a photo from a catalog and tape it to the fridge. The familiarity of seeing your object of desire every day often breeds contempt for spending money on it. And it's much cheaper to experience that contempt before you buy rather than afterwards.

☐ Use What You Already Own

Fringers follow this creed: "use it up, make it last, wear it out, or make it do." In other words, you can burn through several blenders in a lifetime; or, instead, you can treat your current blender with the utmost respect it so rightfully deserves. I don't know what you own, so forgive some more war stories from my own experience:

- *Televisions.* My Sony Trinitron, circa 1989, still works and interferes with the purchase of an HDTV. There's something cool about owning a TV that's old enough to order itself a beer (come to think of it, maybe that's why the picture's so blurry). While I think things over, prices continue to drop.

- *Printers.* My laser produces streaky pages, but until the toner empties I make do with poor quality and use the library's machines whenever I need perfection.

- *Grill Covers.* The Weber's vinyl cover looks worn after six winters, but some black duct tape applied in a geometric design converts it into a unique artwork. This temporary fix buys time to find a low–priced replacement.

- *Odds and Ends.* Some items enjoy useful afterlives. In our house, worn kitchen sponges assume new duties as bathroom scrubbers. Empty jars see new service as storage containers. Old toothbrushes move into auto detailing.

- *Clothes.* Go closet shopping. Your old duds have been stashed away for so long that they'll now seem new.

☐ Make it Yourself

This saves money sometimes, but not always. Just try to make bookshelves for less than IKEA charges—no can do. Consider these situations where you *can* craft your way to savings:

- *Household Cleaners.* Revisit chemistry class by mixing your own cleaners. Common ingredients include white vinegar, borax, and baking soda. Search online for "homemade household cleaners." Important safety note: never mix bleach with ammonia.

- *Personal Care Products.* Search online for recipes to make mouthwashes, toothpastes, deodorants, and soaps.

- *Bottled Water.* Filter water yourself.

- *Greeting Cards.* Bypass Hallmark with construction paper or emailed greetings. Visit eGreetings.com or 123Greetings.com.

- *Meals at Work.* Not only are brownbag lunches cheaper, they usually take less time to prepare than visiting a deli at the noontime rush.

- *Herbs.* If you spend more than $15 a year on fresh herbs, plant some seeds in a pot, add water, and watch your assets grow.

- *Comforter Covers.* Sew two sheets together for a product that looks as nice as the store–bought version.

- *Hummingbird Food.* Forgo the packaged stuff. Mix one cup sugar to four cups of boiling water. Let cool. Serve. I've used this recipe for years and never received any complaints.

☐ Get it for Free

We live in a wealthy society where our affluence often produces effluence in the form of FREE stuff. Any fringer can list many favorite giveaways. Here are some of mine.

- *Used Stuff.* Make that a cofFREE maker, if you please. Visit Freecycle.org or check out the FREE section on Craigslist.org.

- *Music.* Visit Pandora.com, Spotify.com, and many others.

- *Movies.* If you have a DVR, make it work overtime whenever premium channels offer FREE movie weekends. Visit OpenCulture.org, FreeDocumentaries.org, and Crackle.com.

- *Shareware.* Visit OpenOffice.org or CNET.com.

- *C–Span.* Visit C-SpanVideo.org for 195,000 hours of content. A search engine finds your favorite topics, people, and books.

- *The Nation's Library.* FREE films and sound recordings abound at the Library of Congress. Visit LOC.gov.

- *Gifts.* If it's acceptable in your family, request your latest object of desire for the next holiday. Or ask everyone for gift cards that you can combine to buy a big–ticket item.

- *Wrapping Paper.* Wrap for FREE with Sunday comics or pages from holiday catalogs. In the Red Sox championship years, I saved copies of the October sports sections (they were black and white and red all over) and used them in December. Try it when your team wins.

□ **Borrow**

Before buying, the frugal few always consider the possibility of borrowing. Lenders are plentiful. The library offers books, DVDs, audio books, and CDs. Some communities sponsor "tool libraries" where, for a small annual fee, you can check out just–the–right–tool for a remodel. (For one example, visit ResourceToolLibrary.org.) Friends and family possess other items. To prosper as a borrower, return everything promptly and offer to lend out your own things.

□ **Trade or Barter**

Look for websites that specialize in specific goods.

- *Media.* Visit Swap.com, PaperBackSwap.com, SwapaCD.com, and SwapaDVD.com.

- *Video Games.* Visit Swap.com and Goozex.com.

- *Cribs and Bibs.* Visit SwapBabyGoods.com and ThredUp.com.

- *Clothing.* Pair up with someone your size and trade. Or visit RehashClothes.com, SwapStyle.com, and BigWardrobe.com.

☐ Rent

Don't buy an extension ladder if you're using it once only. Rent instead. Many rental centers display photos of their inventory online. Also, check out peer–to–peer sites like Zilok.com, which match renters with owners. They're like dating services for table saws. Rent sports equipment for new activities: kayaks, snowboards, mountain bikes, etc. Consider rentals for party supplies, recreational vehicles, medical equipment, and formal clothing. If your need for a vehicle is sporadic, check out car share programs like ZipCar.com. Rental companies—Hertz and Enterprise among them—now offer by–the–hour rates as well.

☐ Flip

As fringers know, flipping isn't just for houses. Sometimes, you can buy pre–owned items, use them awhile, and then resell them. Like rentals, this works well for short–term needs: chain saws, paint sprayers, step ladders, wedding dresses, prom dresses, maternity wear, and baby clothes. A flip often costs less than a rental. And sometimes, you can even resell for a profit. One warning: you bear the risk of not finding a buyer, so investigate the resale market's strength beforehand. (EBay provides data on recent sales; visit the advanced product search feature and check the box for "completed listings.")

☐ Try Group Buynamics

If a fringer caught you perpetrating a purchase, you might hear this: "why don't you have one of your groups buy it instead?" You can join forces with others in many ways:

- *Volume Discounts.* When buyers transact as groups instead of individually, quantity purchases become much easier. Go in with others on sides of beef and fifty–pound bags of pinto beans.

- *Direct Buying.* Wholesalers ignore individuals. But you receive ample attention if you join forces with friends to shop for six units of the same big–ticket item.

- *Warehouse Club Memberships.* I often hear singles lament that they don't buy enough to justify the annual fee. This minor hurdle is easily cleared: they can band together with others and designate one shopper to act for all. Afterwards, everyone can meet somewhere to divvy up the bounty—paper towels and otherwise.

- *Shared Intelligence.* Open book club meetings with the latest frugal tips. Introduce friends to great new products.

*   *   *

You've now reviewed ten frugal alternatives to making a purchase. That wasn't too hard, was it? You may even think that this list contains nothing new, and that, on occasion, you've even chosen some of these tactics yourself. But the key is this: you probably haven't opted for these alternatives very consistently. With checklists, you embed these frugal options into all your transactions. And over the course of your next 100 purchases, you'll select them more often than ever before.

A short summary of this chapter appears below and as part of the concise products buying checklist in Appendix 1. Pick a dollar threshold—$50 works well, $25 works better—and use the checklist each time you face a purchase above that level.

Remembering to use your checklist is easy. Anytime you're about to spend—before you open a wallet, grab a checkbook, or pull out a credit card—you'll recall the best knock–knock joke ever and know it's time to consult a checklist. As time passes, you'll probably have your own ideas. Write them down in the spaces provided and let other checklisters know about your insights at FrugalFringe.com. If you ever need a refresher about your alternatives to buying, simply reread this chapter.

STRATEGY NO. 1:
DON'T BUY ANYTHING

☐ **avoid the purchase** [address my need without buying]

☐ **wait until later** [season's end, next sale, new models]

☐ **use what I already own** [repair, fix, upgrade, closet shop]

☐ **make it myself** [filtered water, cleaners, work lunches]

☐ **get it FREE** [Freecycle, C–Span, ManyBooks.net]

☐ **borrow** [library, friends, neighbors]

☐ **trade or barter** [media, toys, duds]

☐ **rent** [tools, sports gear, tuxedos]

☐ **flip** [buy, use awhile, resell at profit]

☐ **try Group Buynamics** [buy with friends]

Add my own ideas here:

☐

☐

☐

2

STRATEGY NO. 2:
BUY SOMETHING ELSE

Let's say you've read the last chapter with a purchase in mind, and that you're still in favor of your first inspiration. If any fringers were present, at this point you'd hear loud howls of outrage. Before letting you continue, they'd pummel you with even more alternatives to—MOOOOOO!!!—disrupt your purchase routine. This chapter distills their next wave of advice into several useful tactics. With these alternatives, you actually get to buy something, but it's not what you first had in mind.

☐ **Buy Used**
Things depreciate. To the frugal few, 'tis a far, far better thing to let someone else pay for that depreciation than to pay for it themselves. The best internet sites for secondhand products are eBay, Amazon Marketplace, and Craigslist. For offline shopping, patronize thrift shops, garage sales (YardSaleTreasureMap.com and Craigslist provide local listings), flea markets, pawn shops, and estate sales (visit EstateSales.org). Here's the best stuff to buy used:

- *Vehicles.* With eBay Motors, AutoTrader.com, and Craigslist, buying used cars is easier than ever (see Chapter 43).

- *Furniture.* Don't pay huge mark-ups to retailers. Buy matched sets at estate sales. Collect unmatched pieces one–by–one at consignment shops and garage sales.

- *Sporting Gear.* After you use golf clubs or skis a couple times, they're no longer new. Buy them secondhand in the first place and earmark the savings for greens fees and lift tickets.

- *Jewelry.* Rings, necklaces, and bracelets are for show, so whenever possible, go faux.

- *Baby Gear.* Kids outgrow clothes, furniture, and toys long before those items ever wear out. Buy pre–owned stuff and invest the savings in tax–advantaged 529 education plans. Kids won't remember the supposed indignity of a secondhand infancy, but years later they'll appreciate the help on tuition.

- *Media.* Buy pre–owned: books, DVDs, CDs, and video games.

- *Nostalgia Items.* So many things you once enjoyed are no longer manufactured. Hunt them down on eBay and own them once more.

- *House Wares.* All that's needed for a first apartment can be had for a song. Use the savings to pay the rental deposit.

- *Building Supplies.* Buy from salvage stores. Locate nearby vendors at Habitat.org/restores or OldHouseJournal.com.

- *Tools.* It won't take many yard sales before you find a great circular saw. Make sure it works and bring it home.

- *Replacement Electronics.* When your cell phone, camera, printer, or MP3 player dies, buy the same model secondhand. The advantages: (1) a low price; (2) no time wasted in figuring out how the replacement works; and (3) no need to buy new accessories (batteries, cases, chargers, memory chips, etc.).

- *Mix and Match.* Buy new prints, but shop for old frames. Snag a funky lamp from the 1960s, but freshen it up with a new shade. Buy pre–owned boots on eBay, but insert new insoles.

Among frugal fringers, secondhand goods are points of honor. Each item provides a tangible reminder that function triumphs over form, and that dings and scratches don't matter if something performs its job well. To nudge yourself into this same mindset, try a short exercise. Think about a few items you purchased used and that performed their jobs admirably. Then keep these items in mind as you read through the list below. When you finish, ask yourself this key question: "with all the benefits that secondhand purchases provide, why don't I buy used more often?"

TEN GREAT REASONS TO BUY USED

1. *Lower Prices*. When you buy used, you save. A $30,000 car costs only $12,000, an $8,000 bedroom set drops to $900, and $500 in books go for $40. In each case, the practical usefulness stays the same as if you had bought brand new. The auto still gets you from point A to point B, the furniture works every bit as well, and the books contain the same old text. The big difference: you've saved $25,560.

2. *Lower Sales Taxes*. The savings don't stop at $25,560—you also avoid the sales tax you would have paid on retail pricing. At an eight percent rate, you pocket an extra $2,045 ($25,560 x 8% = $2,045).

3. *Lower Ownership Costs*. Big ticket items like cars come with the extra baggage of annual ownership taxes and insurance premiums. The amounts you pay vary depending upon where you live. In my neck of the woods, buying the used car mentioned above sidesteps about $1,700 in taxes and insurance over the next five years. This boosts the overall savings to $29,305—not too shabby for three measly purchases.

4. *A Planet Saved*. Buying secondhand is recycling at its best. When you buy a used set of dishes, you not only save the plates themselves from the landfill, but also the bulky packaging you would have tossed out had you bought at retail. And wait, there's more: one less set of plates gets manufactured overseas, shipped to a USA port, railroaded to a warehouse, and trucked to a local store. Instead, a neighbor drives the plates a few miles to the thrift shop and you cart them back from there.

5. *Local Economies Supported*. Whenever you buy at a thrift store or garage sale, you buy local. The money doesn't fly offshore; it stays—for now, at least—in your own community.

6. *Good Causes Advanced*. Buy from non–profit stores operated by the likes of Goodwill Industries, and the money you spend meets a good end by funding community services.

7. *Ownership Anxieties Lowered*. Whenever I buy something new, I expend enormous energy trying to protect my precious acquisition. Despite my best efforts, the harsh realities of a cruel world crash in. The first few scratches and dents prompt much loud wailing and gnashing of teeth. But when these same inevitabilities inflict themselves upon my used stuff, life goes on with nary a hitch. It's like this: a Riedel wine glass shatters and all is tragedy; its thrift shop counterpart meets with the same sorry fate, and one simply grabs another glass and keeps on drinking. If possessions are like chains around our necks, then we all might as well don lighter chains. Secondhand stuff weighs on us less.

8. *Walmart Gets Beat at Its Own Game*. If you dislike Walmart, perhaps you express your disdain with visits to more expensive stores. Instead, take a stand by buying secondhand. This costs you less than Walmart (and far less than the higher-priced competitors you've been using), gets you better quality goods (anything used has enough durability to have survived at least one prior owner), and doesn't drain any dollars away from your local economy (one reason many dislike Walmart in the first place). If, on the other hand, you *love* Walmart, then probably what you love best are its low prices. Resellers are even more loveable, because they undercut Walmart in the same way Walmart once undercut all those mom-and-pop stores that used to line Main Street. Isn't sub-retail karma great?

9. *Recreational Shopping Improved*. When you switch from retail to resale, you still get much of the same consumer high, but it harms you less because you pay less. Secondhand purchases are the shopping addict's equivalent of nicotine patches.

10. *Novelty Added*. Used boutiques change their inventories daily. And whenever you buy, you take some of that novelty home to roost. Let others overfill their lives with whatever ho-hum the box stores hawk this season. You march to the beat of a different drummer. With each secondhand piece you acquire, your home, your clothing, and your accessories become all the more unique— just like you.

☐ **Buy the Flawed**

Frugal fringers pay less by choosing to overlook cosmetic defects. After all, it's what's on the inside that counts. Shop for floor models, demos, scratch–and–dents, returned items, blemished products (clerks often have authority to grant discounts for loose stitching or other flaws), reconditioned electronics (visit TigerDirect.com), seconds (visit SierraTradingPost.com), remnants (granite countertops, construction materials), unpopular colors, and all their various brethren.

☐ **Buy Other Technologies**

Before swooping in on any purchase, fringers ask whether something altogether different might do the job for less. Examples:

- *Music.* It's not unusual to download the *Greatest Hits of Tom Jones* for $9.99, but you can also buy a used CD, cassette, or record of the same content and transfer it to your computer for practically nothing. (Under copyright laws, you must limit any copies to your own personal use and maintain possession of the original format from which the copies were made.)

- *Motorboats.* Canoes, kayaks, and rowboats consume no gas, require less storage space, and bestow invigorating exercise. Proceed down your stream merrily.

- *Snow Blowers.* Try this plan: (1) blow off the blower and buy shovels; (2) get those you live with to move the shovels; and (3) keep your labor force on the job with copious quantities of hot cocoa, an effective fuel which happens to cost much less per gallon than gasoline.

- *Weights.* Dumbbells cost less than machines and, according to experts, provide better workouts.

- *Travel Organizers.* These opaque pouches with zippers cost as much as $20. Resealable bags cost pennies and you can see what's inside them.

- *Bath and Kitchen Gadgets.* Choose razors and toothbrushes over their electric equivalents. Buy manual can openers, mixers, and knife sharpeners. Hand tools cost less and last longer.

- *Consumer Electronic Cases.* Whenever you buy a device, the seller pushes a variety of encasements. Almost always, these are overpriced. Having slashed its margins on the main item, the seller hopes for bigger profits on peripherals. Look elsewhere. An official Kindle cover costs $40, but a $2 bubble wrap mailer does the same job for next to nothing.

- *Wine.* Boxed wine tastes great. The packaging costs less and vintners pass some of the savings on to you.

- *Mattresses.* Don't spend big on new mattresses and box springs, buy toppers instead.

- *Noise Cancelling Headphones.* You could spend $300 on this popular fix for cacophonic airplane cabins. But for $0.99, load your MP3 player with an hour–long white noise track from Amazon. Choices include ocean surfs, summer rains, and even windy prairies. Or go cheaper yet. For $0.25, travel with a pair of foam earplugs. Unlike bulky headphones, these thrifty fixes don't take up space in your carryon bag.

☐ Buy Other Models

Frugalists prize pared–down models, discontinued items, and close-outs. Some cases in point:

- *Flat Panel TVs.* Look for smaller screens that lack 3D—a dimension you might not care about anyway.

- *All–In–One Printers.* If a printer includes a fax function that you'll never use, ask whether the manufacturer offers a fax-free version—don't pay extra for features you don't need.

- *Luxury Items.* Whenever you indulge in luxuries, do so on a small scale. Buy bath oils and microbrews instead of day spas and cognacs.

- *The Next–to–Last Generation.* When the latest iWhatever hits the shelves, prices for past versions plummet. Unless the newest release offers compelling upgrades, buy the older model and save.

☐ Buy a Part Instead of a Whole

Whenever anything breaks or wears out, diehard fringers first consider replacing a part instead of the entire item.

- *Computer Upgrades.* Replace failed DVD players or hard drives, but keep the CPU.

- *Off Road Vehicles.* Drop in a new motor, but keep the same snowmobile or ATV.

- *Furniture.* Redo the upholstery, retain the couch.

- *Small Appliances.* Replace the carafe, keep the coffee maker.

☐ Buy Generic

Store brands don't advertise, so they don't pay admen. As fringers know, the happy result is lower prices. Sometimes, house brands even provide better quality. Costco's Kirkland label earns high ratings for a diverse range of products. Generics are increasingly popular. According to the Nielsen Company, they now account for 22.3 percent of all grocery sales, which is up 1.8 percent since right before the Great Recession.

☐ Buy Multipurpose Merchandise

Look for versatile products that address several needs at once.

- *Laptops as Desktop Replacements.* A powerful laptop eliminates any need for a separate desktop. Why buy both when one does the work of two?

- *Netbooks as Tablets.* Screens detach from keyboards to act as tablets (search the web for "hybrid or convertible laptops").

- *Coats.* Why buy one coat for winter and a lighter one for fall and spring? Overcoats with removable liners cover three seasons with a single purchase.

- *Convertible Pants.* Zippers let you convert from long pants to shorts to long pants again, all on the fly. REI.com sells several types. Best pants story: on a hot day in Vatican City, a friend had been standing for hours in line to get into St. Peter's Basilica. When he finally reached the entrance, a guide said he couldn't enter because he was wearing shorts. A couple quick zips later, the shorts became longs and admission was gained. Let's hope we all get through the pearly gates so easily.

- *Kitchen Knives.* Those matching knives look very impressive in their wooden block, but do you really need nine of them? Figure out which ones are the most versatile. Buy those and equip yourself for a fraction of what a full set costs. In the process, you also free up precious countertop space.

- *Yoga Mats.* They double as pads for sleeping bags.

- *Portable Heaters with Fans.* Kill two small birds with one small appliance: heat in the winter and cool in the summer.

- *Two–Way Shop Vacs.* This contraption works as both a vacuum and leaf blower. In the vernacular of Generation X, it not only "sucks," it also "blows." And, dude, you end up with two tools for the price of one!

CODA: SMART PHONES

You'll be tempted by these electronic versions of Swiss army knives, where a single handset takes the place of a camera, GPS, MP3 player, and wristwatch. But run the numbers, including the initial cost and monthly fees. You may find it's cheaper to juggle devices.

❑ **Stack Tactics to Save More**
Combine two or more of the above tactics for even greater savings. For instance, if you've chosen a multipurpose product, you can buy it secondhand for a boost in savings. If you've decided on a freezer with slightly fewer features, take home one of the floor models.

*   *   *

The summary below collects these alternatives, which all reappear as part of the concise checklist in Appendix 1.

STRATEGY NO. 2:
BUY SOMETHING ELSE

- ☐ **buy used** [eBay, Goodwill, yard sales]
- ☐ **buy the flawed** [seconds, dents, demos, returns]
- ☐ **buy other technologies** [shovels for snow blowers]
- ☐ **buy other models** [fewer features, gen3 not gen4]
- ☐ **buy a part instead of a whole** [upgrades, disk drives]
- ☐ **buy generic** [bleach, batteries, frozen veggies]
- ☐ **buy multipurpose merchandise** [heater/fans, 2–way vacs]
- ☐ **stack tactics to save more** [combine two or more of the above]

    Add my own ideas here:
- ☐
- ☐
- ☐

3

STRATEGY NO. 3:
RESEARCH THE PRODUCT

If your initial purchase idea has run the gauntlet of the first two chapters and survived, now's the time to evaluate it in greater depth. This is no easy task. If you search for "coffeemakers" on Amazon, for example, you're confronted with more than 23,000 results. Faced with such sensory overload, how do you decide which product is best? As any fringer could tell you, the answer is research—not too much of it—but enough to improve the odds of scoring quality merchandise at low prices. This chapter presents five tactics: (1) read product reviews and, for big ticket items, buying guides; (2) ask around; (3) try before buying; (4) consider hidden ownership costs; and, in certain circumstances, (5) revisit the alternatives listed in the first two chapters.

☐ **Read Buying Guides and Product Reviews**
Spending less doesn't mean that you buy the cheapest products, especially ones that break or underperform. Instead, spending less means spending smart so that you get full value for every dollar relinquished. This requires research.

> ☐ *Read Buying Guides.* For big-ticket items like appliances, electronics, and power tools, learn the basics. On the web, search for your product and the phrase "buying guide," as in "dishwasher buying guide." At the library, read the *Consumer Reports Buying Guide*, which is published annually and covers dozens of product categories.

> ☐ *Visit Consumer Search.* ConsumerSearch.com collects reviews from web and print sources and recommends specific models. If the site evaluates your product, your analysis is largely completed. Reviews are arranged under logical categories—

electronics, home and garden, kitchen and food, fitness and sports, computers and internet, family and pets, health and beauty, and automotive. *Time* magazine named Consumer Search as one of the fifty best websites for 2009.

❑ *Read Consumer Reports.* Support the cause of good consumerism by subscribing to the magazine or website (ConsumerReports.org). If this seems too costly, reduce your research expenses by periodically reading issues at your local library. *Consumer Reports* contains no ads and is published by Consumers Union, a nonprofit worthy of any fringer's philanthropy (see Chapter 19).

❑ *Visit Amazon.* Search for products on Amazon.com and sort the results by "bestselling." Usually, consumers are wise, and the top–listed items make good choices for quality and value. Each listing includes customer reviews, but beware: some grumps cast aspersions on even the best of products. Don't be scared off by a few negative comments.

❑ *Visit CNET.* Head over to CNET.com whenever you shop for electronics—televisions, computers, printers, tablets, cameras, MP3 players, and cell phones. Look for editor's choices that spotlight the top picks in each product category.

❑ *Look at YouTube.* Uploaded videos show the product in actual use. Beware of postings that are thinly disguised ads. Visit YouTube.com.

❑ *Search the Web.* For most purchases, the above sources provide ample information. But if you thirst for still more data, search online for the product's name, manufacturer, model number, and the word "review."

❑ *Consult Product Specific Sources.* Consult hyper–specific authorities that might have reviewed your product. Look at blogs, club websites, online specialty stores, and enthusiast magazines (*Photography Magazine, Stereophile, Sound and Vision* and *Cook's Illustrated*).

☐ Ask Around

When you shop for appliances, electronics, or software, consider online discussions. Search for your product along with the phrases "chat room," "forum," and "discussion board." Sound out your friends—they're consumers too. They likely have some opinions (again, don't be scared off by one bad comment, but be *very* scared if you hear it repeatedly). Ask detailed questions:

☐ *"Which features were useful, and which were useless?"*

☐ *"Is any feature missing that should have been included?"*

☐ *"How's the durability and reliability? Any breakdowns?"*

☐ *"Would you buy it again, or something else instead? Why?"*

☐ *"Any other opinions?"*

☐ Try Before You Buy

Whenever you can, take the product out for a trial run before spending. Consider these audition techniques:

☐ *Play with Floor Models and Demos.* If the store displays your product, run it through its paces.

☐ *Sample Samples.* Warehouse clubs regularly offer these enticements—eat up before you buy up. And many stores accept returns of half-eaten foods, so if you try a product for the first time and don't like it, you can still get a refund.

☐ *Visit Fitting Rooms.* Try on clothes to save yourself the hassle of a later return.

☐ *Borrow.* Return the favor by lending out your own stuff.

☐ *Rent.* If you're about to pay $15,000 or more for a particular make and model of car, rent one first so that you can learn more about it (see Chapter 17). Also rent before you buy expensive tools and sports equipment. You can even rent mattresses: the next time you travel, book a hotel that features whichever model you like and sleep it over for the night.

☐ *Buy Used.* Before you drop $150 on a new bread maker, buy one for $10 at the thrift store. If your idea is half–baked, you haven't spent much, and you can always donate it back. You even might find the used model works so well that you don't have to spend more on a new one.

☐ *Read Owner's Manuals.* Hold a virtual audition by reading the manual before you buy. Find them at manufacturer websites, ManualsOnline.com, or search the web for the make, model number, and the word "manual."

☐ *Make Use of Trial Periods, Money Back Guarantees, and Liberal Return Policies.* These policies let you back out of any unsatisfactory purchases. Be sure to factor in shipping costs.

☐ **Consider Hidden Ownership Costs**
Typical culprits include installation, storage, accessories, servicing, subscriptions, disposal, repair, energy use, insurance premiums, licenses, ownership taxes, and components (cartridges, filters, and batteries). Favor products that cost less to own. Some cases in point:

- *HDTVs.* They look awesome, but don't forget all of the other costs: (1) wall mounts or cabinets; (2) subscriptions to HD channels; (3) upgraded sound systems; (4) Blu–Ray players and disks; (5) HDMI cables; (6) energy usage (gas plasma sets especially); (7) faster internet connections for online content; and (8) disposal costs for your old TV.

- *Kitchen Gadgets.* Beware of products with frequently replaced components: flavor pouches for single–serving coffee makers, seedpods for hydroponic planters, and canned syrups for brew–at–home cola machines.

- *Printers.* Over time, the cost of toner dwarfs the cost of a new machine. To stay out of red ink, seek printers with low operating costs.

- *King–Sized Beds.* If you go big, you pay more for headboards, bed frames, mattresses, mattress pads, pillows, pillowcases, sheets, blankets, and comforters.

- *Replacement Decking.* Wood decks require frequent waterproofing or staining. Eventually, they wear out. Composite materials cost more up front, but they last longer and demand much less upkeep.

- *Hot Tubs.* Spas soak you twice. Don't forget the post–installation costs: (1) chemicals and test kits; (2) utility costs; (3) filters; (4) insulated covers that you replace every few years; (5) repairs to frozen pipes and other failed parts; and (6) disposal costs once you finally decide to ditch it all. Maybe you'll be less steamed if you accept these as the costs of restorative soakings at 102⁰F.

□ **Consider Repeating Strategy Nos. 1 and 2**

As you research, you might discard your first inspiration in favor of another product. If this happens, backtrack to Chapters 1 and 2 and run your latest idea through the listed tactics. Why? Typically, you save much more from those alternatives than you do by following the herd of mainstream consumers into malls and box stores (where they're milked for all they're worth). The choice is yours. You can become some retailer's idea of a cash cow; or you can jump the fence to greener pastures where the dollars grow in great profusion.

*   *   *

STRATEGY NO. 3:
RESEARCH THE PRODUCT

☐ **read buying guides and product reviews** —
   ☐ for big ticket items, read buying guides [search web]
   ☐ ConsumerSearch.com, *Consumer Reports*
   ☐ Amazon reviews and bestseller lists
   ☐ CNET, for electronics
   ☐ YouTube [video demos]
   ☐ web reviews [search for name, model no., "reviews"]
   ☐ sources unique to this product [magazines, clubs, blogs]
☐ **ask around** [friends' opinions, chat rooms]
☐ **try before I buy** [loaners, rentals, demos, samples]
☐ **consider hidden ownership costs** —
   ☐ install/set–up
   ☐ disposal [old TVs, tires]
   ☐ storage
   ☐ service and upkeep
   ☐ accessories [cases, rechargers]
   ☐ frequently replaced components [filters, toner]
   ☐ energy use
   ☐ insurance
   ☐ fees, subscriptions, licenses
   ☐ tax impacts [ownership taxes, deductions, credits]
☐ **consider repeating Strategy Nos. 1–2**
   Add my own ideas here:
☐
☐
☐

4

STRATEGY NO. 4:
FIND LOW PRICES

Once you find the product that best fits your needs, look around for the best deals. As any frugal fringer will tell you, the internet provides an indispensible guide. Follow these tactics: (1) shop around for the lowest prices; (2) time your purchase to coincide with sales; (3) check for "special offers" on prices; (4) seek out "deal sweeteners" on terms other than the price itself; (5) look for opportunities to "stack" sales, special offers, and deal sweeteners; and (6) weigh the transaction costs, including the value of your own time. This structured approach achieves great bargains on quality goods, and does it consistently.

□ **Shop Around for the Lowest Prices**
Shop at price comparison sites such as Google Shopping, Yahoo! Shopping, or PriceGrabber. The results won't include every vendor, so always visit the sites of specific online stores that likely stock your item.

If you're willing to spend more time, extend your search beyond the internet. Read catalogs and Sunday newspaper supplements (to see the latter online, visit ShopLocal.com). Call up stores or go shopping. If you own a well–featured cell phone, download various apps— Google Shopper, RedLaser, ShopSavvy—that let you compare prices by simply scanning barcodes.

□ **Synchronize Purchases With Sales**
The precise moment you decide to buy might not coincide with a sale. Delay your purchase. While you wait, continue to search the web for lower prices. Sign up at price comparison sites (see above) to receive emails about price drops. Also, many products hit sales racks at predictable times, such as when new models arrive or inventories turn over. To discover the best moment to pounce, ask your web

search engine this question: "when is the best time of year to buy [insert name of product category here]?" Mark your calendar with the results and don't buy until then.

☐ Look for "Special Offers"

Sometimes, a seller drops prices for everyone with a sale. But this means that careless buyers who might otherwise pay full retail pay less and, as a result, revenues lag. To avoid such a catastrophe, sellers employ various devices. Let's call them "special offers." Basically, special offers differentiate between buyers—those willing to put in extra work enjoy a price break and those unwilling to do so pay more. Check for these whenever you shop and be among the few who snag the lower price.

- *Coupons and Codes.* Popular sites include RetailMeNot.com, CouponCabin.com, and CouponSherpa.com.

- *Group Discounts.* If you belong to AAA, AARP, or any professional groups, your organization may already have negotiated a discount for you. Don't count on sellers to remind you of this—after all, they want you to pay more, not less. Be proactive. Most groups publish lists of discounting retailers. Your checklist reminds you to look at these whenever you shop.

- *Rebates.* Rebates are like salmon swimming upstream—only a few complete their journey and reach the happy spawning pools of consumer checking accounts. Sadly, many rebates die before their journey ever begins, because buyers never hear about them in the first place. Other rebates make it further, but consumers: (1) forget to mail forms; (2) fail to enclose sales receipts; or (3) never cash the check. Manufacturers love rebates. With so many chances for buyers to flounder, guess who ends up happy? Whenever you come across a rebate, help it leap over all the artificial obstacles.

- *Volume Discounts.* These fall into three basic categories. First, sellers discount prices for bulk purchases of same item—buy one get one FREE (BOGO) offers or discounts on cases. These usually are good deals. Second, sellers offer price breaks for complete sets (kitchen knives, cookware, bedroom furniture, DVD collections). These provide good deals as long as the buyer has a real need for each separate part of the set. Third, sellers create various package deals such as computers bundled with printers, HDTVs combined with Blu–Ray players, and cameras sold with memory chips. Often, these deals deliver little value because sellers use the promotion to dump unpopular inventory.

- *Discounts for Preferred Form of Payment.* Whenever you use credit cards, merchants pay processing fees to card issuers. To avoid these fees, they may offer discounts for purchases with cash or store–issued cards. Such deals produce significant savings on more expensive items.

- *Deal–a–Day Websites.* With Groupon and Living Social, you don't find the products, they find you. Once you sign up, you receive daily emails about special offers. By inspiring more purchases, however, these sites can turn anyone into a deal-obsessed overspender. Fight the urge to splurge. Buy only what you need and run every offer through Appendix 1.

☐ Seek Out "Deal Sweeteners"

Manufacturers, vendors, and even interested third parties like credit card companies offer benefits in addition to or apart from lower prices. Read the fine print first. Such "deal sweeteners" come in many flavors.

- *Freebies.* Sellers offer FREE shipping, installation, accessories, components, subscriptions, and upgrades.

- *Loyalty Programs.* As you make purchases, you accumulate credits for future transactions, such as reward points or card punches (buy nine sandwiches and your tenth is FREE!).

- *Credit Card Rewards and Other Benefits.* Sellers aren't the only ones who try to influence your purchases. Credit card companies earn fees on every transaction, so to increase card use, they offer buyer rewards. Many cards also offer extended warranties, breakage insurance, and refunds for post–purchase price drops (see Chapter 49).

- *Financing Deals.* Sellers sometimes dangle offers such as zero percent financing or no payments for six months. If you can pay these off as scheduled without penalty, they might prove worthwhile. But if there's any risk you can't pay on time, decline the offer and buy later when you have enough cash.

☐ **Look for "Stacking"**

You receive the best deals whenever a product hits the sales rack at the same time that special offers and deal sweeteners are pending. The checklist reminds you to watch for these savings bonanzas.

☐ **Weigh Transaction Costs**

Don't forget sales taxes (Chapter 20), delivery charges, handling fees, and shipping insurance. These add up fast on big–ticket items or repeat purchases. Find online stores that ship for FREE at FreeShipping.org. Consider too the value of your own time. Ask yourself whether the savings are worth the effort based upon the amounts at stake. This assessment is inherently personal. Some spend many happy hours in the study of pumpkin pie fillings. Most, however, toss the Libby's can into the shopping cart and move on.

*   *   *

STRATEGY NO. 4:
FIND LOW PRICES

☐ **shop around** —

    ☐ search price comparison sites

    ☐ visit web stores not listed on comparison sites

    ☐ search for low prices offline [call stores, read ads]

☐ **delay buying until sales arrive** [search web: "best time to buy xx"]

☐ **look for "special offers" on prices** —

    ☐ coupons and codes

    ☐ group discounts [consult lists of discounting sellers for each of my groups]

    ☐ rebates

    ☐ volume discounts

    ☐ discounts for preferred form of payment

    ☐ deal–a–day websites [Groupon, LivingSocial]

☐ **seek out "deal sweeteners"** [terms other than price] —

    ☐ freebies [delivery, accessories]

    ☐ store loyalty programs [rewards, gift cards]

    ☐ credit card benefits [rewards, extended warranties, price protection]

    ☐ zero percent financing

☐ **look for "stacking"** [sales+special offers+deal sweeteners]

☐ **weigh transaction costs** [sales taxes, shipping, my own time]

Add my own ideas here:

☐

☐

☐

5

STRATEGY NO. 5:
PICK A LOW PRICE SELLER

In most cases, sellers adopt fair policies, give ample product support, and back up their warranties. In the worst cases, sellers lie, fail to deliver, and ignore their customers. To limit unhappy purchases, fringers weed out bad sellers *before* they buy. This strategy consists of five tactics: (1) run background checks; (2) review the seller's policies, especially on returns and price matches; (3) investigate the quality of the seller's product support and customer service; (4) once you pick a seller, search for discounted gift cards; and (5) explore your chosen seller's willingness to negotiate.

☐ **Run Background Checks**

Look at these factors when you compare the sellers who have the lowest prices.

☐ *Consider Your Own Experience.* If you've bought from this store several times and it offers the lowest price, then you can skip the research. But if the lowest price comes from an unfamiliar seller, investigate further.

☐ *Ask Friends.* The people you know and trust are consumers too. Ask what they think about your prospective seller.

☐ *Assess Customer Feedback.* Before you buy on the internet, make sure the seller has received ample customer reviews and high ratings. Google Shopping evaluates sellers on a five-star scale. Similar ratings appear on eBay, Amazon Marketplace, and eOpinions.com. Before you buy from an unfamiliar physical store, check out the Better Business Bureau (BBB.org). If the ratings are low, choose another seller even if—gasp!—it charges more. That's better than suffering massive heartburn later.

☐ *Consider the Seller's Time in Business.* The longer a merchant has been around, the more likely it treats customers well.

☐ **Review the Seller's Policies**
Perform this due diligence if the prospective seller is new to you.

☐ *Look for Extended Warranties.* Some sellers and credit card companies extend warranties for FREE.

☐ *Seek Out Price Matching Before the Sale.* Suppose you have a favorite store, but one of its competitors offers the item you want for less. If your preferred store matches prices, present proof of the competitor's offer and ask for the same deal. Bonus: if your favored vendor matches the price, you don't need to run the less familiar competitor through a background check.

☐ *Seek Out Price Matching After the Sale.* Find out whether your prospect honors price drops that occur within a stated time after purchase. Some credit cards offer this as well.

☐ *Find Out Policies on Back Orders.* If the product has sold out, you might be able to get a rain check.

☐ *Consider Credit Card Surcharges.* Retailers in 40 states now have the legal right to pass along card processing fees to customers. Favor sellers that don't impose these surcharges.

☐ *Know Policies for Returns/Exchanges.* Here's what to look for:

• *Permissible returns.* Some sellers bar all returns and others bar them on certain products only: DVDs, CDs, etc.

• *Deadlines.* Some sellers disallow returns after a stated period of time.

• *Requirements for original receipts and packaging.* Rules may vary depending upon the particular product involved.

• *Nature of refunds.* Will the seller return your money (preferred), issue a store credit (okay), or limit you to an exchange for the same item (least preferable)?

- *Fees.* Most online stores charge for return shipping. Some physical stores impose restock fees or other bogus charges.

☐ **Research Product Support and Customer Service**
Consider whether the seller or manufacturer supports its products. Too often, no safety net exists post–purchase and if something goes wrong, you're on your own. Look for toll free numbers and repair centers. For customer service ratings, visit *Consumer Reports*, JD Power, or the American Customer Satisfaction Index (TheACSI.org).

☐ **Once You Pick a Seller, Look for Discounted Gift Cards**
Several sites sell unused gift cards to familiar stores for slightly below face value. It's a good way to save 5–20 percent more. Visit GiftCardGranny.com, PlasticJungle.com, or GiftCardRescue.com.

☐ **Once You Pick a Seller, Consider Haggling**
Based on prior research (see Chapter 4), you already know that little room exists for a lower price. Still, if you want to squeeze the last nickel from your chosen seller, consider negotiations.

☐ *Plan Ahead.* Decide upfront what price you want to pay. Print out low prices from the internet for later use when dickering.

☐ *Play Nice.* If you're at a store, don't speak so loudly that nearby customers are inspired to start their own bargaining sessions. Show respect. Be cheerful, courteous, and kind. Smile.

☐ *Haggle.* There are millions of ways to negotiate. For starters, consider these examples:

- *"Will you match your competitor's price?"* It's show and tell time. Pull out your website printouts.

- *"Will you match your competitor's price?"* It's show and tell time. Pull out your website printouts.

- *"What price applies when this goes on sale?"* Followed by "can I have that deal now so I don't have to drive back later?"

- *"What price do loyalty club members get?"* More subtle than asking "what's the best deal you can give me?"

- *"I'm seesawing between buying this new or used."* You don't expect to get the secondhand price, of course, but this moves discussions in your favor.

- *"May I please speak to your manager?"* If a sales clerk can't offer the price you want, move up the chain of command. Supervisors usually have greater bargaining authority.

☐ *Explore "Deal Sweeteners."* If a seller won't dicker on price, it might on some other term of sale. Make a specific request: FREE accessories, installation, or delivery.

☐ *There's No Sale Until You Say So.* If you've haggled but there's still no deal, bow out respectfully. Leave a card so the merchant can call you later if it reconsiders. Say thank you.

*   *   *

STRATEGY NO. 5:
PICK A LOW PRICE SELLER

☐ **run background checks** [past dealings, friends' experience, customer feedback, time in business]

☐ **review the seller's policies—**
  - ☐ extended warranties
  - ☐ price matching before *and* after the sale
  - ☐ rain checks and back orders
  - ☐ surcharges for credit card purchases
  - ☐ returns/exchanges

☐ **research product support** [repair sites, parts availability, updates]

☐ **research customer service** [JP Power, *Consumer Reports*, theacsi.org]

☐ **once I pick a seller, look for discounted gift cards** [*e.g.*, PlasticJungle.com]

☐ **once I pick a seller, consider haggling** [on prices, deal sweeteners, shipping costs]

Add my own ideas here:

☐

☐

☐

6

STRATEGY NO. 6:
AVOID PITFALLS

Most fringers approach purchases with extreme trepidation. As each new transaction looms, they worry whether they're about to stumble into a painful pitfall. Here's a list of the typical disasters. Sidestep them and save.

☐ **Refuse to Pay Interest on Consumer Purchases**
If there's anything worse than a sales tax of 9.5 percent, it's 15 percent in credit card interest. Don't borrow except for houses, educations, and, only if you must, cars. If you can't afford particular objects of desire without financing them, revisit Chapters 1–2 for cheaper alternatives that don't plunge you into debt.

☐ **Buy the Right Size**
Buy more than needed, and you waste money. Buy less than needed, and the upgrades demand more cash. In order to save, get in touch with your inner Goldilocks—don't buy too big, don't buy too small, and strive always to buy the size that's "just right."

- *Furniture.* Sectional sofas look nice in show rooms, but for your small cave, a loveseat looks nicer.

- *SUVs.* You live in Miami and it never snows. Buy a sedan.

- *Computers.* Don't splurge on costly gaming machines if you only surf the internet and process words.

- *Pets.* Apartments are bad for St. Bernards. Think Chihuahuas.

☐ **Avoid Stuff That Ends Up Owning You**
Beware high maintenance products like motorboats, RVs, ATVs, snowmobiles, hot tubs, swimming pools, lawn tractors, and their ilk. If it has a motor in it, think twice.

☐ Sweep Away Dust Gatherers

If you doubt your future need for a product, borrow or rent one first. My foremost dust–gatherer was an electric pasta maker. Did you know they sell perfectly good rigatoni in grocery stores?

☐ Never Pay Extra for Prestige

Pay extra for quality, but don't pay more for the name alone. Cheaper brands often perform every bit as well and sometimes better than their luxury counterparts.

☐ Beware of Buying too Cheap

You want the most bang for your buck, but that doesn't always mean paying the lowest price. I've suffered through dollar store bungee cords that didn't stretch, cheap popcorn that never popped, and weak tools that splintered when confronted with their first tough job. Avoid these messes. Seek quality at value prices.

☐ Decline to Serve as an "Early Adopter"

The sooner you buy into new technologies, the more you spend. These products have short shelf lives, so prices plunge quickly. Wait.

☐ Reject Fads and Short–Lived Trends

Let others buy pet rocks and eight-track tapes; you can do without.

☐ Read Agreements Before Signing Them

Contracts are binding. If you sign first and read them later, your cart is misplaced relative to your horse.

☐ Say No to Middlemen Who Add No Value

Even at this late date, middlemen somehow survive. God bless 'em. If you buy from one who adds value, then maybe you *should* pay extra. If not, then maybe he or she should find another line of work.

☐ Plan Ahead for Big Ticket Purchases

Beware rarely bought items—carpets, flooring, mattresses, and autos. Sellers enjoy a huge advantage because they conduct many more negotiations than you do. To level the playing field, anticipate that your infrastructure eventually fails. If your furnace has started to show its age, research replacements now. Don't be forced into a hasty decision when it dies next winter.

☐ **Beware of Deals "Too Good To Be True"**
If the price seems far too low, make sure it's not a scam.

☐ **Sidestep the "Bait and Switch"**
In this ploy, sellers lure shoppers with low prices (the "bait") and then push them into other products that deliver higher profits (the "switch"). Success depends upon the buyer's willingness to act impulsively. You never fall for this if you've researched enough to know precisely what you want and how it meets your needs.

☐ **Forgo Bells and Whistles**
Impose a heavy presumption against paying more for upgraded features, extended warranties, or luxury add–ons. Typically, these line sellers' pockets and deliver no added value to buyers.

* * *

STRATEGY NO. 6:
AVOID PITFALLS

☐ **refuse to pay interest on products** [revisit strategy nos. 1–2]

☐ **buy the right size** [measure twice, buy once]

☐ **avoid stuff that owns me** [spas, RVs, ATVs]

☐ **sweep away dust gatherers** [pasta makers]

☐ **never pay extra for prestige**

☐ **beware of buying too cheap** [seek values, not lowest prices]

☐ **decline to be an "early adopter"** [newest iWhatevers]

☐ **reject fads** [Beanie Babies]

☐ **read contracts before signing them**

☐ **say no to middlemen who add no value**

☐ **plan ahead for big ticket items**

☐ **beware of deals "too good to be true"**

☐ **sidestep the "bait and switch"**

☐ **forgo bells and whistles**

    Add my own ideas here:

☐

☐

☐

7

STRATEGY NO. 7:
FOLLOW UP

You're past the cash register and have in hand your latest object of desire. Had any fringers witnessed your purchase, they'd be crestfallen over the flagrant sacrifice of innocent dollars. But don't worry about that. Because you've used the preceding—MOOOOOO!!!—strategies, you've found a solid product at a great price. However, as any frugalist would tell you: *don't let up too early*. Protect yourself from future losses with these post–purchase tactics.

☐ **Confirm the Terms of Sale**
When you buy at a store, before you leave the premises look at the receipt and confirm its accuracy. Make sure you have the correct item—the right model, size, color, etc.—and that you haven't been overcharged. When you take a delivery, run all these checks before the truck leaves your driveway.

☐ **Inspect for Imperfections**
When you unpack your purchase, look for defects, malfunctions, scratches, and dents.

☐ **Register With the Manufacturer**
Do this to receive notice of recalls and product updates. Hint: you don't have to answer survey questions about your income.

☐ **Retain Receipts, Packaging, and Manuals**
Keep sales slips and boxes in case of a possible return. File away manuals for future reference.

☐ **Monitor Price Drops**
For a month or so after buying, monitor ads and websites for lower prices. Many sellers match any price drops that occur within a few weeks after purchase. Some credit cards offer similar protection (see Chapter 49).

☐ **Visit Chat Rooms**

After you buy, chat rooms provide useful tips about items big (vehicles, appliances, computers) and small (computer peripherals, software). After I bought a used Toyota RAV4, I discovered it had the worst designed cup holders ever—so oversized that all but the biggest cups jostled about. At a RAV4 chat room, several posters recommended some after–market inserts. I bought them and can now drink and drive—nonalcoholic beverages only, of course.

☐ **If You Really Love It, Buy Duplicates**

If it's a great product, perhaps you should buy extras. This protects you in case the manufacturer ceases business or halts production.

☐ **Make the Item Last**

Follow manufacturer guidelines and common sense in operation, storage, cleaning, maintenance, and repair.

☐ **Keep Motivated With a "Checklist Savings Log"**

Finally, each time you complete a purchase, enter your savings into a "checklist savings log" that tracks your progress and reinforces your *SL☑N!* habit. After all, you've just stashed away money that most consumers would have willingly surrendered. It's time to celebrate with a modest use of metrics. For details about logs and other motivational tools, read Chapter 47.

* * *

That's it! In seven chapters, you've learned to operate a checklist that guides you through any purchase of merchandise. A compact summary of the entire system appears in Appendix 1. Feel free to make a copy and take it with you whenever you shop. It's more sedate than most fringers, and it still delivers big savings.

STRATEGY NO. 7:
FOLLOW UP

☐ **confirm terms of sale** [check receipt, shipping manifest]

☐ **inspect for imperfections** [dings, defects, malfunctions]

☐ **register with manufacturer** [for recalls, upgrades, news]

☐ **retain receipts, packaging, manuals** [returns, resale, taxes]

☐ **monitor price drops** [seller or credit card might match]

☐ **visit chat rooms** [vehicles, appliances, software]

☐ **buy duplicates** [if item discontinued]

☐ **make the item last** [know rules for operation, upkeep]

☐ **keep a "checklist savings log"** [see Chapter 47]

Add my own ideas here:

☐

☐

☐

PART II

LINE ITEM
CHECKLISTS

PART II OVERVIEW

At this point, you're no longer a frugal newbie. You've read the introductory chapters. You've learned how to use a checklist to buy products. Now you're ready to extend the SL☒N! system to all your household expenses.

In Part II, SL☒N! takes the form of a guidebook. Consult it whenever you're about to pay for any line item listed below. Just don't read the checklists all at once—maybe you've got some drying paint to watch instead.

Chapter 8:	Miscellaneous Services
Chapters 9–14:	Recreation
Chapters 15–18:	Travel
Chapter 19:	Charitable Giving
Chapters 20–21:	Governmental Expenses (Taxes, Postage)
Chapters 22–24:	Utilities
Chapters 25–28:	Telecommunications
Chapters 29–31:	Insurance
Chapters 32–36:	Healthcare
Chapter 37:	Groceries
Chapters 38–44:	Autos
Chapters 45–46:	Housing

8

MISCELLANEOUS
SERVICES

According to the 2011 CES, most spending on services goes for auto repairs and home remodels—both of which merit their own checklists (see Chapters 41 and 46). For now, let's focus on more routine services. These tend to cost less, get hired more often, and take less time to complete. They involve formal bids only rarely. Examples include barbers, dry cleaners, tutors, carpet cleaners, watch repairers, computer geeks, plumbers, and daycare centers.

As with the products buying checklist, this chapter summarizes the advice you might receive if any frugal fringers weighed in on your miscellaneous hires. To keep you organized, their advice appears in a system of six strategies:

(1) avoid the service completely;

(2) avoid the service in part;

(3) run background checks;

(4) find low rates;

(5) avoid common pitfalls; and

(6) follow up the hire.

Appendix 2 distills all of this into a very serviceable checklist.

8.1 Avoid the Service Completely

Here's a smorgasbord of alternatives to evade the entire hire.

☐ **8.1.1 Skip Discretionary Services**
So many niches sap away our riches: fitness trainers, masseuses, manicurists, pedicurists, event planners, auto detailers, errand

services, and professional organizers. All these services are discretionary. Sidestep them and save.

☐ 8.1.2 Delay and Hire Later

Simply procrastinate. This lets you seek out second opinions and gives you more time to shop around. If you need a repair, for example, buy yourself some time with duct tape, patches, or glue. Sometimes, a stopgap fix even provides a long–term solution.

☐ 8.1.3 Replace High–Cost Services With Low–Cost Products

A reliable product often undercuts the cost of a service.

- *Safe Deposit Boxes.* Don't pay bank rentals year after year; instead, install a home safe.

- *Private Schools.* Buy a home in a good public school district and ditch tuition costs.

- *Lawn Services.* Supplant grassy yards with sparse xeriscapes. Visit LessLawn.com.

- *Exterminators.* Rid yourself of this pesky expense. Set mousetraps yourself.

- *Caterers.* Purchase takeout instead.

- *Upholsterers.* Buy slipcovers.

- *Dry Cleaners.* Use home kits from Custom Cleaner, Dryel, or FreshCare.

- *Hair Stylists.* Replace beauty salons with home dye kits; replace barbershops with clippers.

☐ 8.1.4 Rid Yourself of Products With High Service Costs

Steer clear of high maintenance products. When you buy washable clothes, you liquefy the cost of dry cleaners. When you choose push mowers, wheelbarrows, and scythes, you avoid small engine repairs. When you play electric keyboards, you save on piano movers and tuners. If your need for a service–heavy product is unavoidable, but only occasional, rent, borrow, or flip. This way, someone other than you pays for upkeep.

☐ **8.1.5 Perform Lower Skilled Services Yourself**
Although big spenders could perform many tasks themselves, they choose to pay someone else instead. Not so with the frugal few, where self–reliance is a way of life.

- *Housekeeping.* It's good exercise and almost anyone can do it.

- *Courier Service.* Hand–deliver packages yourself; scan and email documents.

- *Home Moving.* Host the modern equivalent of a barn raising. Invite able bodied friends.

- *Lawn Care.* Dust off the mower; get some exercise.

- *Chimney Sweeping.* Obtain the brushes from a rental center.

- *Carpet Cleaning.* Rent a machine and save $300–$500 off professional cleaning.

- *Window Washing.* Buy the same tools that experts use.

- *Painting.* With time and patience, you can do it yourself.

☐ **8.1.6 Study Higher Skilled Services and Do Them Yourself**
We live in a golden age of DIY. Well–produced videos show instead of tell us how to do things we've never attempted before. Tap into this informative treasure trove and expand your skills set.

- *Music Lessons.* Buy instructional DVDs on eBay.

- *Life Coaches.* Self–help books abound; visit the library or Amazon for choices.

- *Bike Repairs.* Visit YouTube.com. Borrow a how–to DVD from your library.

- *Interior Decorating.* Buy DIY software from Amazon or borrow books from the library

- *Tax Preparation.* Join the IRS's Volunteer Income Tax Assistance (VITA) program and grow your knowledge as you help others. Visit VITA-Volunteers.org.

- *Legal Forms.* Prepare basic legal documents yourself. For how-to books, visit Nolo.com. For software, visit LegalZoom.com.

- *Real Estate Brokers.* The standard commission on a $300,000 house is $18,000. DIY and save. Visit HomesByOwner.com. For the latest how–to books, visit your library.

8.2 Avoid the Service in Part

With these alternatives, you save by restricting the amount of work the service performs.

☐ 8.2.1 Hire, but Do Some of the Work Yourself

Mix and match someone's expertise with your own sweaty efforts.

- *Tree Removal.* Hire expert lumberjacks to drop large conifers without severing power lines. Once the pines lay supine, do the grunt work: trim, cut, split, and stack.

- *House Painting.* Your home has high peaks that make painting a sketchy job. But you can still tackle the lower work yourself. Negotiate a deal where the painter takes responsibility for the high stuff only and you cover the rest.

- *Window Washing.* Same idea as painting: hire experts for hard-to–reach areas and handle the lower windows yourself.

- *Service Travel.* If you drive your computer to the repair center, you sidestep the technician's travel expenses.

- *Carpets.* Move furniture and pull up old rugs before the installers arrive.

- *Moving.* A truck delivers a large bin, which you fill with belongings. Later, it hauls the bin to your new home, where you offload the contents. Visit UPack.com or Pods.com.

☐ 8.2.2 Hire, but Procure Materials Yourself

Services simply buy whatever they need and pass along the cost, often with hefty markups. You have far greater incentives to control expenses than they do. Get involved in procurement, and save big.

- *Caterers.* Borrow tables and chairs from your VFW or church, and you won't have to pay the caterer to rent them for you.

- *Movers.* Supply the boxes yourself. Visit a grocery store or UsedCardboardBoxes.com.

- *Computer Upgrades and Bike Repairs.* Find quality parts on the internet and take them to experts for installation.

- *Lawn Services.* If you already own a lawnmower, hire a neighborhood kid instead of a well–equipped professional.

☐ 8.2.3 Hire Advisors, and Do the Actual Work Yourself

Retain a service for expert advice only.

- *Landscaping.* Hire knowledgeable designers, but shoulder the burden of moving rocks and shrubbery.

- *Lawyers.* Most household budgets can't sustain the burden of legal fees. However, if you're embroiled in small litigation and don't want to give in, retain an attorney for advice about how to represent yourself.

- *Interior Decorators.* Pay them to recommend the best colors, textures, and materials. Armed with their advice, you can move forward from there.

- *Certified Public Accountants.* Hire them for any complicated tax issues, but complete the return yourself.

☐ 8.2.4 Hire Less Often

If you visit a barber every other week, you spend $4,680 over a decade. If you visit only once a month, you save $2,340. In between trips to the barber, trim the hair yourself (that's cutting back, quite literally). This tactic works for many common services:

- Manicures
- Pedicures
- Hair Dyeing
- Lawn Service
- Pool Cleaning
- Carpet Cleaning
- Pet Grooming
- Personal Chefs
- Chiropractors
- Personal Trainers
- Yoga Classes
- Golf Lessons
- Baby Sitters
- Dry Cleaning
- Housecleaners
- Car Washes
- Auto Detailers

A caveat: don't skip services to maintain your most valuable property (houses, vehicles) or to protect your health (dental checkups, physicals). Never go cheap on that which is most precious.

☐ 8.2.5 Hire Basic Services Only
Services love to add bells and whistles that line their pockets, but add little value for consumers. Decline extras and save.

- *Car Washes*. Have them wash the exterior, but forgo any undercoating, vacuuming, and detailing.

- *Barbers*. All you need is a haircut, so go without shampoos or special styling.

- *Lawn Services*. Have the service cut the grass, but decline its offers to spray and fertilize.

☐ 8.2.6 Practice Preventative Maintenance
In the long run, regular maintenance costs less than major repairs. Follow owner's manuals. Find additional advice for upkeep at chat rooms, forums, and discussion boards.

8.3 Run Background Checks

Whenever you hire a service, the most important task is to find someone honest and able. Dishonesty or shoddy workmanship inevitably costs more than whatever was saved by picking the cheapest option.

☐ 8.3.1 Look for Customer Feedback

- ☐ *Consider Your Own Experience*. If you hired someone in the past and liked the results, stick with who you know.

☐ *Seek Recommendations.* People you trust are the next best source of information. Ask for the gritty details. Here are some examples:

- *"Were you satisfied with the quality of work?"*

- *"Was the work completed on time?"*

- *"Were you satisfied with the level of communication?"*

- *"Was there a written contract?"*

- *"Was there a good overall working relationship?"*

- *"If there were any disputes, were they handled well?"*

- *"Were there any negotiations on rates or job pricing?"*

- *"Is there anything else I should know?"*

☐ *Read Internet Reviews.* Various websites provide—or purport to provide—unbiased customer feedback. Although your own experience or friends' advice works best, review sites work better than phonebooks. AngiesList.com boasts a large database that rates all kinds of services, but it charges a monthly fee for access. One frugal approach: join for one month only, research any services you might need for the next few years, and then cancel your subscription.

☐ *Visit the Better Business Bureau.* Before hiring anyone for the first time, check with the BBB. Avoid services that receive frequent complaints.

☐ *Check Out the Service's References.* Any service should be able to provide a list of satisfied customers. Call several and ask the same gritty questions listed above.

☐ **8.3.2 Hold Tryouts**

Audition services before you spend on a large scale. For example, attend a few spin classes before you hire the leader as your personal trainer. And retain a plumbing service for small repairs before you hire it for any major projects.

☐ 8.3.3 Review Samples of the Service's Work

Ask to see examples of workmanship. Many services maintain portfolios on DVDs or websites.

☐ 8.3.4 Review Qualifications

☐ *Consider the Time in Business.* Check how many years the service has been around. Dishonest or incompetent operators don't survive for long.

☐ *Look for Trade Memberships, Certifications, and Licenses.* Many trades regulate themselves by issuing proof of competency such as diplomas or certificates. Governments license a wide variety of vocations; visit your state's official website.

☐ *Know the Level of Specialization Required.* If your needs are straightforward, hire generalists. If they're complicated, hire specialists.

☐ *Know the Level of Experience Required.* For easier jobs, hire the young and eager who are in the early stages of their careers. For tougher tasks, favor those with greater experience.

☐ 8.3.5 Learn the Service's Policies

The more expensive the service, the more you should study its policies.

☐ *Review the Contract.* Read over the forms, including any warranties and guaranties. Favor services that provide greater protections.

☐ *Ask Who Performs the Actual Work.* Is it the owner or unlicensed underlings? If it's underlings, investigate their qualifications. After all, you have to live with the results of their work.

☐ *Watch for Unusual Fees.* Ask for a complete list upfront.

☐ 8.3.6 Weigh Your Own Time Costs

Don't become overly enamored with the research process. The less costly the service, the less time you should spend vetting it.

8.4 Find Low Rates

After you locate qualified services, find out which ones offer the lowest prices.

☐ **8.4.1 Shop Around**

☐ *Compare Prices on Your Shortlist of Prospective Services.* Ask for their hourly rates and also whether they impose any unusual fees, including surcharges for credit card payments (see 8.3.5).

☐ *Ask Friends.* Find out if they've hired a similar service and what they paid for it.

☐ *Seek Special Offers on Prices.* Some examples:

- *Introductory Rates.* Many services offer discounts to first–time customers.

- *Coupons.* Commonly used to promote oil changes, haircuts, and carpet cleanings.

- *Group Discounts.* AAA, AARP, and similar groups publish lists of services that offer member discounts. The checklist reminds you to review these before you hire.

- *Volume or Loyalty Discounts.* Such as discounted gift cards, point programs, and punch cards (buy nine haircuts and your tenth is FREE).

- *Form of Payment Discounts.* Pay cash if the discount exceeds the value of your card's rewards.

- *Deal–A–Day Websites.* Sign up for LivingSocial.com and Groupon.com.

☐ *Seek Deal Sweeteners on Terms other than Price.* Fee waivers, freebies, free estimates, etc.

☐ *Avoid High Overhead Operations.* The costs of fancy offices, new trucks, and big operations get passed on to customers. Favor providers with good reputations and modest infrastructures.

☐ 8.4.2 Haggle

☐ *"Can you match your competitor's rates?"* Show written proof of other offers.

☐ *"If I commit to use your service more often, would you lower your rate?"* Negotiate a volume discount.

☐ *"I know you have overhead, but can you get closer to the online rate?"* Bring printouts of website prices.

☐ 8.4.3 If Warranted, Seek Bids in Writing

Don't bother with bids for inexpensive tasks, but for larger projects, seek written offers.

☐ 8.4.4 Consider Online Services

Consumers have warmed to web–based stockbrokers, matchmakers, and travel agents. Check out these other online services.

- *Tax Advice.* Visit HRBlock.com or TurboTax.com.

- *Computer Repairs.* With remote access software, experts take control of your computer and fix any problems as you watch. Visit OnlineComputerRepair.com, ComputerGeeksOnline.net, AskPCExperts.com, or BoxAid.com.

- *Fitness Training.* Visit inerTrain.com.

- *Tutoring.* Real teachers help school kids at prices that undercut local learning centers. Visit Tutor.com, SkillsTutor.com, SmarThinking.com, TutorVista.com, or HomeworkHelp.com.

- *Piano Lessons.* Scale down this expense at ZebraKeys.com.

- *Expert Advice.* Precise information can help you decide whether to hire or DIY. Take a picture of your problem and post it along with your questions. Visit JustAnswer.com to receive online opinions from mechanics, doctors, plumbers, electricians, and others.

☐ 8.4.5 Consider Trainees, Students, and Responsible Teens

Many schools offer teacher–supervised services for less, including those for dental hygienists, barbers, and veterinarians. Submit your legal problem to a law school clinic. Scour the neighborhood for youngsters who walk pets or care for lawns.

☐ 8.4.6 Share Services With Others

Split the cost of babysitters with neighbors. Sign up with friends for golf lessons. Jointly hire personal trainers. Band together with others and negotiate volume discounts on tuxedo rentals. (Once again, it's Group Buynamics in action.)

☐ 8.4.7 Anticipate Emergency Hires

Emergencies can derail the best laid savings plans. If you wait until a crisis actually hits, you play Russian roulette with the prices. Plan ahead. For each foreseeable service you might need, find several candidates in case your first choice is unavailable in your hour of need. Copy this chart, fill it up with telephone numbers, and tape it to your fridge.

Service	Option 1	Option 2	Option 3
A/C and Furnace			
Appliances			
Computers			
Electrical			
Handyman			
Plumber			
Auto Body			
Auto Repair			
Dentist			
Doctor			
Baby Sitter			
Veterinarian			

☐ 8.4.8 Trade or Barter Services

Exchange your own expertise for someone else's: tax returns for brake jobs, prepared meals for housekeeping, kid watching for the same in return. Naturally, the IRS wants to get involved, and the tax complications are more than annoying. To dip your toe into the morass, download IRS Publication 525. Consult a tax advisor.

☐ **8.4.9 Insure**
You can buy all kinds of insurance to cover routine services, but usually you're better off creating an emergency fund for the inevitable small disasters. Insure for major risks only: health, home, auto, and, if you have dependents, your life.

- *Vision.* Instead of buying insurance, follow Chapter 35.

- *Dental.* Don't buy coverage; instead, use the dental care checklist (see Chapter 36).

- *Major Repairs.* For large appliances, buy reliable brands and self–insure for any breakdowns.

- *Legal Services Insurance Plans.* Unless your interaction with the law is constant, pay for lawyers as the need for them arises.

8.5 Avoid Pitfalls

☐ **8.5.1 Require a Physical Address**
Beware of local businesses that only list a P.O. Box—it's often a red flag for a sham operation. Before you hire, drive past headquarters and look for signs of a legitimate business: equipment, parking, foot traffic, etc. (In contrast, small online service providers commonly use P.O. boxes, and it's not a red flag if you see ample positive reviews.)

☐ **8.5.2 Never Hire Anyone Who Contacts You First**
Beware of anyone who knocks on your door. You decrease your chances of hiring a fraudster if you identify prospects based upon thorough background checks.

☐ **8.5.3 Avoid Quick Hiring Decisions**
Don't rush; adhere to the checklist.

☐ **8.5.4 Hire the Right Level of Specialization**
Generalists charge less. Hire specialists only for complex projects.

☐ **8.5.5 Hire the Right Level of Experience**
Hire experts for complex work; otherwise, hire the young and eager.

☐ **8.5.6 Avoid Unnecessary Hires**
Plan ahead to meet your true needs and seek second opinions.

☐ **8.5.7 Never Pay for Work That Isn't Performed**
Whenever possible, try to observe any work in progress.

☐ **8.5.8 Decline Oversells and Upsells**
Beware of project creep. Favor the original scope of work over spontaneous suggestions that increase your costs.

☐ **8.5.9 Read Contracts Before Signing Them**
Always read contracts before you sign. If you see unclear language, seek help from a trusted friend or advisor.

☐ **8.5.10 Never Use Debt to Fund Discretionary Services**
Don't pay interest on discretionary services. Do without or DIY.

☐ **8.5.11 Research all Recommendations**
Services often make referrals in exchange for kickbacks from those they recommend. Don't accept any referrals that you haven't run through the gauntlet of this checklist.

☐ **8.5.12 Beware of Deals "Too Good To Be True"**
Beware of extremely low offers. They're often red flags for fraud.

8.6 Follow Up

Minimize future hassles with these tactics.

☐ **8.6.1 Inspect Work**
Check the workmanship. If anything's amiss, have it made right.

☐ **8.6.2 Oversee Touch Ups**
Make sure the service performs any fixes to your liking.

☐ **8.6.3 Check for Math Errors**
Yes, you've hired someone smarter than a fifth grader, but check anyway. Make sure the correct rates and hours have been applied.

☐ 8.6.4 Monitor Sales Taxes

Most jurisdictions don't charge sales taxes on services, so they shouldn't appear on the bill.

☐ 8.6.5 Agree to the Form of Payment

Discuss whether discounts are available for payment in cash. If not, pay with plastic and reap the rewards.

☐ 8.6.6 Don't Pay Until You're Satisfied

Your best leverage for quality work is the final installment.

☐ 8.6.7 Build a Long–Term Relationship

If you're 100 percent satisfied, show your appreciation. Say thank you, offer to make recommendations, or, if appropriate, leave a tip.

☐ 8.6.8 Make the Work Last

Ask your service provider for advice about upkeep.

☐ 8.6.9 Retain Paperwork

Keep a file in case of future disputes. This information also helps if any friends ever need the same service.

☐ 8.6.10 Consider Possible Tax Impacts

Services with potential tax ramifications include auctioneers, movers, stockbrokers, real estate brokers, and tax preparers. Consult your tax advisor.

☐ 8.6.11 Keep Motivated With a "Checklist Savings Log"

Finally, each time you complete a hire, enter your savings into a "checklist savings log" that tracks your progress and reinforces your SL☒N! habit. After all, you've just stashed away money that most consumers would have willingly surrendered. It's time to celebrate with a modest use of metrics. For details about logs and other motivational tools, read Chapter 47.

* * *

You now have at your fingertips a frugal system for hiring miscellaneous services. For a condensed version that reduces all this into a few pages, see Appendix 2.

9

RECREATION:
GENERAL RECREATION

Recreational costs are discretionary. If your job disappeared tomorrow, they would be among the first line items to hit the chopping block. But even in good times, it makes sense to save. According to the 2011 CES, the average household spends $2,572 on this line item, so saving 20 percent frees up about $500. Consider these strategies.

9.1 Use the Products Buying Checklist

Whenever you buy equipment for recreation or entertainment, follow Appendix 1. Rent, flip, trade, borrow, or buy secondhand.

9.2 Apply Guidelines for Low Rent Rec

You don't have to spend big to have big fun. Whenever you pay for leisure, follow these frugal principles.

☐ **9.2.1 Analyze Your Hourly Cost**
When a three hour river rafting trip costs $90, you recreate at a rate of $30 per hour. When a six hour mountain hike costs $6 in gas, your rate plummets to $1 per hour. If you enjoy rafting 30 times more than hiking, then river trips provide a solid value. But if you enjoy both activities about the same, hike more and raft less.

☐ **9.2.2 Recreate Locally**
The fewer miles you travel to your entertainment, the less you incur in car depreciation and gasoline (see Chapters 38–39).

☐ **9.2.3 Disfavor Access Fees**
If the activity requires a user fee, avoid paying it (legally, of course) or switch to other activities that don't involve such charges.

☐ 9.2.4 Minimize Equipment
Less stuff means less spending.

☐ 9.2.5 Limit Injuries
Mishaps interfere with employment, increase medical costs, and limit your fun. If you frequently pay doctors to put you back together, try something more sedate.

☐ 9.2.6 Pick Activities With Tangible Benefits
Hike to improve your cardiovascular system, read to expand your mind, and volunteer to feed your soul.

9.3 Consider Lower Cost Alternatives

Audition cheaper recreation. You may find you actually prefer it for reasons other than savings. If you ski downhill, for instance, try cross–country skiing. Some advantages: no lift lines, fewer out–of–control skiers, closer parking, better aerobic exercise, and lower risks of injury. Best of all, day passes at Nordic centers cost $16 instead of the $95 that downhill areas charge. Check each activity below on which you're willing to experiment.

	Activity	$$$	$$	$	FREE!
☐	Sport Events	Pro	Semi–Pro	College	TV
☐	Live Theater	Tour company	College	High School	Job as usher
☐	Water Sports	Speedboat	Sailboat	Kayak, canoe	Swim
☐	Gourmet	Wine tasting	Beer festival	Chili cook–off	Samples
☐	Music	Concert	CD/download	Convert LPs	Radio
☐	Gambling	Casino	Lotto	Poker night	Websites
☐	Movies	Theater	Matinee	RedBox.com	Library
☐	Camping	Lake cabin	Motor home	Trailer	Tent
☐	Bowling	Ten–pin	Leagues	Candlepin	Bocce ball
☐	Kids in water	Water park	Public pool	Local beach	Sprinklers
☐	Theme Parks	Six Flags	State fair	County fair	Seesaws

9.4 Seek Discounts

☐ 9.4.1 Recreate Off–Peak
Avoid peak prices by avoiding peak crowds. Ski and golf on weekdays. Attend matinees.

☐ **9.4.2 Seek Group Discounts**

Join local clubs for your favorite activities and gain access to bargains galore. AAA and AARP members also enjoy many price breaks.

☐ **9.4.3 Clip Coupons**

Buy local entertainment coupon books. Search the internet for deals.

☐ **9.4.4 Go to College**

Local universities sponsor lectures, films, and recitals at rates that even students can afford.

☐ **9.4.5 Buy Recreation Gift Cards**

Your warehouse club sells them for 20 percent below face value.

☐ **9.4.6 Buy in Bulk**

Many venues discount volume purchases.

9.5 Choose Between PAYG and Flat Rates

The marketplace often presents you with a choice to either: (1) pay a flat rate charge; or (2) pay based upon your actual usage, also known as "pay as you go" (PAYG). When the decidedly unfrugal face this decision, they choose with little forethought. Frugal fringers, on the other hand, weigh the pros and cons carefully (obsessively, even). Follow this cheat sheet to find the best values.

☐ **9.5.1 For Heavy Use, Pay the Flat Rate**

If you're an avid concertgoer or sports fan, buy season tickets instead of tickets to individual events.

☐ **9.5.2 For Light Use, Pick PAYG**

PAYG is the best choice if you partake on rare occasions only.

☐ **9.5.3 For Medium Use, Cut Back and Select PAYG**

If your participation falls in a gray area between heavy and light use, it presents you with a valuable savings opportunity. Obviously, this activity isn't a major passion. Otherwise, you'd do it more often. So cut back a little. Some examples:

- *Golf Club Memberships.* Replace them with this blend: (1) practice greens and chipping areas (FREE); (2) driving ranges (cheap); (3) disc golf (FREE); (4) hikes with backpacks instead of golf bags (FREE); and (5) PAYG golf at quality courses with low greens fees (cheap).

- *Annual Ski Passes.* Get your outdoor winter fix from several sources: (1) backcountry skiing (FREE); (2) cross–country ski centers (cheap); (3) outdoor rinks (cheap); (4) pond hockey (FREE); (5) snowshoeing (FREE); and (6) PAYG downhill with discounted day passes (cheap).

- *Season Tickets to Pro Sports.* If you plow mega dollars into the local franchise, hire substitutes instead: (1) watch the sport at lower levels (minor leagues, development leagues, colleges); (2) support less popular sports (professional lacrosse, soccer, arena football); (3) follow your team on TV or radio; (4) play the game yourself; and (5) buy bleacher seats to single games.

9. 6 Consider Recreation/Entertainment for Profit

Pick activities that cut household expenses or produce extra income.

☐ 9.6.1 Trade Collectibles
Buy low and sell high: antiques, baseball cards, stamps, vinyl records, stamps, coins, first editions, and prints.

☐ 9.6.2 Investigate Investments
Learn to invest and save on brokers and financial advisors.

☐ 9.6.3 Become a Guide
If you love to kayak, fish, or hunt, turn your avocation into a part–time vocation.

☐ 9.6.4 Grow a Garden
Shrink your waistline along with your food bill.

☐ 9.6.5 Give Lessons
Offer your expertise to local health clubs (yoga, aerobics, spinning) or community colleges (business law, musical instruments).

☐ 9.6.6 Tinker for Pay
If you like motors, pursue a sideline in small engine repair.

☐ **9.6.7 Get Crafty**
Sell your works at artisan co–op stores or Etsy.com.

☐ **9.6.8 Picture Yourself Making a Profit**
If you enjoy photography, line up gigs at weddings and other events. Sell nature photographs online or at gift shops.

☐ **9.6.9 Make Beautiful Music**
If you're a performer, moonlight at clubs and coffeehouses.

☐ **9.6.10 Trade Work for Play**
Greens fees add up, so serve as a course marshal for minimum wages plus FREE rounds. The same approach works for museums (guide), musicals (usher), bowling alleys (lane attendant), ball parks (beer vendor), and ski areas (patrol member).

☐ **9.6.11 *Spend Less Now!***
Frugality delivers great deals on products, services, and monthly bills. That's enough to brighten anyone's day. And when it's all said and done, isn't that exactly what you want from a hobby?

10

RECREATION:
HEALTH CLUBS

With regular workouts, you stay fit and control medical bills. Because of this, gyms provide a healthy value. But that doesn't mean you can't also trim some fat here.

10.1 Avoid Monthly Dues

Health clubs present a big savings opportunity because the average membership costs about $500 per year. Cobble together several alternatives, and you can dodge this monthly hit to your finances.

☐ **10.1.1 Rent Apartments With Gyms Attached**
Many apartment complexes include workout rooms. Live there and skip the club membership. If your current place lacks a gym, band together with other tenants and ask the manager to fill a spare room with cardio machines and free weights. If your landlord oversees other properties, ask if any of them have fitness centers you might use.

☐ **10.1.2 Outfit Home Gyms**
For cardio exercise, hunt for used Nordic Track ski machines, which burn calories fast because they work both the lower and upper body. Find them online or at garage sales for about $25. For strength training, look for used dumbbells and benches. Parents offload this excess weight as soon as the kids leave home.

☐ **10.1.3 Outfit Ultra–Portable Gyms**
If you lack room for cardio and dumbbells, use Appendix 1 to run the $200 TRX suspension trainer through its paces. The TRX has received rave reviews, but beware of secondhand equipment because the manufacturer has recalled two early models. For details, visit TRXTraining.com.

☐ **10.1.4 Substitute DVDs for Classes**
Borrow workout videos from friends or libraries. These provide cheaper motivation than classes.

☐ **10.1.5 Visit Friends With Home Gyms**
Workouts with partners deliver better results. So you don't overburden anyone, visit several different buddies each week.

☐ **10.1.6 Exercise Outdoors**
In winter, snowshoe, skate, or ski. In other seasons, walk, hike, jog, kayak, rollerblade, or bike.

☐ **10.1.7 Visit Parks**
Many parks feature Par Courses, Fit–Trails, or Vita Courses. These provide stations for pull ups, pushups, crunches, and the like. Look also for outdoor basketball courts, tennis courts, bike trails, rinks, and nature trails.

☐ **10.1.8 Switch to PAYG**
Drop the gym membership, but visit occasionally at the daily rate.

10.2 Slash Monthly Dues

If you still want to belong to a club, consider these tactics.

☐ **10.2.1 Join Public Rec Centers and YMCAs**
They cost less than private gyms and often provide better facilities.

☐ **10.2.2 Join at Local Campuses**
Perspire for less at college health centers.

☐ **10.2.3 Join Smaller Clubs**
If you don't swim or play tennis, you don't need pools or tennis courts. Join a studio club (Curves or Snap Fitness).

☐ **10.2.4 Buy Limited Memberships**
Some clubs offer lower rates if you exercise at off–peak hours or agree to stay off the tennis courts.

☐ **10.2.5 Search for Special Offers**
Clubs run frequent specials. Visit their websites.

☐ 10.2.6 Seek Reimbursements

Your health insurer or employer might pay part of your club dues in order to contain its health care costs.

☐ 10.2.7 Seek Member Discounts

Check for discounts at the websites of any groups to which you belong. This includes warehouse clubs. As I wrote this, Costco featured a two–year certificate to a national chain of fitness centers for only $350.

☐ 10.2.8 Shop at Month's End

At many clubs, the sales force must meet quotas. You get better deals if you join late in the month.

☐ 10.2.9 Ask for Price Matching

Club A charges lower dues, but club B is closer to home so you would prefer to join there. Ask club B to match club A's price.

10.3 Beware the Contract

Health clubs are notorious for one–sided contracts that work you over before you ever start working out. Bad agreements are costly, so take precautions.

☐ 10.3.1 Try Before You Buy

If you join a club you hate, you'll waste money because you'll never visit. Ask for a trial membership.

☐ 10.3.2 Read Before Signing

Never rely on what a salesperson tells you. The written words trump any oral promises.

☐ 10.3.3 Skip Enrollment Fees and Pre–Pays

Ask the club to waive these charges. To document the waiver, cross out any mention of the fees or prepays, enter your initials near the cross–out, and write in "WAIVED BY CLUB" before you sign.

☐ 10.3.4 Know the Length of Membership and Renewal Terms

Does the contract bind you for a full year or for even longer? When your initial term expires, do you switch to a month–to–month membership or do you automatically renew for a full year?

☐ 10.3.5 Know Your Cancellation Rights (Under Contract)

Does the agreement discuss whether you can cancel if you lose your job, suffer an injury, travel abroad, or move away?

☐ 10.3.6 Know Your Cancellation Rights (Under Statute)

The laws of many states guarantee the right to cancel within a few days after you sign a health club contract. To see whether your state grants this remedy, run this internet search: "health club cancellation rights [enter your state here]."

☐ 10.3.7 Retain a Copy

Useful in any later disputes, especially if the contract contains handwritten changes.

11

RECREATION:
PETS

Pets enrich our lives, and they also enrich breeders, kibble makers, and, most expensively, veterinarians. I've shepherded two geriatric cats through their final months, and I know firsthand the staggering costs. It's hard to go cheap when a friend of many years puts up a good fight and a chance exists for more time. Believe it or not, I've opened the wallet wide and paid out thousands. When such strong emotions drive my spending, I say "ouch," and try to make it back elsewhere (perhaps recovering from the veterinarian by becoming more of a vegetarian, see 37.7.8).

11.1 Consider Lower Priced Alternatives

☐ **11.1.1 Buy Animatronics**
For options, visit the "Toys and Games" department at Amazon, look under "Electronics for Kids," and click "Electronic Pets."

☐ **11.1.2 Go Micro: Habitats**
Ant farms, sea monkeys, butterflies, lady bugs, praying mantises, frogs, and earthworms all make great starters for young pet seekers. Visit "Toys and Games" at Amazon, look under "Learning & Education Toys," and under that click "Habitats."

☐ **11.1.3 Go Small: Aquariums**
Fish and fish food cost less than dogs and dog food.

☐ **11.1.4 Go Rodents!**
Hamsters, gerbils, and hedgehogs make good pets if they stay in their containers. Escapes become major adventures.

☐ **11.1.5 Play Chicken**
Chickens produce fresh eggs, which saves you scratch as they peck and scratch. Visit BackYardChickens.com or UrbanChickens.org.

□ 11.1.6 Join Slytherin

Trade fur for scales. Snakes and small reptiles hang out in their terrariums for much less than dogs or cats hang out in your house.

□ 11.1.7 I Know Why the Caged Birds Sing

Because they're so cheep! Adopt finches, canaries, or parakeets.

11.2 Borrow Your Pets

□ 11.2.1 Visit

Satisfy your family's pet cravings with visits to zoos, butterfly pavilions, and aquariums. Attend dog shows and county fairs. Send kids out to play with neighborhood dogs.

□ 11.2.2 Install Feeders

Attract hummingbirds, robins, sparrows, and, inevitably, squirrels. Indoctrinate youngsters: because they roam freely, these wild pals are much cooler than dogs or cats.

□ 11.2.3 Go Bird Watching

If birds bypass your family roost, roust everyone out to see the birds.

□ 11.2.4 Take Part Time Jobs

Older kids get their pet fix when they walk dogs, clerk at pet stores, assist in veterinary offices, or work at kennels.

□ 11.2.5 Volunteer

Help at animal shelters or zoos. Who needs pets when you hang out with lions, tigers, and bears?

□ 11.2.6 Furnish a Foster Home

You shelter abandoned pets pending their placement elsewhere. Beware: fostering often leads to adopting.

□ 11.2.7 Pet Sit for Friends

If you like someone's dog or cat, care for it when the owner travels.

□ 11.2.8 Train Service Dogs

Train a puppy to become a service animal. Typically, this takes 12 to 20 months. As you help those in need, you sidestep all kinds of end of life medical issues (the most expensive and emotional aspects of pet ownership). Visit AssistanceDogsInternational.org.

11.3 Follow the Products Buying Checklist

For pets and supplies, follow the system in Appendix 1 and these additional tips.

☐ **11.3.1 Get Sheltered Pets**
Breeders charge. Many shelters offer free pet days.

☐ **11.3.2 Visit Online Pharmacies**
If your veterinarian uses its in–house pharmacy as a profit center, flee to the lower prices at 1-800-PetMeds.com, PetCareRx.com, or DiscountPetMedicines.com.

☐ **11.3.3 Shop at Discount Stores**
At Walmart and Target, generic dog and cat medicines sell for $4.

11.4 Follow the Miscellaneous Services Checklist

Follow the strategies in Appendix 2 and these added ideas.

☐ **11.4.1 Use OTC Remedies**
Bypass vet visits with medicines for heartworms, ticks, and fleas.

☐ **11.4.2 Hire Young Entrepreneurs**
Neighborhood kids usually undercut the rates adult providers charge to walk dogs and pet sit.

☐ **11.4.3 Visit Animal Shelters**
Many provide discounted vaccinations and reproductive fixes.

☐ **11.4.4 Skip Pet Insurance**
Consumer Reports concludes that most pet owners come out ahead if they skip this coverage. Run the numbers for yourself. Visit ConsumerSearch.com/pet-insurance to see the top–rated plans.

12

RECREATION:
BOOKS AND MAGAZINES

According to the CES, the average household spends $115 per year on reading materials. Why bother with a checklist for such a smalltime expense? Because reading remains one of the cheapest forms of entertainment ever. If you borrow a great book from the library, read it, and talk it over with friends, you've spent dozens of hours and enriched your life for a total cost of *zero*. Repeat this process 30 times per year and you're left with precious few hours for malls and restaurants. No wonder so many fringers are avid readers.

12.1 Read Books for FREE

☐ **12.1.1 Borrow Hard Copies**
Visit friends or the library.

☐ **12.1.2 Borrow E–Books**
Visit your library's website to see whether it lends over the internet. Borrow e–books at eBookFling.com, which takes advantage of Kindle and Nook's FREE two–week loan policies. Since titles are delivered by email, you avoid all postage costs. Similar sites: BookLending.com and LendInk.com.

☐ **12.1.3 Download E–Books**
Books published before 1923 reside in the public domain and can be downloaded for FREE. Visit Gutenberg.org. A great site for Kindle formatted books is ManyBooks.net, which offers FREE titles that otherwise might cost $0.99 or more on Amazon. Search online for "best sites to download free [enter your e–book format here] books."

☐ **12.1.4 Consult Reliable Websites**
Locate information for FREE online.

☐ 12.1.5 Read Books That Travel

My library supports BookCrossing.com, in which you take home one of the program's clearly–labeled paperbacks, read it, and then leave it in a coffee shop or other public space for someone else to enjoy. You can even enter the book's i.d. number at the website and track its journey around the world.

☐ 12.1.6 Swap and Trade

Trade with friends and try PaperBackSwap.com, which offers about five million paperbacks, hardbacks, and audio books. The site is easy to use: register and list at least ten books. In exchange, you receive two credits good for ordering books from other members. When someone orders a book from you, mail it via media mail—this costs as little as $2.41—and receive another credit. Similar sites: BookMooch.com and TitleTrader.com.

☐ 12.1.7 Download Audio Books

Download MP3 files of public domain books at LibriVox.org, OpenCulture.com, or LiteralSystems.org.

☐ 12.1.8 Browse FREE Book Bins

Find them at thrift shops and used book shops.

☐ 12.1.9 Seek Books as Gifts

Request bookstore gift cards as presents for holidays and birthdays.

12.2 Buy Used Books

☐ 12.2.1 Buy Online

Popular online stores for used books include Amazon Marketplace, eBay.com, Alibris.com, AbeBooks.com, and Biblio.com. To find more stores, search the "best sites for used books" or for the author and title of any book you seek.

☐ 12.2.2 Shop at Used Book Stores

Browse secondhand shops for cheap and fun entertainment.

☐ 12.2.3 Attend Used Book Sales

Many service groups host annual book sales. Find dates and locations at BookSaleFinder.com or BookSaleManager.com.

☐ **12.2.4 Flip**
Resell, swap, or donate your books for a tax deduction.

12.3 Read Magazines for FREE

There are many ways to peruse magazines without committing the deplorable act of actually paying for them.

☐ **12.3.1 Read at the Library**
The periodicals department offers a wide variety of current issues.

☐ **12.3.2 Read Online**
More than 8,000 magazines host websites. Look online for your favorites and see how much content they post. If liberality prevails, cancel your subscription and read for FREE. (Don't worry that you might sink magazines with this tactic. Most of their revenue comes from advertising, and you see plenty of that on the websites.)

☐ **12.3.3 Visit Google Books**
Books.Google.com offers a large database of magazines, including the full run of *Life*. Search for your favorite places, movie stars, or sports teams. Browse old advertisements. Other archived titles include *New York Magazine*, *Men's Health*, and *Kiplinger's*.

☐ **12.3.4 Borrow**
Libraries often lend older issues for at–home reading. So do friends.

☐ **12.3.5 Browse Recycle Bins**
Find recent issues at your neighborhood recycling center.

☐ **12.3.6 Sign Up for FREE Copies**
Some publishers offer trial subscriptions at no cost.

☐ **12.3.7 Convert Miles to Magazines**
If you're down to a precious few frequent flyer miles, redeem them for subscriptions before they expire. Visit MagsForMiles.com.

☐ **12.3.8 Seek Subscriptions as Gifts**
If hints are palatable among your gift givers, suggest your favorite magazines.

12.4 Read Magazines for Less

□ **12.4.1 Cancel Unread Subscriptions**
If you don't read them, cancel now and pocket the partial refund.

□ **12.4.2 Buy Used**
Acquire recent copies at thrift shops and garage sales.

□ **12.4.3 Share Subscriptions**
You agree to get *The Economist*. She agrees to get *The New Yorker*. Every other week, you meet to discuss issues and trade them.

□ **12.4.4 Shop Around**
The cheapest subscriptions often come from online vendors. Visit Amazon.com/Magazines, Subscription.com, and Magazines.com.

□ **12.4.5 Look for Coupons and Discount Codes**
A sample internet search: "coupons or discount codes *People*."

□ **12.4.6 Subscribe to the Internet or E–Book Version**
Digital content sells for less because there's no paper or postage.

□ **12.4.7 Buy Multi–Year Subscriptions**
For established publications only; start–ups can become belly–ups.

□ **12.4.8 Stay a New Subscriber Forever**
Instead of renewing, let subscriptions lapse and re–subscribe later at low introductory rates. If you miss any issues, catch up at the library.

□ **12.4.9 Never Buy Single Copies**
Always carry reading material. If you're at the airport, look for abandoned copies on seats and in recycle bins.

□ **12.4.10 Seek Group Rates**
Take advantage of lower rates for students, seniors, and other groups.

□ **12.4.11 Buy the DVDs**
Many publishers sell their entire stock of back issues on searchable DVDs, including *National Geographic*, *Mad Magazine*, *The New Yorker*, and *Rolling Stone*. Buy the DVDs used on eBay and get a lifetime of content for pennies an issue.

13

RECREATION:
DINING OUT

Without question, Americans love restaurants. According to the 2011 CES, the average household paid $2,620 for food consumed away from home. For *SL⊠N!*'s purposes, however, the real question is how much do you scarf down? To figure that out, you need to cook up your own statistics.

If you use credit cards to pay for all your dining, then you can look at your online statements. A year's worth of data is optimal, but even a single month gives a good snapshot. If your credit card records are incomplete, track your dining expenses for the next 30 days. Every time you visit a coffee shop, fast food joint, or corner deli, pocket the receipt—it's your record of where you ate and how much you paid. When the bill is split with friends, jot down your share on the receipt or leave yourself a voice mail. For a realistic baseline, spend in line with your current habits.

Once you collect the dining data, chart the facts. How often do you dine out? How many breakfasts, lunches, dinners, snacks, and coffee runs? Whose meals do you pay for? How much is your yearly burn rate? (If you only have one month's data, multiply by 12 for a rough estimate.) In addition, list your main reason for each meal: (1) socializing; (2) convenience (time constraints, failure to plan, too late to cook); (3) hunger; (4) tasty food hard to duplicate at home (sushi, Thai, exotic presentations); (5) entertainment (live music, people watching, TV sports); (6) atmosphere; (7) service (pampering, hospitality); (8) celebration; (9) habit (the usual hangouts); (10) novelty; and (11) any other reason.

As an example of a working chart, here's one for the decidedly unfrugal Jane Dough.

Jane Dough
April Dining Out

No.	Where	Who	Amount	Reason
1	McDonald's	Family	$ 27.12	Hungry
2	Deli	Me	$ 8.97	Convenience
3	Applebee's	2 of us	$ 42.98	Date night
4	Deli	Me	$ 7.97	Convenience
5	King Leo's	Family	$ 72.36	Tasty food
6	Bob's BBQ	Family	$ 61.15	Tasty food
7	Morton's	2 of us	$ 101.56	Celebrate raise
8	Subway	Me	$ 6.17	Convenience
9	Deli	Spouse	$ 7.39	Convenience
10	Starbucks	Spouse	$ 6.24	Caffeine habit
11	Wendy's	Me	$ 5.39	Convenience
12	Pizza	Family	$ 35.10	Entertainment
13	Anthony's	Spouse	$ 4.89	Convenience
14	Deli	Spouse	$ 7.57	Socializing
15	McDonald's	Spouse	$ 4.97	Hungry
16	McDonald's	Me	$ 4.29	Hungry
17	Bill's Tavern	2 of us	$ 34.02	Entertainment
18	Bob's BBQ	Earl & I	$ 25.00	Socializing
19	Deli	Me	$ 8.12	Convenience
20	McDonald's	Kids	$ 15.80	Convenience
21	Deli	Me	$ 7.50	Convenience
22	Diner	Family	$ 62.30	Entertainment
			$ 596.86	

Jane's chart reports April dining of almost $600, and this suggests an annual burn rate of about $7,200. Let's just say that, once again, Jane has ample room for improvement. But back to you. Once you make your own chart, use the data in two ways. First, seek to understand your reasons for dining out and use that knowledge to reduce restaurant visits. Second, when you do venture out for a meal, adopt new habits that cut costs. A portable checklist that summarizes both strategies appears in Appendix 3.

13.1 Reduce Restaurant Visits

If you visit restaurants four or more times per week—in other words, if you're a typical American diner—substitute some of your meals out with meals in. Here's a modest example. A chicken dish at a casual restaurant chain comes with rice, sautéed veggies, and costs about $12. Add alcohol and your cost bumps up to $17. But there's more. You need to leave a 20 percent tip for your server—don't go cheap on someone else who works for a living—so this adds $3.40. In addition, the tax man insists on his due: 8.5 percent on $17 is another $1.44. This brings your total bill to $21.84—but, hey, at least it tastes like chicken. In contrast, the same meal at home costs you only $2.63: $0.89 for a half pound chicken breast, $0.15 for a scoop of rice, $0.59 per serving of vegetables, and $1.00 for a beer from the fridge. By the way, you don't tip at home and, in many places, you don't pay sales taxes on groceries. Cook at home one time, and you save $19.21. Skip the weekly meal for a full year and you save about $1,000, or $2,000 if you pay for two diners.

As you salivate over these savings, look at your data. For each meal, focus on the main reason you visited the restaurant. Several good alternatives can meet your needs for much less.

☐ 13.1.1 Socialize Elsewhere
Economize with takeout, delivered pizza, pot lucks, dinner parties, or progressive dinners (one course consumed at each home). Gather your after–work crowd at happy hours and coffee shops. Did you dine out on work days so you could hang out with friends? It's just as pleasant to meet them at the park for a brownbag lunch. Or socialize without restaurants. Join book clubs or schedule friends for at–home workouts (see 10.1.5).

☐ 13.1.2 Switch to Other Conveniences
Bulk cook on weekends so that during the week you can plunk leftovers into the microwave. The BBQ is great for this—it's lit anyway, so you might as well grill a few extra chicken thighs for later feasting. Another idea: in the morning, throw a few ingredients into a slow cooker so that a fragrant home cooked meal awaits your return. It's like living with your parents again, only your mom

doesn't yell at you to make your bed. Do you buy sandwiches on workdays in order to save time? Instead, make a sandwich in the morning—it's quicker than standing in line for one at a crowded deli. Forget to pack lunch? Buy yogurt and fruit at a downtown convenience store. Although it costs more than a home-packed meal, it's still cheaper than a full-priced sandwich.

☐ 13.1.3 Try New Hunger Games
Did you eat fast food because you were starving? A better choice for wallet and waistline: food caches. In your car or purse, stash some energy bars. These tide you over without nearly as much damage—fiscal or physical. At work, convert a spare desk drawer into a pantry. Stock it with apples, soup, tuna—you get the idea.

☐ 13.1.4 Consider New Paths to Specialized Cuisines
Learn to cook your favorite cuisines with cookbooks from the library or online recipes. For esoteric dishes, try pre-packaged products (your grocer sells $2 stir-fry kits that are ready in 15 minutes). If home preparation falls short of the restaurant original, you still can save by choosing takeout instead of a sit down meal.

☐ 13.1.5 Create Atmosphere Elsewhere
For upscale ambience at home, light candles and turn on the stereo.

☐ 13.1.6 Pamper for Less
Trade chef services with other household members. You can also cook large batches so that you labor once only, but receive several meals in return. Visit your grocer's deli counter for takeaway ribs, meatloaf, and salads. Visit your warehouse club for ready-to-eat rotisserie chickens, which somehow cost less than uncooked fryers.

☐ 13.1.7 Ditch the Dining Habit
Are you a restaurant rat? Discover a new habitat. For date nights, download popular recipes and cook at home. Visit Epicurious.com.

☐ 13.1.8 Seek Newer Novelties
Do you like to visit new places? Mix up locales for less by using your formal dining room. Set up a table in the backyard. Host a picnic at a nearby park.

The above tactics reappear in Appendix 3, which takes two distinct approaches. The first approach organizes tactics according to your primary reason(s) for dining out. The second approach lists the leading alternatives to restaurants. Whichever framework works best for you, use it whenever you feel the urge to splurge for meals away from home.

13.2 Spend Less at Restaurants

Sometimes, even the most saintly fringer yields to temptation and dines out. Whenever this happens to you, choose from among these *a la carte* options.

☐ 13.2.1 Match Eateries to Occasions

Dinners at nice places create special memories. However, you should go big only on truly big (and rare) occasions. Frequent fine dining is nothing but a habit, and a costly one. If you suffer from this expensive routine, give yourself a break from the nicest restaurants for a few weeks to gauge how often you really need to see cloth table linens. You may find that you can switch to more casual places without major sacrifice.

☐ 13.2.2 Choose Value Alternatives

You don't have to downshift to less–than–fine greasy spoons. Instead, pick restaurants that offer good quality at value prices. For example, P.F. Chang's China Bistro provides great food in upscale dining rooms, but it also operates a similar no frills chain: Pei Wei Asian Diner. Pei Wei offers many of P.F. Chang's dishes, but at lower prices. Is it only a coincidence that Pei Wei is pronounced "pay way," as in "pay way less?"

☐ 13.2.3 Help Kids Eat Free

For listings of local restaurants that offer FREE kids' meals, visit MyKidsEatFree.com.

☐ 13.2.4 Visit Restaurants Without Waiters

You can have as much fun at limited service restaurants that don't require tipping, among them: Whole Foods, Corner Bakery Cafe, Au Bon Pain, Qdoba Mexican Grill, and Wahoo's Fish House. This saves you 15–20 percent on every visit.

☐ 13.2.5 Look for "Special Offers"

If you owned a restaurant, how would you retain high–paying customers and still attract cheapskates to fill the open seats? The options are many. Frugal diners know them and eat for less.

- *Off–peak Dining.* Some restaurants charge less for late lunches, early dinners, or midweek meals. Find the discounts and enjoy your prime rib during off–prime hours.

- *Discounted Gift Certificates.* Buy them at warehouse clubs, Restaurant.com, PlasticJungle.com, GiftCardGranny.com, and GiftCardRescue.com.

- *Coupons, Daily–Deal Sites, and Entertainment Books.* Find dining deals at Groupon.com and LivingSocial.com. In most metro areas you can buy entertainment books loaded with restaurant deals. Keep one in your car.

- *Senior and Student Discounts.* If you fall into these favored groups, patronize places that bestow discounts.

- *Memberships.* For each of your groups, keep lists of discounted eateries in your car.

- *Frequent Diner Rewards.* Discover places that reward loyalty and register as a frequent diner.

☐ 13.2.6 Skip Items

Lower your bill by declining the typical extras: appetizers, soups, salads, sides, drinks, and desserts.

☐ 13.2.7 Eat Bread to Save Bread

It's easier to skip items with a FREE basket of rolls. Ask for refills.

☐ 13.2.8 Share Dishes

Many restaurants charge "plating fees" to discourage shared dishes. When you come across such places of parsimony, tell them "no thanks, the only one here who gets to be parsimonious is *me*" and take your business elsewhere. Another sharing idea: look for restaurants that serve "family style," where groups eat for less.

☐ **13.2.9 Eat Appetizers Only**
If the restaurant serves oversized appetizers, order one as a meal.

☐ **13.2.10 Eat at the Bar**
Some places offer smaller meals at the bar for less.

☐ **13.2.11 Use Doggie Bags**
Order big servings and box up the remainders for a second meal.

☐ **13.2.12 Know Your Plastic Rewards**
Math question: if one of your cards offers three percent cash back for restaurants and another offers one percent, which should you use?

☐ **13.2.13 Limit Sales Taxes**
In many metro areas, rates vary widely. Dining in cheaper tax districts saves you 1–5 percent (see 20.1.2).

☐ **13.2.14 Compute a Fair Tip**
One small savings point: tip only on the meal's pre–tax value. Also, when using a coupon or other discount, tip on the amount the meal would have cost had you paid full price. This is fair to your waiter. Don't make others subsidize your personal quest to spend less.

* * *

A summary of these tactics appears in Appendix 3. If you like, make a copy and take it with you.

14

RECREATION:
DRINKS OUT

The mark–ups on beer, wine, and liquor at bars are enough to sober up anyone. A typical $1 bottle of domestic ale costs $4, and a $2 glass of wine fetches $8. And that's before you tip. Consumer news flash: whenever you buy drinks out, you're getting soaked and heavily so. Pour over these strategies before you hit the bars.

14.1 Drink Out Less

☐ 14.1.1 Stay Away From Bars
Socialize at less expensive venues: coffee shops, museums on free days, high school sporting events, etc.

☐ 14.1.2 Drink After Work at Work
In *Boston Legal*, every episode ended with Messrs. Shatner and Spader enjoying their after work drinks at the office. Those guys were savvy savers. *If permitted*, hoist the Friday libations at work.

☐ 14.1.3 Drink at Home
Invite friends over for pizza and beers. Split the costs.

☐ 14.1.4 Carry Flasks
The trusty flask hasn't gone the way of raccoon coats and flivvers. But don't be a bad cheapskate who sneaks pours at bars. Do, however, tell friends to meet you somewhere for sodas with supplements—and it's your treat.

☐ 14.1.5 Drink Sodas Only
Just because you're at a bar doesn't mean you must have alcohol. Drink cokes instead. Your cost for a couple of hours, with tips, drops from $10–$20 to $4–$5.

☐ **14.1.6 Pursue Better Drinking through Nursing**
Drink slow. Take one sip of alcohol and then one sip of water.

☐ **14.1.7 Place Limits**
If you can give yourself hard–line rules and follow them faithfully, commit never to consume more than one drink per night.

14.2 Shop Around

There's beer pong, there's quarters, and then there's the pauper of drinking games—finding the best deals on alcohol.

☐ **14.2.1 Visit Happy Hours**
Save 50 percent or more at happy hours. To find them in your neighborhood, visit Happy-Hour.com or DailyHappyHour.com.

☐ **14.2.2 Find Discount Bars**
If bar banners promote $2 draws, meet buddies there instead of places that sell the same beer for $4.

☐ **14.2.3 Tour Breweries and Wineries**
And try the FREE samples.

☐ **14.2.4 Clip Coupons**
Buy a local entertainment coupon book and use it. Check the internet for deals before you head out the door.

☐ **14.2.5 Order Specials**
Monday it's Guinness, Tuesday it's Coors. Make it a habit: always ask "what's on special?"

☐ **14.2.6 Call in Relief Pitchers**
Beer by the pitcher costs less than individual glasses.

☐ **14.2.7 Go Small**
Order twelve ounces instead of full pints.

☐ **14.2.8 Try Samplers**
If you're about to imbibe in something new, ask for a sample first.

☐ **14.2.9 Hunt Down Promos**
Certain bars always seem to host liquor companies that dispense hats, tee–shirts and other freebies. Search their websites for events.

14.3 Avoid Driving While Influenced

A drunk driving charge hits the pocketbook hard, with tow trucks, impoundments, attorneys, fines, and auto premium hikes. You also risk injury to yourself and others. It's easy to keep the possible consequences in mind as you read this, but it's difficult after three drinks. Resolve never get into the driver's seat if you've had more than one. Keep your resolution by having a solid exit strategy in place before you ever enter the bar.

☐ **14.3.1 Drink Locally**
Pick bars within easy walking distance of where you live.

☐ **14.3.2 Designate a Driver**
Drink with a trusted teetotaler who can get you home safely.

☐ **14.3.3 Take a Cab**
Know in advance which nearby hotels have cabstands; program your cell with phone numbers for taxis. Consider the on–demand car service Uber.com (see 44.1.4).

☐ **14.3.4 Know Bus and Subway Schedules**
Public transportation is better than the drunk tank.

☐ **14.3.5 Accept Ride Vouchers**
In many cities, innovative programs offer FREE rides on the big drinking nights: New Year's Eve, St. Patrick's Day, July Fourth, and Halloween.

☐ **14.3.6 Invest in Alcohol Breath Analyzers**
A recent search for these on Amazon yielded 174 results. When shopping, follow the system in Appendix 1.

☐ **14.3.7 Get a Room**
Hotels are expensive, but they cost much less than a charge of drunk driving. To save on lodging, see Chapter 16.

15

TRAVEL:
AIRFARES

Once upon a time, flying was fun. Not so much lately, especially with security hassles, crowded flights, and fee–crazed airlines. Whenever airports beckon, don't wing it—save with these strategies.

15.1 Don't Buy Airline Tickets

☐ **15.1.1 Redeem Miles**
From airline loyalty programs or reward cards (see Chapter 49).

☐ **15.1.2 Take Stay–Cations**
For your next break, remain home. Visit your library and check out local travel guides. Make lists of places and activities.

☐ **15.1.3 Take Road Trips**
The interstate provides a speedy conduit. You paid the taxes, so reap the benefits. Visit CostToDrive.com, where you can compare the cost of flying to the cost of driving your particular make and model.

☐ **15.1.4 Travel by Bus or Train**
There's ample legroom. Wi–Fi is FREE. You don't have to turn off electronic devices. The vibe soars high above the mood at the airport. And the tickets cost much less. Bus fares from New York City to Washington, D.C. currently average $19 (visit BoltBus.com).

15.2 Stay Flexible

☐ **15.2.1 Travel at the Right Time of Year**
Fly in the opposite direction of the migrating flock and save.

☐ **15.2.2 Travel at the Right Time of Week**
Some airlines impose surcharges for flying on popular travel days. You save if you're flexible enough to travel at other times. Rule of thumb: the cheapest days to fly are Tuesdays, Wednesdays, and

Saturdays. Exceptions exist, so when you shop for tickets, study fares closely.

☐ 15.2.3 Travel Late at Night
Book "redeye" flights that leave late at night and arrive early next morning. If you possess the rare ability to sleep on planes, you can reward yourself with huge savings.

☐ 15.2.4 Sign Up for Fare Alerts
Apply for these at travel sites and receive notice of the latest deals via email, Facebook, or Twitter.

☐ 15.2.5 Increase Layovers
Direct flights usually cost more. If you have time to spare, schedule one or more connections.

☐ 15.2.6 Land at Nearby Airports
Check for lower fares at less popular airfields.

☐ 15.2.7 Travel to the Deals
Let the market tell you where to vacation and journey to where the bargains bloom.

☐ 15.2.8 Seek Overbooked Flights
Gate personnel dangle lucrative payoffs to volunteers who agree to give up their seats and fly later. Some flexible travelers deliberately book themselves onto crowded flights and hope to get bumped. If you're interested in this, search the web for "how to find overbooked flights."

15.3 Shop Around

☐ 15.3.1 Shop Early
The longer you shop, the more likely you find low fares. Start early and keep notes.

☐ 15.3.2 Shop Midweek
Recent reports claim that the price of airfares dip to their lowest point on Tuesday afternoons. But by the time you read this, Wednesday mornings might be better. So ask the internet oracle this

question: "when is the best time to shop for airline tickets?" The most recent answer shall guide thee.

☐ 15.3.3 Visit Aggregator Sites
You can make separate visits to Hotwire, Travelocity, and Expedia; or you can view them all at once at "travel aggregators" such as Kayak.com, Mobissimo.com, or Momondo.com.

☐ 15.3.4 Shop for One Seat at a Time
Here's a great tip from FareCompare.com: always look for one seat only, even if you need two or more tickets. The reason? Sites are programmed to report only those prices that accommodate all requested seats. So if you shop for three tickets, and lower prices happen to exist for only one or two, you're never informed. By shopping for one seat at a time, you get to see the lowest fares. When you're ready to buy, open multiple purchase screens to assure that everyone gets on the same flight.

☐ 15.3.5 Sign Up for Price Alerts
If you think that prices will drop before you're ready to buy, register with alert services such as FareCompare.com, Yapta.com, or AirFareWatchDog.com. These sites will email you about any price changes.

15.4 Cross–Check before Booking

Consider visits to these other sources before you finally book.

☐ 15.4.1 Cross–Check With Carrier Websites
Travel sites are intermediaries, so you might find a better deal if you buy direct from the airline itself.

☐ 15.4.2 Cross–Check With Discount Carriers
The cheapest airlines don't always pay to post on travel websites, so before you book, visit Southwest.com, Spirit.com, and JetBlue.com.

☐ 15.4.3 Cross–Check With Travel Agents
Any agents who survive at this late date do so because they deliver value. Before booking, check to see if one can find you a lower price. If you fly often, build a mutually profitable relationship.

15.5 Consider Alternative Buying Approaches

☐ 15.5.1 Bundle Up

Sometimes you can save if you book airfare, hotels, and rental cars all at once. Run the numbers.

☐ 15.5.2 Package Your Vacation

Vacation packages are common for resorts or group tours. This collapses most of your vacation spending into a single purchase. Visit TravelZoo.com or SmarterTravel.com. Package buyers are popular targets for scams. Vet unfamiliar vendors before you book.

☐ 15.5.3 Try Group Buynamics

If you need ten or more tickets, contact airline group desks. Alternatively, save yourself the legwork and call a travel agent.

15.6 Avoid Price Gouges

☐ 15.6.1 Escape Baggage Fees by Packing Light

Ultra–light hiking has inspired a similar movement in leisure travel. Pack everything into a single carryon. For a complete rundown, visit 1Bag1World.com. Some space savers:

- *Lightweight Clothes.* Avoid heavy sweaters, blue jeans, and sweatshirts. If your trip requires bulky clothing, wear it onboard. You can always cram your parka into the overhead bin or underneath the seat in front of you. Specialized travel clothing weighs less and dries quickly, features which make it great for travel. Visit REI.com or CoolmaxFabric.com.

- *Convertible Pants and Shirts.* Find several examples at REI.com.

- *One Pair of Shoes Only (and You're Wearing Them).* Lightweight low hikers are comfortable and versatile.

- *Washing Plans.* You can pack lighter if you launder mid–trip. Some options: friends with washers, lodging with laundry rooms, and hotels with sinks (after washing, roll up wet clothing in bath towels and squeeze).

- *Compressible Bags.* These reduce mass, but cause wrinkles.

- *Resealable Bags.* Leather shave kits are bulky.

- *Small Souvenirs Only.* If you must buy oversized trinkets, pay to ship them home.

☐ **15.6.2 Fly Airlines That Don't Charge Baggage Fees**
Southwest Airlines, for one. JetBlue checks one bag at no charge. Some airlines waive fees if you book with certain credit cards.

☐ **15.6.3 Ship Ahead**
FedEx or UPS might ship to your destination for less than airlines do. Visit ShipGooder.com or ShippingSideKick.com.

☐ **15.6.4 Carry Food and Water**
Pack enough kibble for your entire flight and any foreseeable delays. Fill empty bottles at water fountains once you clear security.

15.7 Follow Up

☐ **15.7.1 Consider Cancellation Insurance**
For big trips, cancellations are costly. Consider insurance. Beware: the policies are riddled with exceptions and customer dissatisfaction is rampant. Understand the terms before buying. To shop policies from multiple companies, visit InsureMyTrip.com.

☐ **15.7.2 Print Your Own Boarding Passes**
This saves time and, in some cases, saves the expense of missed flights and rebooking fees.

16

TRAVEL:
LODGING

Everyone likes to save on hotels. These strategies get low rates without too much complexity.

16.1 Choose Alternatives to Hotels

Mix and match tactics work great with this line item. If your vacation lasts two weeks, you can stay in hotels for several nights and sleep elsewhere the rest of the time. Hotels are pricey, so the strategy that saves the most is the strategy that avoids them the most. You have many frugal options.

☐ **16.1.1 Choose Friends and Family**
Although this lodging usually is FREE, remember that fish and guests smell after three days. Break up your visit by staying a couple nights when you first arrive and a couple nights before you leave. In between, bunk elsewhere.

☐ **16.1.2 Swap Houses**
Trade a stay in your home for a stay in someone else's. Visit these sites: HomeExchange.com, HomeForExchange.com, HomeLink.org, Intervac-HomeExchange.com, or RoofSwap.com.

☐ **16.1.3 Sleep on Free Couches**
Visit CouchSurfing.org, a FREE site which matches people who travel with people who have couches or, in many cases, spare rooms. Read reviews of sleeping quarters and hosts.

☐ **16.1.4 Sleep on Less Than Free Couches**
AirBNB.com resembles CouchSurfing.org, except that you pay for the lodging. The site now books more room nights than the Hilton Hotel chain and serves more than 8,000 cities. Reviews of rooms and

hosts are included. Similar sites provide a similar experience: Roomorama.com and BedandFed.co.uk (Ireland and England only).

☐ **16.1.5 Stake Out Campgrounds**
Pitch a tent and sleep on rock hard surfaces at rock bottom rates.

☐ **16.1.6 Bunk in Cabins**
KOA pitches its rustic cabins as falling somewhere between tents and hotels. The lodging is priced accordingly. Visit KOA.com to look and book.

☐ **16.1.7 Go to Night School**
Dormitories offer good sleeps in campus settings. No online clearinghouses exist, so you have to identify colleges at your destination, call them up, and ask whether they rent.

☐ **16.1.8 Visit YMCAs and YMCA Camps**
There are 2,600 locations nationwide, but only 130 of them still sport living quarters. Visit YMCA.net to see whether the outpost at your destination offers rooms. Reportedly, it's fun to stay at the YMCA.

☐ **16.1.9 Overnight at Hostels**
Book at Hostels.com, HostelBookers.com, or HostelWorld.com. You can do this even if you're no longer a student.

☐ **16.1.10 Stay at Bed and Breakfasts**
These often provide better values than hotels and you always start the day with a meal. Hence the name. Check out listings at BedandBreakfast.com or in travel guides (which usually review the better B&Bs).

☐ **16.1.11 Consider Vacation Rentals**
At resorts, book condos or vacation homes. Good sites include: VRBO.com, FlipKey.com, and HomeAway.com. For visits to cities, check out the local Craigslist, which includes a section under "housing" for "vacation rentals."

☐ **16.1.12 Try Group Buynamics**
For vacations with friends, rent houses together instead of paying for separate hotel rooms.

CODA: RVS FOR VACATIONS

Once I dreamed of roaming the country for less in a modest motor home. I figured on free overnight stays in Walmart parking lots and inexpensive onboard meals. But when I pulled the numbers together, they proved that the same trips in the Prius would cost much less — even if we stayed at three star hotels and ate at upscale restaurants. Why? Mostly, it came down to the huge initial cost of motor homes (even used, they're expensive), awful gas mileage, hulking taxes, massive insurance premiums, and scary repair bills. The economics start making sense only if you're willing to sell your house and live nomadically (see 45.8.4).

16.2 Stay Flexible

☐ 16.2.1 Book Off–Season
Try Vail in late spring or Martha's Vineyard in winter.

☐ 16.2.2 Shop for Rooms Midweek
Weekend shoppers pay higher prices, so shop on weekdays.

☐ 16.2.3 Vacation in Recessions
Bargains abound whenever the economy hits rough patches. Save your biggest trips for low spots in the destination's business cycle.

☐ 16.2.4 Skip Special Events
Hotels fill up fast for conventions, college reunions, or sporting events. Check local websites to see whether you're scheduled to visit at a busy time when prices are high. If so, change your dates.

☐ 16.2.5 Subscribe to Travel Alerts
If you request, many travel sites will send you emails about the best last second deals to your favorite destinations, including Orbitz.com, Hotwire.com, and Priceline.com.

☐ 16.2.6 Book Outliers
Stay away from city centers and save on room rates and taxes.

☐ 16.2.7 Stay Flexible on Destinations
Pick vacation spots based upon low prices.

☐ **16.2.8 Stay Flexible on Quality Levels**
If you only need a bunk for the night, a two–star place works fine.

☐ **16.2.9 Consider Boutiques**
Smaller hotels offer great values, but they can't afford to list on major travel sites. Find them at HotelSweep.com.

☐ **16.2.10 Share Rooms**
You can save if you're flexible about the number of sleepers per room. A suite or rollaway bed costs much less than another room.

☐ **16.2.11 Avoid Weekends**
Prices jump on weekends, so favor alternatives to hotels on Friday and Saturday nights (see 16.1).

16.3 Research Online, but Haggle With the Front Desk

Many online sites help you shop hotel prices, including Expedia.com, Hotwire.com, and Orbitz.com, to name a few. Basically, these sites are middlemen that collect fees from hotels for each referral. When you call the hotel's front desk directly, you often get lower prices. (Don't bother with a 1-800 reservations number, because the operators don't have the power to deal that on–site employees do.) Choose from among these openers.

☐ **16.3.1 *"Are Any Group Discounts Offered?"***
Most hotels offer discounts to AAA or AARP members, members of the military, government employees, alumni groups, seniors, students, and others.

☐ **16.3.2 *"Will You Match Your Competitor's Price?"***
Obtain a low quote from a hotel in which you have less interest and see whether your preferred hotel will match that price.

☐ **16.3.3 *"Can I Get a Lower Rate With Your Loyalty Program?"***
If you're not already a member, ask to join.

☐ **16.3.4 *"What Does Your Least Expensive Room Cost?"***
Many hotels have problematic rooms that they rent out for less, including rooms with dormers, poor views, or elevator noise. Ask

about "suite connector" rooms, where hotels open the sitting areas of unsold suites and rent them out for cheap.

☐ **16.3.5 *"What if I Changed Dates or Stayed an Extra Night?"***
Work some alternative scenarios into the negotiations.

☐ **16.3.6 *"May I Speak With Your Manager, Please?"***
Sometimes the desk clerk lacks authority to bargain. If so, climb up the next rung of the ladder.

☐ **16.3.7 *"Help! I'm too Shy to Haggle!"***
If so, visit HotelsCombined.com, an aggregator that searches all major travel sites, *plus* the websites of individual hotels. You won't get as good a rate as you would at the front desk, but you might undercut the travel sites.

16.4 Research at Hotwire, but Bid at Priceline

First, price hotels at Hotwire.com. Note the cheapest option at your desired quality level, as shown by the assigned number of stars. Second, go to Priceline.com and bid at least 20 percent below the lowest Hotwire price. If your bid wins, you know you've scored a great price. If your bid fails, you can rebid immediately by making a small change to your criteria (such as a new star level or location). Otherwise, the system locks you out for 24 hours, and you're left to making slightly higher bids until at last you succeed.

16.5 Reserve Early, Revisit Before the Cancel Deadline

Book a good price that allows you a penalty–free cancellation at least 48 hours before arrival. Mark the cancel deadline on your calendar. Right before time expires, repeat strategy no. 16.3 or 16.4 to see if any better deals have emerged. If you find a lower price, lock it in and cancel the reservation.

16.6 Look for Special Offers and Deal Sweeteners

This takes more time, but sometimes yields lower rates. On a recent car trip, we picked up hotel coupon books at rest areas as we neared our nightly stops. Our savings averaged $35 per room.

Special Offers:

- Coupons and codes
- Group discounts
- Rebates
- Volume discounts
- Cash Payment discounts
- Deal–a–Day websites

Deal Sweeteners:

- Freebies
- Loyalty programs
- Credit card rewards
- Discounted gift cards

16.7 Book at the Last Second

As night falls and vacancies remain, rates plummet. Play a friendly game of chicken with hotels by not booking before 6:00 p.m. This game isn't for the faint of heart, however, because you risk a night without a room. Have in place a solid backup plan, such as one of the hotel alternatives in 16.1. Casually mentioning your backup at the front desk might help, as in something subtle like "Hey there. We were on our way to the campground on Highway 79 when we noticed your vacancy sign—what's your best price for a room tonight?"

16.8 Avoid Price Gouges

Like other businesses, hotels charge fees and add–ons. Know these usual suspects and dodge them whenever possible:

- Mini bars
- Gift shops
- Phone charges
- In–room movies
- Parking fees
- Excessive lodging taxes

- Vending machines
- Bottled water in room
- Wi–Fi charges
- Room service
- Valets
- Resort fees

16.9 Follow Up

☐ **16.9.1 Check for Belongings**
Save yourself the cost of replacing personal items.

☐ **16.9.2 Check the Bill**
Study it carefully before leaving. With hotels, billing mistakes are common and difficult to fix once you leave the premises.

17

TRAVEL:
RENTAL CARS

These transactions always follow a predictable sequence, so you probably spend according to ingrained habits instead of frugal practices. Use these strategies to steer clear of high rates.

17.1 Plan Ahead

☐ 17.1.1 Consider Alternatives

Don't assume you need to rent. Other transportation may work well enough, especially in cities. Read travel guides for available options. Visit HopStop.com for public transit details and walking directions (in 86 cities and growing). Substitutes for rental cars abound:

- Buses
- Trains
- Taxis
- Borrowed cars
- Bike rentals
- Boats or ferries
- Subways
- Light rail
- Hotel shuttles, van services
- Bike shares
- Car shares (Zipcar.com)
- Sidewalks and hiking trails

☐ 17.1.2 Know Your Insurance Coverage

Learn beforehand how your insurance covers rental car accidents.

- *Coverage for Business vs. Personal Travel.* Many auto policies cover personal travel, but not business trips. For work travel, buy the rental agency's waiver of vehicle collision/damage and seek reimbursement from your employer.

- *Collision and Comprehensive.* If you own an older car, perhaps you've dropped this coverage (see 30.2.1). That's a good idea for your 1992 Honda, but not for a 2013 Kia rental. Your credit card might fill the gap. See below.

- *Deductibles.* If you carry a high deductible on your auto insurance (see 30.2.5), you're at risk for that amount when you rent. Your credit card might fill the gap. See below.

- *Credit Card Insurance.* Most credit cards supplement your auto policy when you use them to pay for car rentals. Learn your cards' policies and favor whichever one gives the best terms.

☐ 17.1.3 Sign Up for Low Price Alerts
Major travel websites announce bargains via email and social media.

☐ 17.1.4 Join Loyalty Programs
All major agencies offer them. If you rent often, sign up.

☐ 17.1.5 Rent Twice
Don't pay for rentals that sit unused while you sightsee. Return the car when you first arrive and rent again for the trip back.

☐ 17.1.6 Try Group Buynamics
Vacation with friends and split the costs.

☐ 17.1.7 Cut the Rental Length
If you're scheduled to arrive late, book a hotel by the airport and pick up your car next morning. If you're departing early, book a hotel near the agency and drop off the car the day before you leave.

17.2 Shop Around

☐ 17.2.1 Check Rental Prices
Shop for rentals at these websites:

- *Aggregator Sites.* Travel sites have proliferated like prairie dogs in predator–free meadows. The solution: aggregators to herd them all. Visit Kayak.com, Momondo.com, or Mobissimo.com.

- *Travel Sites.* Best accessed through aggregator sites, see above, they include Hotwire.com, Travelocity.com, and Orbitz.com.

- *Regional Rental Agencies.* Regional agencies such as Ace, Fox, Midway, and Triangle may undercut the price of national chains. Search prices at CarRentalExpress.com.

- *Rental Agencies away from Airports.* Lower rates beckon, but be sure to factor in your costs of getting there and back.

☐ **17.2.2 Reserve Economy Cars Only**
When gas prices spike, the smallest cars leave the lot first, so you'll likely receive a FREE upgrade anyway.

☐ **17.2.3 Seek Discounts**
Round up the usual suspects: coupons, promo codes, warehouse clubs, loyalty programs, and member deals (AAA, AARP).

☐ **17.2.4 Cross–Check Aggregator Results With Rental Agencies**
You may get better rates direct from the rental agencies themselves.

☐ **17.2.5 Reserve Early, Shop Again Before the Cancel Deadline**
This tactic has four steps: (1) reserve a car several weeks before your trip at a good rate; (2) docket the cancel deadline on your calendar; (3) before the deadline expires, search for better deals; and (4) if you find a lower rate, book it and revoke the prior reservation.

☐ **17.2.6 Reserve Early, and Later Bid Less on Priceline**
If your bid wins, cancel the old reservation.

17.3 Save at the Rental Agency

☐ **17.3.1 Pack Smart**
Save money and time with these items: driver's license, credit card, receipt/itinerary (for online rentals), digital camera, GPS device (or map), and a copy of this checklist.

☐ **17.3.2 Decline Insurance**
You've planned ahead, so you already know you're covered. Don't pay twice.

☐ **17.3.3 Decline All Upgrades and Extras**
Stick to the basics and save.

☐ **17.3.4 Agree to Return a Full Tank**
Almost always, it's cheaper to return a full tank than to pay the rental company to top it off for you.

☐ **17.3.5 Photograph the Car**

Take a short video or several photos to prove the car's condition when you picked it up. Zoom in on any damage to keep the rental company from sticking you with liability later.

17.4 Drive Around

☐ **17.4.1 Note Nearby Gas Stations as You Leave the Lot**

You'll want to visit one of them when you return the car.

☐ **17.4.2 Know Where You're Going**

A good navigator or GPS system saves time and gas.

☐ **17.4.3 Use the Gasoline Checklist**

Most tactics work equally well for rentals. See Chapter 39.

17.5 Drop Off

☐ **17.5.1 Fill the Tank**

To avoid fees, top off at a gas station as you near the rental lot.

☐ **17.5.2 Arrive on Time**

Most agencies impose penalties for late returns. If you're tardy, plead for a waiver.

☐ **17.5.3 Check for Personal Items**

And save the replacement cost.

☐ **17.5.4 Check the Receipt**

Confirm its accuracy before you leave the lot. It's much tougher to resolve disputes if you wait until you get back home.

☐ **17.5.5 Photograph the Car Again**

In case the agency tries to stick you with damage that occurs after you return the car.

☐ **17.5.6 Retain Paperwork**

Keep contracts and photos for a few weeks in case of any disputes.

18

TRAVEL:
ROAD FOOD

When travelling, it's easy to overspend at restaurants. Manage food costs and waistlines with these simple strategies.

18.1 Book Lodgings That Save on Food

☐ **18.1.1 Book Rooms With Kitchens**
With a small kitchenette, you can eat in.

☐ **18.1.2 Seek Refrigerators and Microwave Ovens**
Even if your lodging lacks a kitchen, you still can save with these.

☐ **18.1.3 Use Coffee Makers**
With access to hot water, you can enjoy instant oatmeal, cup–o–soups, and freeze–dried dishes (visit REI.com).

☐ **18.1.4 Book Lodgings With Free Breakfasts**
Start the day with a big FREE meal and eat light afterwards.

18.2 Map Out Cheap Eats in Advance

Plan ahead to cut your food costs.

☐ **18.2.1 Find Restaurants**
Travel guides sort eateries by price range. Make a list of top values.

☐ **18.2.2 Locate Your Warehouse Membership Clubs**
Lunch at outposts of Costco, Sam's Club, or BJ's. Or pick up rotisserie chickens to go.

☐ **18.2.3 Pinpoint Groceries and Dollar Stores**
Map these out beforehand, or travel with a GPS device.

◻ **18.2.4 Visit Sub–Priced Sandwiches**
When split in half, a twelve–inch sandwich at Subway feeds two heroically for the price of one.

18.3 Pack to Save on Food

◻ **18.3.1 Carry Water Bottles**
Hydrate for less. When flying, fill up at water fountains after you pass through security.

◻ **18.3.2 Stock Portable Pantries**
For car travel, stock a box with snacks and quick road meals. For flights, pack a few items in your carryon, including energy bars and just–add–hot–water meals.

◻ **18.3.3 Pack a Rice Cooker**
In *The Pot and How to Use It*, movie critic Roger Ebert suggested travelling with a three–cup rice cooker. The compact device fits easily into your carryon bag and cooks not only rice, but also oatmeal, chicken, and other savory fare.

◻ **18.3.4 Use a Cooler**
If driving, pack a hard–sided cooler. Stock it with drinks and snacks. If flying, pack a soft sided cooler—it collapses down to fit into luggage. If you don't have room to pack a cooler, buy one from a thrift store at your destination, use it as you travel, and donate it back before you head home (and don't forget to take the tax deduction if you itemize).

◻ **18.3.5 Favor Reusable Ice**
Ice is messy and sometimes you even have to pay for it. If your room has a refrigerator, it likely includes a freezer with enough space to refreeze your ice packs.

◻ **18.3.6 Clip Coupons**
Before your trip, visit the websites of local eateries and print their coupons. Join the Groupon and Living Social sites for your destinations.

◻ **18.3.7 Pack the Restaurants Checklist**
Take along a copy of Appendix 3 and follow it.

18.4 Avoid Price Gouges

□ 18.4.1 Don't Spend at Airports

Vendors know they hold you hostage and overcharge at will. Local governments pile on with sky–high sales taxes. Fight back. Stash your bag with enough food to cover the trip and any delays that might strand you at the terminal. For convenient protein, pack beef jerky as your carryon carrion.

□ 18.4.2 Skip Hotel Shops, Convenience Stores, and Gas Stations

Once again, you're held captive to high prices; visit grocers or dollar stores instead.

□ 18.4.3 Avoid Vending Machines

If you vend, you overspend. Pack water bottles and energy bars.

19

CHARITABLE GIVING

Frugality produces an abundance that makes for easy gifting. But that doesn't mean fringers give nonprofits a free ride. The same attitude that drives their household spending also drives their philanthropy. In both cases, they demand value. For a fringier approach to charity, consider these strategies.

19.1 Run Background Checks

The CES reports that households donated an average of $1,721 in 2011, which represents 3.9 percent of the typical budget. Given the large amounts involved, it makes sense to vet nonprofits with the same attention you give to products and services.

VETTING THE EASY WAY: ONLINE CHARITY REVIEWS

☐ **19.1.1 Visit Charity Navigator**
CharityNavigator.org evaluates the financial health of more than 5,500 charities and issues ratings based on a four–star system.

☐ **19.1.2 Visit the Better Business Bureau**
Charities open their books to the BBB, which rates them under several accountability standards. Visit BBB.org/us/charity/.

☐ **19.1.3 Visit CharityWatch**
This site rates over 500 charities on an A to F scale and publishes the results in its Charity Rating Guide. Visit CharityWatch.org.

☐ **19.1.4 Visit Philanthropedia**
Currently, more than 3000 experts have contributed to reviews of 560 nonprofits in 36 categories of causes. Visit MyPhilanthropedia.org.

☐ **19.1.5 Visit GiveWell**
This site conducts in-depth research to identify a few nonprofits that deliver stellar returns on donations. Visit GiveWell.org.

VETTING THE HARDER WAY: DIY BACKGROUND CHECKS

☐ **19.1.6 Read a Brochure**
Any legitimate charity publishes materials that discuss its mission.

☐ **19.1.7 Visit Guide Star**
GuideStar.org posts data on more than 1.8 million nonprofits.

☐ **19.1.8 Check State Registries**
Many states require the registration of charities. Avoid gifts to unregistered nonprofits. At best, they don't have their act together enough to comply with the law; at worst, they're frauds. Visit nasconet.org/documents/u-s-charity-offices/.

☐ **19.1.9 Note the Charity's Time in Service**
The newer the nonprofit, the more you should investigate it.

☐ **19.1.10 Search the Web**
The charity you like may have a record of laudable works or abject mismanagement. A quick search provides fast answers.

☐ **19.1.11 Review Financials**
According to Charity Navigator, charities should spend no more than 25 percent of collected dollars on administration and fundraising. If your charities overspend in these areas, reconsider your support. There might be better places to send your money.

☐ **19.1.12 Check the Recent Track Record**
Favor charities that can boast of recent accomplishments, as opposed to those that rest on their laurels.

☐ **19.1.13 Start Small**
Giving a little motivates you to monitor the charity more closely.

☐ **19.1.14 Best of all, Volunteer**
When you donate time, you learn firsthand about the nonprofit's operations. There's no better way to run a background check.

19.2 Get the Most Bang for Your Benevolent Buck

Make sure your charity receives the full benefit of your contribution.

☐ 19.2.1 Avoid Gifts by Credit Card
When you use plastic, the charity pays processor fees to your credit card company. When you pay by check, it receives full value.

☐ 19.2.2 Avoid Gifts of Greenbacks
Cash contributions are easily lost or stolen. They're also difficult to prove in tax audits.

☐ 19.2.3 Seek Out Dollar Matches
Ask the charity whether any large donors match contributions.

☐ 19.2.4 Give Earlier in the Year
Many wait until year's end to give, but charities often have unmet needs at other times. Investigate whether you can deliver extra value by donating when contributions lag.

☐ 19.2.5 Give Goods
Donate merchandise instead of money. If you use the products buying checklist (Appendix 1), you probably can find a lower price than the charity could—and this itself delivers added value.

☐ 19.2.6 Make Gifts in Honor of Friends and Family
Acknowledge others with contributions to their favorite charities. Funnel more money to your favorite nonprofits by asking for donations in lieu of gifts.

☐ 19.2.7 Spread the News
This way, you inspire others to give. So tell friends about your favorite causes and post positive opinions at CharityNavigator.org.

19.3 Maximize Tax Benefits

The more deductions you receive, the more you can afford to donate. Important: consult your tax advisor before you take these actions.

☐ 19.3.1 Assess Whether You Can Itemize this Year
Under current tax laws, only itemizers can deduct charitable contributions. If you're close to qualifying for itemization, accelerate any donations slated for the next year into the current one so that you meet the necessary threshold.

☐ 19.3.2 Confirm Deductibility in Advance

By law, you can't deduct unless your charity registers with the IRS as a "qualified organization." The IRS lists qualified organizations in its "Exempt Organizations Select Check," an online search tool located at IRS.gov. If your charity is listed there, your contributions qualify for a deduction.

☐ 19.3.3 Deduct Car Expenses

You can deduct a standard mileage rate for unreimbursed travel in connection with charitable work. The rate varies each year and the rules are complicated. See IRS Publication 526.

☐ 19.3.4 Give Appreciated Stock

If you donate appreciated stock from a taxable account, you avoid paying capital gains (currently 15 percent for most wage earners) and still receive a deduction for the stock's full market value. Most large charities have systems in place to handle such gifts.

☐ 19.3.5 Contribute to Donor–Advised Funds

With this approach, you make an irreversible donation to the fund, claim an immediate deduction, and then later—maybe years later—recommend to the fund's trustee what amounts should be donated where. Such funds offer many advantages. For example, you can gift appreciated stock and funnel the proceeds to smaller charities, many of which lack the capability to accept such gifts directly. For details, visit Vanguard.com, Schwab.com, and Fidelity.com.

19.4 Avoid Pitfalls

Americans give billions each year to charities. Predictably, scammers seek to siphon off some this largesse for themselves. Frustrate the fraudsters by following this short list.

☐ 19.4.1 Avoid Impulsive Giving

Especially after natural disasters. Vet first; give later.

☐ 19.4.2 Ignore Telemarketers

At best, the charity pays inflated fees to third party solicitors. At worst, the telemarketers are outright frauds. Bypass intermediaries and give directly.

□ **19.4.3 Reject High Pressure Tactics**

Legitimate charities don't lean on people for donations.

□ **19.4.4 Beware of "Thanks for Your Pledge" Scams**

Don't converse with callers who thank you for pledges you don't recall making. It's a common fraud.

□ **19.4.5 Beware of Soundalikes**

Double–check the name and website address. Many dubious operations choose monikers that mimic those of legitimate charities.

19.5 Follow Up

□ **19.5.1 Keep Payment Records**

Retain all paperwork that proves your payment, including any cancelled checks or credit card statements. Consult your tax advisor.

□ **19.5.2 Keep Charity Acknowledgements**

In order to deduct a cash donation of $250 or more, you need a letter from the charity that lists what you gave and whether you received anything of value in return. You need the same type of letter when you deduct noncash gifts valued between $501 and $5,000. See IRS Publication 526. For noncash gifts over $5,000, you need a written appraisal that complies with IRS Publication 561.

□ **19.5.3 Photograph Noncash Gifts**

Take a photo or video of what you give and use it later to help value the property for tax purposes.

□ **19.5.4 Monitor Your Charities**

Make sure they continue to follow the principles that caused you to donate in the first place. If any drift off course, give elsewhere.

20

GOVERNMENTAL: TAXES

In 2012, according to The Tax Foundation, total taxes paid to federal, state, and local governments accounted for 29.2 percent of the nation's gross income. Much of this burden is hidden from view, because governments use agents to do most of their collecting. Merchants tack on sales taxes when you buy goods, employers withhold income taxes from your paycheck, and mortgage lenders charge a little extra each month to cover property taxes. Such indirect collecting can lull you to sleep about how much you actually pay. But you should scrutinize taxes as much as any other household expense. For when it comes to this unpopular line item, either you pay attention, or else you pay more to the government.

20.1 Minimize Sales Taxes

Sales taxes aren't complex. Governments impose them by requiring sellers to collect from buyers a specified percentage of merchandise sales. Depending upon where you shop, your purchase can trigger sales taxes from multiple sources—the state, the county, the city, and possibly even from special districts which fund such extras as public transit and stadiums. The amount you pay depends upon how many jurisdictions are involved and where they set their respective rates. According to the Sales Tax Clearinghouse, as of 2012, 23 states averaged combined sales tax rates of 6.85 percent or higher. Wherever you live and whatever your sales taxes, fight back with these tactics.

☐ **20.1.1** *Spend Less Now!*
At an eight percent tax rate, spending $3,000 less on goods saves you $240. So follow Appendix 1: find alternatives to buying, shop around for low prices, and avoid common pitfalls. The large cherry on top of your savings sundae will be all the sales taxes you never had to pay.

□ 20.1.2 Shop Where Taxes Are Lower

If you live near a city, you're within driving distance of several different tax districts. Rates can vary by as much as five percent. This is a big deal. Buy a big–ticket item for $2,500, and saving five percent adds $125 to your coffers. Spend $2,000 this year at restaurants, and five percent works out to $100. Spend $900 at discount stores, and five percent is $45. From these three examples alone you save $270. Think about how much you'd save if you checked for lower taxes on all your shopping.

□ 20.1.3 Shop on Tax Holidays

Many locales offer "holidays" during which taxes on particular items are suspended temporarily. The most popular time for these suspensions occur in the fall when families shop for back–to–school items. Happily, these holidays coincide with big sales, so delay your purchases of qualifying products until then.

□ 20.1.4 On Big–Ticket Items, Choose Pick Up or Delivery

For items that require delivery, you're taxed based upon where the item is sent, and not where it's purchased. If the sales tax is lower where you live than at the store, have the item dropped off at your home (provided the tax savings exceed any delivery charges). Conversely, if sales taxes are lower at the store, borrow a friend's truck and pick it up yourself.

□ 20.1.5 Repair Instead of Buy

Most jurisdictions don't impose taxes for services provided by the likes of tailors, mechanics, and electricians. If you live in or near such a place, that's one more reason to fix what you own instead of buying a replacement.

CODA: BYPASS SALES TAXES ALTOGETHER

I didn't list this as a tactic because of the thorny legal and ethical issues. As tax rates have soared, many consumers have sought refuge by patronizing sellers who aren't required to collect sales taxes, such as out–of–state websites and Craigslist users. Under most state tax codes, however, if a given seller hasn't collected a sales tax, then the buyer by law must pay something called a "use tax," which the state charges to recoup its lost sales tax revenue. Many states include a line on their income tax forms urging the payment of use taxes. But most filers ignore the requirement, and most states lack the enforcement resources to press the issue. To comply with the law, calculate your use tax and remit what you owe.

20.2 Minimize Income Taxes

You enter complicated territory when you deal with state and federal income taxes. Although *SL☑N!* doesn't cover tax planning in any great detail, you can save thousands if you take advantage of basic opportunities. Important: consult your tax advisor before you pursue any of these tactics.

☐ **20.2.1 Fund Tax Advantaged Retirement Accounts**
The federal government rewards you for payments into traditional IRAs, Roth IRAs, and 401k's, to name a few. Fund these accounts to slash your tax burden and boost your net worth.

☐ **20.2.2 Fund Other Tax Advantaged Accounts**
The feds also recognize other specialized accounts—including 529 College Savings Plans, Health Savings Accounts, and Flexible Spending Accounts (for healthcare and dependent care expenses).

☐ **20.2.3 Act on Governmental Incentives**
Governments often offer tax breaks for socially desirable spending. In 2009, for instance, I learned: (1) that the IRS would let me deduct the sales tax on any new vehicles I bought that year; (2) that my home state would issue a $2,880 tax credit for buying a new hybrid; and (3) that the "Cash for Clunkers" program would pay $4,500 for my 1998 Ford Explorer (170,000 miles with a bad transmission). Faced with these programs, which overlapped more than a little, I surrendered my Explorer (19 MPG rating) and replaced it with a new Prius (50 MPG rating). I saved $7,500 upfront, and since then I've saved thousands more on gas. Governments dream up new programs like this all the time, so keep your eyes peeled.

☐ **20.2.4 Convert Consumer Debt into Deductible Debt**
If you refinance your home mortgage, use some of the proceeds to pay off car loans and credit card accounts. This saves money. Not

only are mortgage interest rates lower than those for consumer loans, mortgage interest is deductible. The downside: refinancings are incredibly complex. For a FREE guide, visit HSH.com and use the "Mortgage Refinancing Starter Kit."

☐ **20.2.5 Combine Business With Deductible Pleasure**
The tax code allows deductions for many business expenses, including meals, sports tickets, and hotels.

☐ **20.2.6 Deduct Mileage**
Travel for business, charity, and medical care may be deductible.

☐ **20.2.7 Time Your Deductible Spending**
If you itemize, many expenses are deductible, including property taxes, mortgage interest, and charities. If you're near the threshold for itemizing, accelerate any future years' deductible expenses into the current year. If you're not close to itemizing, postpone any deductible expenses until after January 1 of the next year.

☐ **20.2.8 Pay With Pre–Tax Dollars**
The IRS allows this for a few expenses only and, once again, the rules are complex. For example, employers can deduct pre–tax dollars from your paycheck and use them to cover your public transportation or parking costs. I had personal experience with this when I last changed jobs. Although my old employer had funded my parking on a pre–tax basis, my new employer didn't, so each month I coughed up $150 to a nearby garage—all paid for with after–tax dollars. Ouch. After several months of this, I found out that my wife's employer let its employees use pre–tax dollars to pay for onsite parking, so I began leaving the car at her building. How much can you save when you use this tactic? The answer depends upon your own top marginal tax rate. At a combined state and federal marginal rate of 40 percent, for example, parking with pre–tax dollars as described above saves $720 per year ($150 x 12 = $1800 x 40% = $720).

20.3 Minimize Real Estate Taxes

If you own real estate, you owe taxes. These tactics apply in most jurisdictions. Check your local regulations.

□ 20.3.1 Buy Less Property
Don't buy more house than you need. The less expensive your property, the lower your taxes.

□ 20.3.2 Live Where Taxes Are Low
If you have a choice of jurisdictions in which to live, favor homes in lower tax districts.

□ 20.3.3 Seek Group Discounts
Many localities tax certain property owners at lower rates, including veterans, seniors, long–term residents, and disabled persons. Call your county clerk or assessor's office.

□ 20.3.4 Deduct Property Taxes
If you itemize, you usually can deduct real estate taxes.

□ 20.3.5 Change Your Property's Designation
Some states tax agricultural land at lower rates than residential or commercial properties. Cultivate an understanding of your local laws and see whether you can harvest a lower tax bill.

□ 20.3.6 Find Valuation Errors
In most counties, an assessor values your property for tax purposes. The assessor looks at many factors, including acreage, building size, construction quality, and the number of bedrooms. Obtain a copy of the assessor's written report—it's usually available from the county clerk—and check its accuracy. If you find mistakes that reduce your tax burden, inform the assessor's office in writing. If the mistakes go uncorrected, appeal to the appropriate review board.

□ 20.3.7 Challenge Comparables
When valuing a residence, the assessor usually selects several recent and nearby sales that he thinks most closely resemble the property in question. These similar sales are known as "comparables." Their selection is an art, not a precise science. You can reach a much lower valuation simply by choosing a different set of comparables. Ask a local real estate broker to supply you with the recent sales data from your neighborhood. Beware: if you mount a challenge, pay close attention to any filing deadlines. If you miss a deadline, you lose your right to appeal.

☐ 20.3.8 Pay on Time

Most counties impose penalties for late payment of property taxes. Mark deadlines on your calendar.

☐ 20.3.9 Pay With Plastic

Check whether you can pay your property taxes by credit card. Beware: many counties charge fees for this privilege that far outstrip the value of any card rewards.

21

GOVERNMENTAL: POSTAGE

Taxes are huge, but postage costs are miniscule. So why bother with this line item? Because you have so many cheap options, that it's hard to remember them all. Each time you're about to—MOOOOOO!!!—pay postage on anything, these strategies deliver real savings.

21.1 Choose Alternatives to Mailing

☐ **21.1.1 Call**
At current long distance rates, you can talk at least 15 minutes before it costs you as much as postage.

☐ **21.1.2 Email**
If you enjoy internet access, an email costs nothing extra. Meanwhile, the price of first class postage jumps every year.

☐ **21.1.3 Scan**
You can mail the paperwork or you can email the .pdf file for FREE.

☐ **21.1.4 Fax**
This is older technology, but it still gets the pages there for less than the cost of postage.

☐ **21.1.5 Avoid Mailing Checks**
Instead, pay online or set up automatic withdrawals.

☐ **21.1.6 Use Invite Websites**
Stamp out the cost of mailing invites with FREE online services such as Evite.com, Pingg.com, PunchBowl.com, or AnyVite.com.

☐ **21.1.7 Use Business Reply Envelopes**
If a company mails you postage–paid envelopes, use them.

☐ 21.1.8 Hand–Deliver

If you attend a lunch to celebrate someone's birthday, deliver the card in person. Distribute cards at holiday parties.

21.2 Shop Around

☐ 21.2.1 Compare Package Shipping Costs

View prices at ShipGooder.com or ShippingSidekick.com.

☐ 21.2.2 Buy Stamps at Warehouse Clubs

Somehow, they manage to sell stamps below face value. Maybe it's something extra you get for your membership fee.

21.3 Buy the Right Size of Postage

☐ 21.3.1 Ship With USPS Priority Mail

Whatever fits in the box ships anywhere in the United States for the same flat rate. Packages must weigh less than 70 pounds.

☐ 21.3.2 Use Third Class Mail

If your letter weighs more than one ounce and you can wait two or three days more for it to arrive, you save.

☐ 21.3.3 Mail Postcards

Cheaper than letters.

☐ 21.3.4 Ship With Media Mail

Ship these items for less: books, sound recordings, recorded video tapes, printed music, and recorded computer–readable media (such as CDs, DVDs, and diskettes).

☐ 21.3.5 Choose Certified Mail

If you need proof of delivery, certified costs less than registered.

☐ 21.3.6 Avoid Overnight Deliveries

Plan ahead. If you wait until the last second, you absolutely, positively pay more.

☐ 21.3.7 Use Postage Meters or Stamps.com

These services are cheaper when you mail large batches.

21.4 Save When Shipping Gifts

☐ **21.4.1 Give Gift Codes**

These ship for FREE because you email them.

☐ **21.4.2 Buy Online and Ship Direct**

Instruct the seller to ship the item directly to your recipient.

☐ **21.4.3 Enlist Local Help**

If a terrific gift for your out–of–state brother weighs a ton, mail his wife a check and ask her to buy it for you locally.

☐ **21.4.4 Buy Presents Small and Light**

Good things in small packages cost less to mail.

☐ **21.4.5 Give Media**

DVDs, books, and CDs all ship for less via media mail.

☐ **21.4.6 Donate in Lieu of Gifting**

A check in honor of your friend or family member costs much less to mail than a parcel (see 19.2.6).

21.5 Use FREE Shipping

☐ **21.5.1 Find Free Shipping**

As of this writing, Amazon ships for FREE on qualifying orders over $25. LL Bean ships everything for FREE except heavy freight. Find the policies of other retailers at FreeShipping.org.

☐ **21.5.2 Consider In–Store Pickup**

Some sites offer FREE delivery to your nearest store. Beware: this might increase your sales tax if the store is located in a higher tax district than your home. Run the numbers.

22

UTILITIES:
HOME ENERGY

I once paid scant attention to this line item. During 2004–2008, as I snoozed, my utility bills averaged $1,930 per year. After that, I undertook some easy steps to save energy. I lowered thermostats, installed CFLs, enabled computer sleep modes, switched to low–flow showerheads, and more. Magically, my bills nosedived. During 2009–2012, the yearly cost fell to $1,470—that's a 24 percent drop (yup, as to this expense, I'd been decidedly unfrugal).

This chapter presents strategies to whittle your energy bills down to size. For your convenience, the strategies follow typical home energy uses as reported by the Department of Energy (DOE):

Energy Use	Share of Bill
Space Heating	31%
Space Cooling	12%
Water Heating	12%
Lighting	11%
Computer/Electronics	9%
Appliances	9%
Refrigeration	8%
Other	8%

Remember one idea that applies to all these categories: whenever you replace anything that uses energy, buy models that slash your operating costs. Visit EnergyStar.gov.

22.1 Cut Heating Costs

☐ 22.1.1 Lower Thermostats
Lower them by 10–15 degrees for eight hours each day and you save about 5–15 percent per year. The precise savings depend upon your home's size and the climate (milder climates yield greater savings).

☐ 22.1.2 Install Programmable Thermostats

Program these to lower the temperature whenever you go to bed or leave for work. Many thermostats allow for seven day programming, so you can set them higher on weekends.

☐ 22.1.3 Seal Off Rooms

If parts of your house receive little use in winter, close them off and lower the thermostat for that zone.

☐ 22.1.4 Seal House Leaks

Look for gaps around windows, pipes, and wire holes. Close them up with caulk, foam, or weather stripping.

☐ 22.1.5 Seal Outlets and Light Switches

Install foam gaskets behind any plates located on exterior walls.

☐ 22.1.6 Vent Rarely

When you run the fan, heated air escapes.

☐ 22.1.7 Block Fireplace Leaks

Close dampers when the fireplace is idle. Consider inflatable inserts to seal chimney flues even tighter. Search the web for "inflatable fireplace inserts."

☐ 22.1.8 Install Indoor Window Insulation

Install clear plastic over windows or patio doors. Apply double-sided tape around the frame, stretch the wrap over the tape, and use a hair dryer to remove wrinkles. This produces a crystal–clear, air-tight barrier. I've experimented with these on several windows and skylights. The results: drafts decreased and the plastic surfaces stayed warm to the touch while untreated windows stayed cold. Search the internet for "indoor window insulation kits." Buying tip: these go on sale every spring.

☐ 22.1.9 Install Outdoor Window Insulation

Install clear plastic over the outside of windows or patio doors. If the aesthetics bother you, install them only on your home's backside.

☐ 22.1.10 Install Window Treatments

Consider honeycomb blinds, thermal shades, and insulated drapes.

☐ **22.1.11 Employ Draft Dodgers**
For exterior doors that stay closed in winter, seal the gap between the door and frame with clear weather strip tape. For doors that see winter use, install insulated draft stoppers along door bottoms.

☐ **22.1.12 Use Passive Solar Power**
Open drapes on south–facing windows to let the sun shine in. At night, close the drapes to retain the warm air.

☐ **22.1.13 Use Portable Heaters**
Heat the room you're in, not the entire house. Energy efficient models feature thermostats or dials to control power consumption.

☐ **22.1.14 Use Electric Blankets or Mattress Pads**
Heat the bed you're in, not the entire bedroom. This tactic doesn't work with some foam mattresses because the extra warmth degrades bedding materials. Check your mattress maker's recommendations.

☐ **22.1.15 Use Heated Throws**
Heat yourself, not the space you're in—they're great for TV rooms.

☐ **22.1.16 Wear Sweaters and Slippers**
Heat yourself, and do it without paying for more energy.

☐ **22.1.17 Schedule Furnace Tune–Ups**
Invest in them annually or every other year.

☐ **22.1.18 Consider Home Energy Audits**
They often turn up new ideas for savings. Check with your utility.

☐ **22.1.19 Add Insulation**
Blow in foam or pile more layers into your attic.

☐ **22.1.20 Add Rugs**
If floors are cold in the winter, throw down area carpets instead of raising thermostats.

☐ **22.1.21 Install Ceiling Fans**
These redirect heat downward; and they're especially effective for rooms with cathedral ceilings.

☐ **22.1.22 Go With the Flow**
Anything that blocks registers, baseboards, or radiators makes your furnace work harder. Move aside furniture and drapes.

☐ **22.1.23 Consult the Feds**
They're from the government and they're here to help! For a reliable site, visit EnergySavers.gov.

22.2 Cut Cooling Costs

☐ **22.2.1 Raise Thermostats to 78⁰F**
Wear shorts and tee shirts. Drink iced tea.

☐ **22.2.2 Install Programmable Thermostats**
Raise the temperature when you're away from home.

☐ **22.2.3 Seal House Leaks**
You pay to cool the air, so keep it from leaking out.

☐ **22.2.4 Use Portable Air Conditioners**
Cool the room you occupy, not the entire house.

☐ **22.2.5 Try Personal Cooling**
Cool yourself instead of the room. Use water misters or cooling wraps that store in the fridge.

☐ **22.2.6 Open Windows and Use Fans**
Cool without air conditioners.

☐ **22.2.7 Install Ceiling Fans**
These direct hot air upwards in summer.

☐ **22.2.8 Use Window Treatments**
Close windows and drapes during the day to keep hot air out. Open them at night to let cool air in.

☐ **22.2.9 Add Insulation**
This cools your house in summer and heats it in winter.

☐ **22.2.10 Keep AC Filters Clean**
Check your manufacturer's recommendations.

☐ **22.2.11 Clear Debris away From Outside AC Units**
This promotes efficient operation.

☐ **22.2.12 Schedule AC Tune–Ups**
Well–maintained air conditioners use less energy.

☐ **22.2.13 Cook Outside on Hot Days**
It's BBQ season anyway.

☐ **22.2.14 Install Attic Fans**
These cool your house at night.

22.3 Cut Water Heating Costs

☐ **22.3.1 Set the Water Heater to 120⁰F**
This provides adequate heat and cuts the risk of scalding.

☐ **22.3.2 Take Showers, Not Baths**
Baths use more hot water.

☐ **22.3.3 Install Low–Flow Showerheads**
Hold a bucket under the nozzle; run the water for 30 seconds. Multiply the volume collected by two. If the showerhead spews over two gallons per minute, replace it with a low–flow model.

☐ **22.3.4 Install Flow Control Valves**
Install them right before the showerhead so that you can cut heated water to a trickle while you lather up. Some nozzles come with this feature already attached.

☐ **22.3.5 Take Shorter Showers**
Longer showers cost more, so: (1) keep your hair short; (2) shave elsewhere; or (3) play a favorite song that lasts less than five minutes and finish before the music ends.

☐ **22.3.6 Take Navy Showers**
Post these instructions by each shower: "CONSERVE ENERGY: WET DOWN, SHUT OFF WATER, SOAP UP, RINSE OFF." If you can convince your shipmates to comply, you're more persuasive than me.

☐ **22.3.7 Shower on Alternate Days**
Keep clean in between with sponge baths.

☐ 22.3.8 Install Faucet Aerators

These cut hot water waste.

☐ 22.3.9 Repair Leaky Faucets

They cost you over time. Fix them.

☐ 22.3.10 Turn Off the Water Heater When Away

Don't pay to heat water during your summer vacation. In colder climates, this isn't an option for winter trips, unless you want to suffer burst pipes and flooding.

☐ 22.3.11 Insulate Hot Water Pipes

If your hot water pipes pass through cold areas—garages, crawl spaces, attics—wrap them in pre–slit foam insulators.

☐ 22.3.12 Install an Insulated Blanket

Effective for older hot water heaters, but newer models are better insulated and unlikely to benefit. A simple test: if the outside of the tank is warm to the touch, then a blanket probably helps.

22.4 Cut Lighting Costs

☐ 22.4.1 Switch to Energy Efficient Light Bulbs

Replace the incandescent bulbs you use most often with compact fluorescent light bulbs (CFLs) or light emitting diodes (LEDs). Note: CFLs cost less than LEDs.

☐ 22.4.2 Switch to Cheaper Holiday Lights

Old style bulbs consume too much electricity; use LEDs.

☐ 22.4.3 Install Timers

For any lights you keep forgetting to turn off.

☐ 22.4.4 Install Dimmers

Dimmed bulbs use less energy.

☐ 22.4.5 Use Three–Way Bulbs

Lamps don't have to blaze away at full power 24/7.

☐ 22.4.6 Install Motion Detectors

These provide security without ramping up energy bills.

☐ **22.4.7 Light the Task, Not the Room**
When you read or sew, don't light the entire room—use a desk lamp.

☐ **22.4.8 Place Workspaces Near Windows**
No one charges for sunlight (yet).

☐ **22.4.9 Turn Lights Off When You Leave a Room**
Your parents whined about this for good reason.

22.5 Cut Computer and Electronic Costs

☐ **22.5.1 Turn Off Idle Peripherals**
Any scanner, printer, or monitor should be turned off unless in use.

☐ **22.5.2 Activate Sleep Modes**
If your PC runs Windows, type the word "power" into the search box located in the upper right corner of the control panel window. Select from the available options.

☐ **22.5.3 Use Tablets and Phones for Entertainment**
These consume much less power than computers or TVs. If you've already bought one—hopefully, by following Appendix 1—favor it for movies, games, and internet usage.

☐ **22.5.4 Use Power Strips**
Many electronics drain power even when they're off (it helps them start faster, but you pay more).

☐ **22.5.5 Use a Kilowatt Meter**
These measure how much energy particular appliances and electronics consume when idle, which motivates you to either unplug them or install power strips. Borrow a meter from your local utility or buy one on eBay for about $15.

☐ **22.5.6 Beware Satellite/Cable Boxes**
According to the National Resources Defense Council, a setup of two HD boxes, one of which records, consumes 446 kilowatt hours per year. That's more energy than most refrigerators use. The fix: connect your boxes to timers so they don't run when you're away from the TV (when you're at work, asleep, or at work *and* asleep).

22.6 Cut Appliance Costs

Everyone in your household uses these energy suckers according to ingrained habits instead of wise practices. Short–circuit the waste. Copy the condensed versions of these savings tactics (see Appendix 4) and tape one to each appliance.

CLOTHES WASHERS

☐ **22.6.1 Disfavor Whites**
The fewer white textiles you own, the less hot water you use.

☐ **22.6.2 Wear Clothes More Than Once**
Wear most of your clothing two or three times before washing. This means fewer loads and garments that last longer.

☐ **22.6.3 Wash Full Loads Only**
The fewer loads you wash, the lower your bills.

☐ **22.6.4 Wash in Cold Water**
Use hot water only for whites or heavy soils. Even then, use cold water for rinse cycles.

☐ **22.6.5 Use Shorter Wash Cycles**
The less time a load takes, the less electricity is used. Slightly soiled fabrics need only six minutes of wash time. Presoak grimy items.

☐ **22.6.6 Cut Back on Extra Rinses**
This cuts water costs as well.

☐ **22.6.7 Wash Off Peak**
Some utilities charge less at certain times. Run your washer then.

☐ **22.6.8 Follow the Owner's Manual**
Adopt its advice to improve efficiency. If you can't find your manual, visit ManualsOnline.com or search the web for your make, model, and the word "manual."

CLOTHES DRYERS

☐ **22.6.9 Favor Fast–Drying Clothes**
Lightweight clothing dries quickly.

☐ **22.6.10 Use Clothes Lines**
Install one outside or a retractable indoor version in your shower.

☐ **22.6.11 Use Drying Racks**
They make for fewer dryer loads.

☐ **22.6.12 Use Plastic Hangers**
When clothes lines and racks fill up, these provide extra capacity.

☐ **22.6.13 Use the Dryer's Moisture Sensor**
This reduces wasteful over–drying.

☐ **22.6.14 Dry Off Peak**
Some utilities charge less at certain times. Run your dryer then.

☐ **22.6.15 Tumble Press**
Some clothes stiffen when air dried. Five minutes on the permanent press softens them up at a very low cost.

☐ **22.6.16 Dry Several Loads in a Row**
This skips the cost of reheating your dryer for each load.

☐ **22.6.17 Clean Lint Traps and Vents**
Clogging interferes with your dryer's efficiency.

☐ **22.6.18 Buy Natural Gas Dryers**
They cost less to operate than electrics.

☐ **22.6.19 Follow the Owner's Manual**
Adopt its advice to improve efficiency. If you can't find the manual, visit ManualsOnline.com or search the web for your make, model, and the word "manual."

DISHWASHERS

☐ **22.6.20 Avoid Washing Dishes by Hand**
If you're stingy with hot water and your machine is inefficient, you might save; but most sources say that fully loaded dishwashers do the job for less. According to EnergyStar.gov, you save about $40 per year with the dishwasher.

☐ 22.6.21 Avoid Pre–Rinsing

Experiment to see whether you can avoid rinsing dishes. Or soak them in cold water instead.

☐ 22.6.22 Run Full Loads Only

And use less energy during the year.

☐ 22.6.23 Wash Off–Peak

Some utilities charge less at certain hours. Run loads then.

☐ 22.6.24 Use Energy Saving Modes

Reset the buttons once, and the machine works cheaper ever after.

☐ 22.6.25 Air Dry

Heating elements consume energy.

☐ 22.6.26 Check Filters and Drains

Clean them regularly to assure peak efficiency.

☐ 22.6.27 Follow the Owner's Manual

Adopt its advice to improve efficiency. If you can't locate your manual, visit ManualsOnline.com or search the web for your make, model, and the word "manual."

STOVETOPS

☐ 22.6.28 Boil Elsewhere

Heat water efficiently in an electric kettle and transfer it into your pot on the stovetop.

☐ 22.6.29 Run the Microwave

It uses less energy than a stovetop.

☐ 22.6.30 Try Hot Plates for Small Jobs

They're more efficient than stove burners.

☐ 22.6.31 Use Smaller Cookware

Larger pots and pans take more energy to heat.

☐ 22.6.32 Cook With Flat Bottoms Only

This isn't a diet tip: if your pot's base is warped, it costs more to heat whatever you cook. Replace damaged cookware.

☐ **22.6.33 Use the Right Sized Burner**
Small pans on oversized burners waste energy.

☐ **22.6.34 Use Vent Fans Sparingly**
Open a nearby window instead.

☐ **22.6.35 Turn Off Burners Early**
Electric burners stay hot long after they're switched off. Use the residual heat to finish cooking.

OVENS

☐ **22.6.36 Use Alternatives**
Ovens suck electricity. Whenever possible, use slow cookers, toaster ovens, microwaves, or pressure cookers.

☐ **22.6.37 Preheat Sparingly**
Most recipes direct you to warm up the oven while you mix ingredients, but if your preparation takes too long, you waste energy. A solution: prepare first, and then preheat. An oven thermometer shows you when the desired temperature is reached.

☐ **22.6.38 Bake Double Batches**
Cheaper than running the oven twice.

☐ **22.6.39 Keep the Door Closed**
Place a meat thermometer's readout by the oven's window so that you can check the food's temperature without opening the door.

☐ **22.6.40 Leave the Door Open**
In winter, open the oven door after cooking to help heat the kitchen.

REFRIGERATOR/FREEZERS

☐ **22.6.41 Use Energy Saving Modes**
All newer models have them.

☐ **22.6.42 Set Refrigerators to 37°–40°F**
Test the temperature with a thermometer placed in a glass of water.

☐ **22.6.43 Set Freezers to 5°F**
Test temperatures with a thermometer.

☐ **22.6.44 Turn Off the Ice Maker**
If you have enough ice, don't pay to keep the maker running.

☐ **22.6.45 Stock Them Full**
Full refrigerators and freezers consume less energy.

☐ **22.6.46 Keep Doors Closed**
Remove items promptly and close the door. Note to self: mercilessly hound anyone who refuses to comply.

☐ **22.6.47 Keep Hot Foods Out**
Let leftovers cool to room temperature before loading them into the refrigerator or freezer—and do it before they begin to spoil.

☐ **22.6.48 Keep Foods Covered**
Uncovered foods release moisture, and humid air costs more to cool.

☐ **22.6.49 Vacuum Coils Regularly**
This evicts energy sucking dust bunnies.

☐ **22.6.50 Maintain Gaskets**
If door seals crack, your unit leaks air and loses efficiency.

☐ **22.6.51 Follow the Owner's Manual**
Adopt its advice to improve efficiency. If you can't find your manual, visit ManualsOnline.com or search the web for your make, model, and the word "manual."

23

UTILITIES:
WATER

If you're on a meter, the less water you use, the less money you spend. Even if you're on a well, conserving water means fewer pump outs for septic tanks and longer lives for leach fields.

23.1 Use Less in Showers and Baths

Follow the same tactics you used to cut your water heating costs (see 22.3). Avoid bathtubs, install low–volume nozzles, take shorter showers—and even take Navy Showers, if you're really committed or need to be committed. One additional tactic:

☐ **23.1.1 Capture Cold Water**
If your shower takes time to warm up, collect the water in a bucket and use it to flush toilets, water plants, or scrub floors.

23.2 Use Less in Toilets

☐ **23.2.1 Put a Bottle in the Tank**
Fill a plastic bottle with pebbles and place it in the flush tank.

☐ **23.2.2 Flush Only When Necessary**
You're at the controls, so you make the call.

☐ **23.2.3 Favor Low–Flush Toilets**
When we redid our master bathroom, we installed a low–flow model. We use it more often than our other toilets because it uses less water.

☐ **23.2.4 Consider Indoor Leaks**
If water runs for over a minute after flushing, you have issues. Visit HomeDepot.com/hdus/en_US/DTCCOM/HomePage/Commerce/Bath/ Toilets_Bidets/Docs/CP1101–ToiletRepair.pdf.

☐ **23.2.5 Consider Outdoor Leaks**
I live rurally amongst many critters. In one easy step, I cut water use *and* mark my territory.

23.3 Use Less From Faucets

☐ **23.3.1 Fix Dripping Faucets**
Leaky faucets waste water.

☐ **23.3.2 Install Faucet Aerators**
Conserve by cutting the water flow.

☐ **23.3.3 Avoid Running Water**
Don't let water run while you brush teeth, shave, rinse dishes, or wash vegetables.

☐ **23.3.4 Limit Garbage Disposal Use**
Less water goes down the drain; and if you're on a well, you don't have to pump out the septic tank as often.

☐ **23.3.5 Buy Fewer and Smaller Plants**
This means less watering.

23.4 Use Less Outdoors

☐ **23.4.1 Collect Water From Gutter Spouts**
Attach rain barrels and use the runoff for lawns or gardens.

☐ **23.4.2 Don't Water Sidewalks and Driveways**
Position lawn sprinklers correctly.

☐ **23.4.3 Run Sprinklers in the Early Morning or After Sunset**
This way, less evaporates.

☐ **23.4.4 Use Alternatives to Sprinklers**
Irrigate with drip lines or soaker hoses. Buy them used.

☐ **23.4.5 Reschedule Irrigation Automatically**
When wired into your sprinklers, a rain sensor tells your system to skip scheduled waterings after downpours.

☐ **23.4.6 Plant Xeriscapes or Native Grasses**

These reduce or even eliminate the need for irrigation. Visit LessLawn.com.

☐ **23.4.7 Cover Bare Ground**

Use chipped wood, mulch, or gravel to cut evaporation.

☐ **23.4.8 Clean Without Water**

Brooms or blowers work well on decks, sidewalks, and driveways.

☐ **23.4.9 Use Nozzles With Automatic Shut–Offs**

The water flow cuts off whenever you release the handle.

☐ **23.4.10 Wash Cars Less Often**

Cut back to every other week and use a car duster in between washes.

24

UTILITIES:
TRASH COLLECTION

Switch from a flat rate payment plan to pay–as–you–go, which trash services call "pay–as–you–throw." PAYT services track your usage with tags, stickers, or specially marked bags. The fewer of these you use, the less you pay.

PAYT delivers enormous savings. During 1997–2008, I paid a flat fee of about $250 per year. When I switched to PAYT and recycled more, my cost shrank to $34—saving me $216 annually. (I still kick myself for not figuring this out sooner.)

24.1 Choose PAYT and Reduce Your Refuse

Call trash services and ask whether they offer PAYT. (Note: many services don't advertise PAYT because they make more money from flat fees—*so you might have to call*.) Once you switch to PAYT, reduce the volume of trash you generate with these key tactics.

☐ **24.1.1 Recycle**
This is a great first step. Most recycle centers accept paper, cardboard, glass, plastics, aluminum, and steel.

☐ **24.1.2 Compost**
Composting is pure magic: you save money as you help grow food. Even if you don't garden yourself, a neighbor might.

☐ **24.1.3 Reduce Yard Trimmings**
Use mulching lawnmowers; plant xeriscapes (visit LessLawn.com).

☐ **24.1.4 Ditch Disposables**
Switch to reusable products: cloth for paper towels, silverware for plastic ware, permanent coffee filters for paper ones, etc.

☐ 24.1.5 Cut Food Waste
For effective tactics, see 37.6.

☐ 24.1.6 Repair and Reuse
Just because it's broken doesn't mean it's ready for the trash heap.

☐ 24.1.7 Sell or Donate
Don't toss items you can convert into cash, or, at a minimum, into healthy tax deductions.

☐ 24.1.8 Practice Responsible Disposal
Watch for annual drives that collect items recycle centers don't accept, including Styrofoam, batteries, paint, tires, and hazardous chemicals. Home Depot takes in expired CFLs. Radio Shack collects dead rechargeable batteries. Best Buy accepts electronics of all kinds—even if you bought them elsewhere. For details, visit BestBuy.com.

☐ 24.1.9 Halt Junk Mail
Yes, you can recycle the paper, but you can also stop most of it before it ever reaches your mailbox. Several websites operate "no mail" lists: CatalogChoice.org, 41Pounds.org, or PrivacyCouncil.org.

☐ 24.1.10 Avoid Excessive Packaging
Favor products in recyclable containers. Buy foods in bulk. Filter your own water. Buy secondhand items that have already shed their packaging.

☐ 24.1.11 Compact
With PAYT, it pays to reduce. Stomp stuff down with your feet. If your service charges $50 to haul away old mattresses and couches, grab utility knives and wire clippers. Recycle the steel coils, feed the wood to the fireplace, and discard the much-reduced remainder.

☐ 24.1.12 Burn, Baby Burn
This works in rural areas, but creates air pollution. Before firing yourself up for this option, check the local regulations.

☐ 24.1.13 Post a Trash Talking Checklist
Remind cohabitants to mind what they toss. See Appendix 5.

CODA: TRASH COMPACTORS AND GARBAGE DISPOSALS

Neither of these provide good options. Compactors cost money upfront, often require specialized bags, and consume kilowatts. Foot stomping works almost as well. Garbage disposals consume water and electricity. And if you're on a leach field, heavy disposal use means more septic tank pumping. Composting works better.

24.2 Cut Costs under a Flat Rate Payment Plan

☐ **24.2.1 Lobby for PAYT Pricing**
You save, and your hauler wins societal brownie points for promoting greener behaviors.

☐ **24.2.2 Schedule Less Frequent Pick–ups**
Some haulers charge less if you put out the trash every other week.

☐ **24.2.3 Split Costs With Neighbors**
Share collection expenses with one neighbor, and cut your costs in half; share with two neighbors, and cut your costs by two–thirds.

☐ **24.2.4 Haggle as a Group**
If multiple trash companies serve your area, band together with neighbors and throw your "collective" business to the lowest bidder.

☐ **24.2.5 Haul it Yourself**
Before undertaking this, account for landfill fees, fuel costs, vehicle wear, and the value of your time. The trash service might be cheaper.

☐ **24.2.6 Join "Trash Pools"**
You and neighbors take turns hauling everyone's refuse away.

☐ **24.2.7 Seek Discounts**
Some services offer price breaks to seniors and the disabled. Ask your trash hauler whether you qualify.

☐ **24.2.8 Burn, Baby Burn**
Reduce your trash pursuant to 24.1 and torch the rest. Check your local regulations.

25

TELECOMMUNICATIONS: PAY TELEVISION

Currently, the average pay–TV subscription runs $86 per month, for a whopping $1,032 per year. Worse yet, these bills continue to jump by about six percent annually, which is more than twice the overall rate of inflation. But here's some good news: you have many ways to watch TV without watching so many of your dollars disappear.

25.1 Pick Alternatives

Cable and satellite providers once held a tightly wrapped cord around our necks. With the onset of new technologies, their grip has finally loosened. If you tap into enough other video sources—many of which are FREE—you might even cut the cord forever, and save yourself about a thousand per year in the process.

☐ **25.1.1 Attach an Antenna**
Local stations deliver high definition content over the airwaves for FREE. To receive signals, all you need is an HDTV antenna. Indoor versions cost as little as $5. Visit AntennaWeb.org, type in your address, and see antenna choices tailored to your neighborhood's signal strength.

☐ **25.1.2 Access the Internet**
New HDTVs and Blu–Ray players display internet content via a wireless home network or Ethernet connection. If your equipment lacks this capability, you can buy a digital media receiver such as the Roku HD player for as low as $50. Alternatively, if you own a decent computer screen, you can watch online content there. Some video sites are free (CBS.com, C-SpanVideo.org, FreeDocumentaries.org, Crackle.com). Although other sites charge, they still cost less than cable or satellite (Amazon Prime, Hulu Plus).

□ 25.1.3 Corner a Kiosk

RedBox.com offers movies and video games. Currently, DVDs rent for $1.20 per day and Blu–Rays for $1.50. Provide your email address and receive a steady supply of promo codes.

□ 25.1.4 Join Netflix

Monthly plans start at $8. Share a subscription with a friend and cut your costs in half. Visit NetFlix.com.

□ 25.1.5 Borrow Video Content

Libraries lend not only movies, but also documentaries, educational films, and entire TV seasons. Borrow DVDs from friends too.

□ 25.1.6 Trade With Others

Visit Swap.com or SwapaDVD.com. Trade with friends.

25.2 Bundle

You might cut your overall costs for television, internet, landline, and cells if you buy them all from a single provider. Run the numbers in advance to confirm your savings.

25.3 Use Your Memberships

Look for cable/satellite deals offered through your warehouse membership club, AAA, or any other groups to which you belong. I went through Costco for my last satellite contract and scored $60 off of the first year's subscription, plus a $180 gift card.

25.4 Try Group Buynamics

If you have roommates, share TV costs. Then you all can fight over who gets the remote. For pay–for–view events, invite friends and split the costs. Some providers pay cash bonuses if you refer new subscribers.

25.5 Avoid Bells and Whistles

Cable and satellite companies are notorious for tacking fees onto monthly bills. Dodge them and save.

□ **25.5.1 Cancel Premium Services**

Drop any you don't use. For any must–see series, wait until you can rent the DVDs. Switch to cheaper packages with fewer channels.

□ **25.5.2 Forgo Pay–For–View**

Movies cost $5 or more when you order them with your remote control, but only $1.20 at Redbox.com.

□ **25.5.3 Sidestep Equipment Rentals**

Don't pay extra for converter boxes or other equipment. Instead, buy them used. Confirm with your TV provider in advance that supplying your own hardware will actually remove the rental fees.

□ **25.5.4 Ditch DVRs**

At $8 or more per month, these costs add up fast. But if you dislike commercials, maybe it's a small price to pay.

25.6 Avoid Pitfalls

□ **25.6.1 Dodge Late Fees**

Arrange for automatic payments and you never have to worry.

□ **25.6.2 Watch Out for Rebates**

Read the fine print whenever you switch providers. Some new customer offers take the form of rebates that must be formally redeemed. If you don't redeem them, you don't save.

□ **25.6.3 Suspend Service During Travel**

Many providers allow you to temporarily suspend your account during lengthy vacations. Take advantage of such policies. Don't pay for TV you're not there to use.

□ **25.6.4 Know When the Contract Expires**

Mark your calendar with the expiry date. When it arrives, renegotiate or cancel (see 25.7 and 25.8). If you do nothing, your bill skyrockets and you commit the grave sin of overpaying.

25.7 Haggle

Competition is intense, so a single phone call often yields savings. Let the operator know what other companies offer new customers and ask for the same deal. Usually, you have to speak to another department before you're connected to anyone authorized to bargain. When haggling, hold out for common deal sweeteners such as three FREE months of movie channels. Until you hear that bonus dangled forth, you haven't heard the best offer.

25.8 Play the Cancel Card

Read this war story and profit. Before I switched satellite services, I called my existing provider and tried to get the price they gave to new customers (I had been with the company for five years). Despite my several threats to cancel, the company refused to budge. So I terminated the service and signed up with their competitor. Within a week, the old service pummeled me with telephone calls offering— you guessed it—the same deal it gave new customers. The lesson: often threats aren't enough, and you have to actually cancel. In fact, some savvy fringers routinely terminate at the end of their contracts and make do with broadcast signals for a few days (see 25.1.1) until the inevitable offers start rolling in. Better yet, if you cancel as you leave on vacations or business trips, you can snag a lower price when you return and not miss any service at all.

26

TELECOMMUNICATIONS: LANDLINES

According to a 2011 industry survey, a basic landline now costs about $500 per year. Back when Ma Bell held a monopoly, you had one choice only. Nowadays, services abound and you have many ways to save.

26.1 Ditch the Landline and Use Cell Phones

More Americans have decided to drop their landlines. According to the National Center for Health Statistics (NCHS), as of the first half of 2007, 14 percent of US households used cell phones only. By the second half of 2011, wireless–only households had jumped to 34 percent. The NCHS suggests that others are poised to join the trend, because in almost one of every six households that still cling to a landline, almost all calls are made wirelessly.

If you haven't already done so, evaluate whether to ditch this relic from the last century. Here's a checklist that helps you make the call. The more often you check the "No" boxes, the more sense it makes to cancel the service.

Should I Keep My Landline?

No.	Factors	Yes	No
1	*My Home's Wireless Signal Is Weak.* Walk around your house and test the reception in several places. If service is spotty, check the "yes" box; if it's strong, check "no." Even if you checked "yes," explore whether you can beef up signal strength with a "cell phone signal booster." Or switch your cell service to a carrier that delivers a stronger signal.	□	□

No.	Factors	Yes	No

2   *My Cell Phone Is Unreliable.* If you suffer from dropped calls, dead batteries, or other cell phone troubles, keep the landline. Or address these problems with: (1) cell chargers that use car batteries, hand cranks, or solar panels; (2) backup batteries or phones (buy them used on eBay); (3) VoIP service through a broadband connection (see 26.2); and (4) separate cell phones for each household member (one of which should work at the crucial moment of need, provided the phone's owner is home).   ☐   ☐

3   *My Household Still Uses a Landline.* If so, perhaps you should keep it. However, if yours is among the one in six households that pay for a landline, but use it rarely, going wireless makes good sense.   ☐   ☐

4   *I Want a Listed Number.* Unless you request otherwise (and pay a fee), your landline number is public information. This lets old friends track you down, but it also exposes you to obnoxious pollsters, dubious charities, and other undesirables. In contrast to landlines, cell phones generally go unlisted.   ☐   ☐

5   *Instant 911 Call Location Is Important to Me.* When you dial 911 on a landline, the dispatcher sees a readout of your address—a helpful feature in an emergency. Cell phones don't offer this capability yet, but you can contact emergency service providers to tell them to list your home address as your cell's default location.   ☐   ☐

6   *Power Outages Are Frequent Where I Live.* Corded phones work without electricity (however, cordless landline phones don't). Cell phones work in power outages too, but they require charged batteries.   ☐   ☐

No.	Factors	Yes	No
7	*I Love to Fax.* If you still use a fax machine, your best bet for reliable service is an analog landline. Cell phones can't transmit faxes. You could, of course, drop the landline and switch to a web–based fax service, but that requires old dogs to learn new tricks, and being an old dog is likely why you still heel to the fax screech.	□	□
8	*Dropping My Landline Triggers New Charges or Interferes With Other Services.* Before you cut the cord, think about the consequences. Without a landline, you might need to buy more mobile minutes or additional cell phones for other household members. Some home security systems won't work without a constant phone connection. Some satellite providers require a landline in order to deliver pay-per-view shows or seasonal sports packages.	□	□

26.2 Ditch the Landline and Use VoIP

Voice over Internet Protocol (VoIP) systems use your internet connection. If you intend VoIP to *replace* a landline, pick a service that lets you call cell phones and landlines, and isn't limited to computer–to–computer calls. Also, pick a service that allows long distance and international calls. Read the latest reviews of top providers at ConsumerSearch.com/voip or *Consumer Reports.* To decide whether to adopt this option, work through this checklist.

VoIP ADVANTAGES

□ *VoIP Is Portable.* If you use landlines and move often, you pay disconnect and reconnect fees. With VoIP, the service moves wherever you do for FREE.

□ *For Premium Phone Service, VoIP Costs Less.* If you load your landline with premiums such as call waiting, voicemail, and three–way calling, your costs can run $700 per year. But with VoIP these premiums are standard (savings versus landlines: $300–$400 per year).

❑ *For Basic Phone Service, VoIP Can Be Cheaper.* If you have a bare bones landline, a switch to VoIP can save you money, but you have to shop around. As of this writing, Vonage's cheapest VoIP service allows unlimited incoming calls and 300 minutes per month of outbound local and long distance calls. This costs $144 per year, plus local taxes and levies. A Vonage competitor, Phone Power, offers unlimited domestic service for about $100 per year. The catch is that you have to pay for two full years upfront. Bottom line: if you now pay for basic landline service, which runs about $350–$420 annually, a switch to one of the cheaper VoIP plans will save you about $175–$225 per year.

VoIP DISADVANTAGES

❑ *VoIP Quality Depends on Your Broadband Quality.* According to ConsumerSearch.com, fiber optic services and cable companies deliver the fastest internet. If you buy your internet elsewhere, use these online testers to predict the likely VoIP quality:

- VoipReview.org/voipspeedtester.aspx

- WhichVoip.com/voip/speed_test/ppspeed.html.

❑ *VoIP Fails During Internet and Power Outages, but Workarounds Exist.* Until recently, a big knock against VoIP was that it wouldn't work in power or internet outages. Nowadays, however, most VoIPs forward incoming calls to your cell phone whenever such lapses occur.

❑ *911 Calls on VoIP Require Advance Preparation.* Depending on the VoIP provider's capabilities, your local 911 operator might not receive a readout of your location and callback number. The FCC requires providers to explain all 911 limitations upfront and to obtain your signed acknowledgement that you understand them.

❑ *VoIP Can't Match the Reliability of Landlines.* Traditional phones are overpriced, but at least they're reliable. Internet connections aren't as trustworthy yet, and that's what VoIP depends upon. It boils down to this: will you accept periodic glitches in exchange for a 50 percent price break on phone service?

26.3 Keep the Landline and Seek Savings

☐ **26.3.1 Switch to a PAYG Cell Phone**

If you keep the landline, it's easier to get by with an inexpensive PAYG cell plan (see 27.1).

☐ **26.3.2 Bundle**

You might cut your overall costs for landline, internet, television, and cells if you buy them all from a single provider. Run the numbers in advance to confirm your savings.

☐ **26.3.3 Shop Around**

Visit Movearoo.com or ConnectMyPhone.com, where you can enter your home address and receive offers from local phone companies.

☐ **26.3.4 Avoid Bells and Whistles**

Stick to basics. Decline extras like voice mail and caller id.

☐ **26.3.5 Use Long Distance and International Calling Cards**

You have to program a 1-800 number and password into your handset, but the savings make it worthwhile. As of this writing, Costco sells a $20 card for 700 minutes worth of stateside calls (at $0.029 per minute) and a $30 card for international calls (at slightly higher rates, which vary by the country called). Visit Yahoo! Shopping or Google Shopping to search for similar cards.

☐ **26.3.6 Use Free Long Distance**

Get FREE long distance and international calls in exchange for listening to a couple of short (10 to 12 seconds) commercials. Visit FreePhone2Phone.com.

☐ **26.3.7 Share With Roommates**

Split landline costs with your housemates—yet another benefit of social living.

☐ **26.3.8 Scour the Bill**

The phone company might charge you for services you never use and don't even know you have. If so, call to have the services removed. Seek a refund for past charges.

☐ 26.3.9 Keep Alert for New Deals

Just because you have a landline now doesn't mean you need one forever. Newer technologies continue to improve. Revisit your options annually to see whether it's time to cut the cord.

26.4 Haggle

If you buy premium services from the phone company, you probably can talk your way into a lower monthly rate. Negotiations might shave a few bucks off your bill, but you pay less—much less—if you choose the barebones service.

If you have basic service, like I do, discounts are unlikely. Still, I took a stab at negotiation. A loyalty department representative told me the price couldn't be dropped since I already had the cheapest package available. I persisted. I asked whether any deals were possible if I paid one year in advance (answer: no), signed a multi-year contract (no again) or switched to PAYG (no here too). Finally, the agent tired and offered four months' service at half price. I accepted, and thereby saved myself $34, which represents 10 percent off my annual bill. Not great, but well worth the short phone call. I'll try the same approach next year—provided I haven't ditched the landline by then.

27

TELECOMMUNICATIONS: CELL PHONES

As of 2011, US consumers accounted for 321 million cell phone subscriptions—that's more than one phone per person. All this service comes at a heavy price. According to JD Power, the average cell phone user pays $78 per month, or $936 per year. For those who choose smart phones with internet access, the cost jumps to $1,500.

Try this three part approach to slash costs. First, if you're a light user—less than 40 minutes per week—shop around for an inexpensive pay–as–you–go (PAYG) phone. Second, if you're a moderate user—between 40 and 70 or so minutes per week—cut your usage enough so that PAYG makes sense. Third, if you're a heavy cell phone user—more than 70 minutes weekly—choose from a smorgasbord of tactics, none of which force you to cut down on any yakking.

27.1 Choose a PAYG Phone

PAYG offers many advantages. You avoid credit checks, contracts, monthly bills, and most of the phone company "gotchas" (late payment fees, overage charges, and termination penalties). Some plans even provide advanced features like call forwarding and internet access. Best of all, rates are low. Under the best deals, if you pay $100 in advance, your phone loads up with 1,000 minutes that don't expire for a full year, which saves you $776 off the average subscription price.

Visit online review sites. ConsumerSearch.com recommends several reliable PAYG services based upon your expected level of use. PrepaidReviews.com provides star ratings of more than 25 PAYG providers. MyRatePlan.com takes a similar approach. As you shop, look at these issues.

- *Activation Fees.* Some companies charge fees to activate phones for the first time. Ask for waivers or choose carriers that don't impose the charges.

- *Daily Access Fees.* Under some PAYG plans, you pay a lower per minute charge, but on any given day that you use the phone, you pay a $1–$3 access fee. If you don't use the phone very often, then this fee structure might make sense. Otherwise, pick a plan that charges more per minute, but doesn't charge you separately for access.

- *Refill Expirations.* Under most PAYG plans, the fewer minutes you buy, the sooner they expire. If you spend $100 upfront, however, your minutes last a full year, and any unused time rolls over if you recharge with another $100 within twelve months.

- *Roaming Charges.* Any cell phone has a designated home territory — a metro area, state, or, under the best plans, the entire country. When you're outside of the designated area and make a call, you're "roaming." Some PAYG plans charge extra for these calls and others don't.

- *Nationwide Long Distance.* If you make frequent calls to numbers outside your home area code, favor plans with FREE nationwide calling.

- *International Calls.* If you expect to travel abroad, including Canada and Mexico, know whether the phone works there and what calls cost.

- *Coverage.* Before buying, check the carrier's call quality at the places you spend the most time. When friends visit your home, have them make calls to test the signal strength of their carriers. And be sure to visit DeadCellZones.com and CellReception.com, where you can type in any address and receive reports of various carriers' reception quality at that precise location.

- *Handset Features.* Choose from among cameras, Bluetooth, keyboards, speakerphone, touch screens, etc.

27.2 Reduce Cell Phone Use and Choose PAYG

If you're a moderate cell phone user, a PAYG plan lies within reach, but to get there, you have to slash minutes. Consider these tactics.

☐ **27.2.1 Rethink Your Cell's Social Life**
Your cell's greatest advantage is its mobility—it lets you schedule meetings on the fly, locate friends in a crowd, and solve all kinds of minor hassles. When it comes to social calls, however, your cell offers no advantages over less expensive options such as face–to–face conversations and landlines. Limit your cell phone's socializing.

☐ **27.2.2 Use Other Phones**
During the day, you're near phones other than your cell: landlines, VoIP lines, or the cells of family members. Use these alternatives whenever you can.

☐ **27.2.3 Time Yourself**
On outbound calls, if the conversation can wait until you can reach a cheaper phone, talk later. On incoming calls, keep conversations short or ask if you can call back at another time on a different line.

☐ **27.2.4 Retrieve Voice Mails on Landlines**
The minutes you save will end up saving you.

☐ **27.2.5 Turn Cells Off**
A phone doesn't have to be on 24/7. The more it's off, the fewer minutes you use.

☐ **27.2.6 Use Email**
Whenever practical, write instead of call.

27.3 Pay a Monthly Bill but Limit Costs

If you're a heavy user, a monthly plan delivers value. With these tactics, you enjoy reasonable bills that don't leave you speechless.

☐ **27.3.1 Ditch the Landline**
If you rely on your cell phone this much, you probably can ditch the landline (see 26.1). Don't pay for redundant services.

❑ 27.3.2 Shop Around
With 321 million cell subscriptions, the US market is saturated. Price wars are near. Research the latest deals at PhoneDog.com, CNET.com, ConsumerSearch.com, and MyRatePlan.com. Or visit BillShrink.com, which reviews your recent call records and suggests cheaper plans based on your actual usage.

❑ 27.3.3 Try Before You Buy
Many carriers offer one–month trials during which you can cancel contracts without penalty.

❑ 27.3.4 Hire a No–Contract Carrier
At StraightTalk.com, for example, you get unlimited talk, data, and text for about $45 monthly—half the price of a typical smart phone.

❑ 27.3.5 Shop at Warehouse Clubs
If you're a member, don't sign any new cell contract until you first review the latest warehouse offers.

❑ 27.3.6 Bundle
Some carriers include a cell phone option in their bundled offers.

❑ 27.3.7 Avoid Extras
Smart phones are expensive. Opt for less trendy handsets that offer great features at lower prices.

❑ 27.3.8 Talk When Talk Is Cheap
If you chat on evenings and weekends, seek plans that offer discounts for calls at those times.

❑ 27.3.9 Text Sparingly
Texting is convenient, but costly. Leave this form of communication to teenagers and the very wealthy.

❑ 27.3.10 Download a Text App
If text you must, limit your costs with an app such as TextPlus.com.

❑ 27.3.11 Use the Internet at Home
Unless you have Wi–Fi at home, surfing via cell costs more. Ride the surf where the surf is cheap, dude.

□ **27.3.12 Call FREE 411**

Call 1-800-FREE-411 and get FREE directory assistance if you listen to a short commercial (about 12 seconds).

□ **27.3.13 Follow Family Planning**

If your household consumes minutes by the truckload, shop at carriers that offer low–cost family plans.

□ **27.3.14 Follow Tax Planning**

If you use your cell phone for business purposes, you may be able to pay for part of the monthly bill with pre–tax dollars. The rules are complicated, so consult your tax advisor.

28

TELECOMMUNICATIONS: INTERNET

According to a 2011 industry survey, the average household pays $552 per year to Internet Service Providers (ISPs). Despite this cost, the internet pays its own way. Newspaper delivery costs $180, but online subscriptions go for $45. Postage runs $50 per year if you pay bills by mail, but nothing if you pay online. Retail stores are pricey, but with internet vendors like eBay or Craigslist you can locate what you need quickly and buy it secondhand for less. Despite these savings, don't deny yourself the frugal pleasure of trimming one of modern life's basic overhead costs. Here are three strategies.

28.1 Consider Alternatives to ISPs

If you surf infrequently, you have several options for finding low–cost access.

☐ 28.1.1 Visit Libraries
Most branches offer computers with FREE broadband access.

☐ 28.1.2 Locate Free Wi–Fi
Many businesses offer FREE internet access to anyone with Wi-Fi enabled devices, including McDonald's, Starbucks, and Panera Bread. Locate hotspots at WiFiFreeSpot.com or JiWire.com. When you use public Wi–Fi, take steps to protect your identity and data. For details, read "10 Tips for Public Wi–Fi Hotspot Security," at PCMag.com.

☐ 28.1.3 If Permitted, Use the Internet at Work
If it's allowed, surf during your breaks.

☐ 28.1.4 Access Free Broadband
Amazon's Kindle includes a basic browser that provides FREE internet via Wi–Fi and, if you pay more upfront, 4G mobile access.

☐ 28.1.5 Consider Free Dial Up

NetZero.net offers up to ten hours of FREE dial–up web surfing each month. At home, use this slow service to access text–based sites that don't require much speed. Visit the library for any sites that require a fast connection.

☐ 28.1.6 Buy PAYG Access

Some phone companies—Virgin Mobile, for one—offer prepaid cards that provide mobile internet access without a contract.

28.2 Cut Back on Internet Use

If your usage is more than light (several hours each week), but less than heavy (several hours each day), cut back and adopt 28.1 above.

☐ 28.2.1 Forgo Video

Rely instead on old standbys like TVs and DVDs.

☐ 28.2.2 Get News, Sports, and Weather Elsewhere

Access these reports for FREE on radio and TV.

☐ 28.2.3 Use Snail Mail

Monitor your finances monthly instead of daily.

☐ 28.2.4 Check Email Less Often

According to experts, this improves your efficiency. Added benefit: it reduces your need for constant internet access. Rely more upon the telephone and face–to–face interaction.

☐ 28.2.5 Use the Sneaker Net

Download large files to disks or flash drives and hand deliver them. It worked during the Clinton years, and it still works now.

☐ 28.2.6 Plan Ahead

Prepare lists of upcoming internet searches. This improves your online efficiency and reduces your need for ISPs.

☐ 28.2.7 Recreate Offline

For video games, buy a used TV gaming console. Rediscover cards and board games. Go for walks, read books, and participate in other activities that don't charge monthly access fees.

28.3 Pay ISPs, but Pay Less

If you spend five hours each day on the internet, a $40 monthly bill works out to 27 cents per hour. That's cheap. But make things cheaper yet with these tactics.

☐ 28.3.1 Bundle
You might cut your overall costs for internet, landline, television, and cells if you buy them all from a single provider. Run the numbers in advance to confirm your savings.

☐ 28.3.2 Shop Around
Locally owned wireless ISPs often offer lower rates. Check the yellow pages for options. Or visit price comparison sites such as WhiteFence.com.

☐ 28.3.3 Don't Buy Speed That You Don't Need
Don't pay for fast service if you rarely visit sites that require broadband access.

☐ 28.3.4 Avoid Duplication
Do you really need both home and mobile internet?

☐ 28.3.5 Share With Neighbors or Roommates
A neighbor's Wi–Fi might spill into your house. Share access and split the costs. Don't use anyone's internet without permission.

☐ 28.3.6 Seek Out Special Offers
Before you hire an ISP, search for special offers and coupon codes.

☐ 28.3.7 Prepay
Some ISPs—particularly dial–ups—offer discounts if you pay a full year in advance. If the ISP goes bankrupt before the year runs out, you'll be out some money, so pay upfront only if the company is well–established.

☐ 28.3.8 Leverage the Technology to Save
Your internet service pays off whenever you access FREE content: music, e–books, audio books, magazines, news, video, sports, streaming radio, and baseball broadcasts (visit MiLB.com).

☐ 28.3.9 Suspend Service During Travel

Many ISPs allow you to temporarily suspend your account when you go on long vacations. Take advantage of these policies. Don't pay for internet you're not there to use.

☐ 28.3.10 Play the Cancel Card

Drop service at each contract's end and go a few days without internet to re–qualify for introductory rates. Alternatively, if you cancel as you leave on vacations or business trips, you can snag a lower price when you return and not miss any service at all.

INSURANCE: HOMEOWNERS INSURANCE

HomeInsurance.com reports that annual premiums now average $917. If you're like most homeowners, it's been years since you last reviewed your policy or shopped around for better deals. As a result, you likely overpay—and nothing hurts a fringer more than that. Avoid the house of pain with these strategies.

29.1 Research the Product

Not only are these policies costly, they're complicated. The typical contract exceeds fifty pages, so it makes sense to educate yourself. The National Association of Insurance Commissioners (NAIC) publishes a "Consumer Guide to Homeowners Insurance." Visit NAIC.org.

29.2 Measure Your Needs

If you buy too much coverage, you overpay, so find the right fit.

☐ **29.2.1 Compute Your Home's Replacement Value**
Buy only the coverage needed to rebuild lost structures (don't insure the land because that survives any natural disaster). Buy more coverage if your home features gourmet kitchens or luxury bathrooms. Use these resources to calculate a value.

- *Free Calculators*. Visit Building-Cost.net or search the internet for "free home insurance calculators."

- *Low–Cost Calculators*. For fancier calculators that cost about $8, visit AccuCoverage.com or HMFacts.com.

- *Local Experts*. Ask a nearby broker or builder to estimate the typical cost per square foot of construction and multiply that number times the size of your home.

❏ 29.2.2 Disfavor Extras

You need insurance, not bells and whistles. Weigh carefully whether to buy coverage for sewer backups, carpet damage, and mold remediation.

❏ 29.2.3 Choose the Highest Deductible You Can Afford

Insure only for major catastrophes that would have a severe—and not merely inconvenient—effect upon your finances. Use some of what you save on premiums to buy inexpensive safety devices: power outage sensors, deadbolt locks, intrusion alarms, security lights, and steel–belted hoses for washing machines. These might even qualify you for further discounts (see 29.3.4).

29.3 Shop Around

Market conditions change constantly. Shop at least every other year.

❏ 29.3.1 Seek Online Quotes

Popular comparison sites include Insure.com and Bankrate.com.

❏ 29.3.2 Visit Insurance Company Websites

Many insurers don't list on price comparison sites, including Geico, Progressive, USAA, Allstate, Amica, and State Farm.

❏ 29.3.3 Call an Independent Agent

Ratchet up the competition. Locate a good deal online and then ask an agent to find you something better.

❏ 29.3.4 Seek Discounts

Look for these deals whenever you pay a bill or shop around for new homeowners policies.

- *Bundles*. If you now pay multiple insurers for home, auto, and life, consider buying from a single company. Run the numbers.

- *Group Discounts*. Look for price breaks if you belong to certain groups—retirees, seniors, veterans, current military, employees of large corporations, AAA, or AARP.

- *High Credit Scores*. If yours is lofty, make an inquiry.

- *Annual Premium Payments.* Some insurers grant breaks if you pay premiums in advance.

- *Safety Features.* Some insurers offer discounts for alarms, deadbolt locks, fire sprinklers, or other similar devices.

- *Structural Features.* Houses made of brick, rather than of straw or sticks, cost less to insure. Seek discounts if you have fire resistant siding, heavy shingles, a reinforced roof, storm shutters, shatterproof windows, earthquake retrofits, or other safeguards that protect your home against natural forces and hard blowing wolves.

- *Updated Home Systems.* New furnaces, air conditioners, hot water heaters, or electrical wiring might trigger discounts.

- *Location, Location, Location.* Seek discounts for proximity to hydrants and fire stations, inclusion in gated communities, or governance by homeowners' associations.

- *Zero Claims.* Some insurers issue discounts to customers who never file claims. If your claims record is spotless, ask for a break on premiums.

- *Loyalty.* At many companies, longtime customers pay less.

- *Credit Card Payments.* Pay with plastic and pocket the rewards, but *only* if you pay off your cards every month (see Chapter 49).

29.4 Pick a Low–Priced Insurer

After you find the best offers, it's time to investigate the insurers that made them.

☐ 29.4.1 Talk With Friends
Ask if they have experience with any of your prospective insurers.

☐ 29.4.2 Research Customer Satisfaction
Some insurance companies pay off claims quicker than others and do it without hassles. Review ratings in *Consumer Reports* and at

JDPower.com. To view customer complaint records, click on your home state at NAIC.org/state_web_map.htm.

29.4.3 Research Company Finances

Buy from solvent insurers only. Check with your state's regulatory agency or private sources such as A.M. Best and Standard & Poor's.

29.5 Follow Up

29.5.1 Keep a File

Maintain copies of your policy, endorsements, declarations page, price comparisons, and buying guides.

29.5.2 Maintain a High Credit Score

At many insurers, those with higher credit scores qualify for lower premiums. Maintain your score by paying bills and loan installments on time. Check with the three major reporting agencies each year to make sure that your credit history is accurate. To request a FREE copy of your report, visit AnnualCreditReport.com.

29.5.3 List Personal Property

If you ever file a claim, you need to prove your loss. Before disaster strikes, make a video of all rooms and closets. Scan receipts of any big ticket items. For FREE software that helps you prepare an inventory, visit KnowYourStuff.org. Keep copies of the data in multiple safe places away from home.

29.5.4 Perform Home Repairs

Homeowners policies typically exclude coverage of losses that stem from neglect or failure to repair.

29.5.5 Avoid Small Claims

A new claim raises your premium and sometimes makes it difficult to obtain insurance in the future. Self–insure for smaller losses and file claims only for major catastrophes.

29.5.6 Avoid High–Risk Stuff

Certain possessions make insurers cringe: pools, trampolines, and aggressive dog breeds. Most companies either charge more to insure these items or refuse to cover them at all.

☐ **29.5.7 Avoid High–End Stuff**

Most frugal fringers don't own furs, high–end jewelry, original art, valuable antiques, and big–time coin or stamp collections. Many insurers cap their coverage for these items, so if you want insurance, prepare yourself to pay higher premiums.

29.6 Buy Insurance Friendly Houses

☐ **29.6.1 Buy a Smaller House**

The smaller the home, the lower your premiums.

☐ **29.6.2 Buy a Newer House**

Older homes cost more to insure, particularly if plumbing and electrical systems are antiquated.

☐ **29.6.3 Avoid High Risk Areas**

Homes located in areas prone to natural calamities—wildfires, mudslides, coastal storms—cost more to insure. So do homes sited in high crime areas or away from fire stations and hydrants.

☐ **29.6.4 Avoid Flood Plains**

Buy a house near a river and you'll pay extra for flood insurance, which typical homeowners policies don't cover.

☐ **29.6.5 Check Insurance Costs Before You Buy**

Ask the seller for a report of the house's insurance loss history, generally contained in CLUE (Comprehensive Loss Underwriting Exchange) or A–PLUS reports. These may disclose conditions that inflate premiums or, in the worst cases, make it impossible to obtain any coverage at all. Homeowners can access CLUE reports for FREE at LexisNexis.com.

30

INSURANCE:
AUTO INSURANCE

The average auto insurance policy costs about $1,200 per year. What you pay depends upon several factors, some of which are difficult to change, including your state of residence, the make and model of your vehicle, and your age. No matter what your own particulars, you still have many good choices available to spend less on this line item. Here are the best strategies.

30.1 Research the Product

Auto policies are complex, so before you shop, read a buyer's guide. The National Association of Insurance Commissioners (NAIC) publishes "A Consumer's Guide to Auto Insurance." Visit NAIC.org.

30.2 Measure Your Needs

If you buy too much coverage, you overpay—so find the right fit.

☐ **30.2.1 Consider Cancelling Collision/Comprehensive Coverage**
Consumer Reports suggests that you drop this coverage if the annual premiums exceed 10 percent of your car's value. To assess value based upon recent market data, visit Kelley Blue Book at KBB.com.

☐ **30.2.2 Consider "Pay–As–You–Drive" or "Usage–Based" Plans**
Look at policies that base premiums upon actual driving habits, including total miles travelled, speeds, and acceleration rates. To qualify, you must agree to outfit your car with a "telematic" device that tracks its every move. Progressive and Allstate offer PAYD policies, as do other companies. This is the insurance of the future and it's available now.

☐ **30.2.3 Ditch Excess Vehicles**
If you own vehicles you don't drive often, sell them.

☐ 30.2.4 Disfavor Extras

You need insurance, not bells and whistles. Decline coverage for roadside assistance, towing, rental car reimbursement, and other small–time risks.

☐ 30.2.5 Choose the Highest Deductible You Can Afford

Use auto insurance to insure for major catastrophes that would have a severe—and not merely inconvenient—effect upon your finances. Ask your agent about the availability of higher deductibles.

30.3 Shop Around

Market conditions change. Shop for policies at least every other year.

☐ 30.3.1 Seek Online Quotes

Visit price comparison sites: Insure.com and Bankrate.com.

☐ 30.3.2 Visit Insurance Company Websites

Many insurers don't list at price comparison sites, but still offer competitive products, including Geico, USAA, Progressive, Allstate, Amica, and State Farm.

☐ 30.3.3 Call an Independent Agent

Ratchet up the competition. Locate a good deal online and then ask an agent to find you something better. If the agent beats the price you found, you save.

☐ 30.3.4 Seek Discounts

Look for these deals whenever you pay a bill or shop around for new auto insurance policies.

- *Bundles.* If you pay multiple insurers for home, life, and auto, consider buying from a single company. Run the numbers.

- *Group Discounts.* Look for price breaks if you belong to certain groups—retirees, seniors, veterans, current military, employees of large corporations, AAA, or AARP.

- *Annual Premium Payments.* Some insurers grant breaks if you pay a year in advance.

- *High Credit Scores.* If yours is lofty, make an inquiry.

- *Safety Features.* If your vehicle has side air bags, anti–lock brakes, or daytime running lights, ask whether any discounts apply.

- *Anti–Theft Devices.* Some insurers lower premiums for autos with anti–theft features.

- *Alternative Fuel Vehicles.* Hybrids or electrics receive price breaks from some insurers.

- *Driving Records.* Fewer accidents and speeding tickets often trigger lower premiums.

- *Defensive Driving Courses.* Ask whether you would receive a discount if you completed a driver's safety course.

- *Good Students.* Many insurers offer discounts for teenage drivers with high grades.

- *Low Mileage.* The fewer miles your vehicle travels each year, the lower your accident risk.

- *Multiple Vehicles.* Check for discounts if you insure more than one vehicle.

- *Non–Drinkers and Non–Smokers.* If you're healthy, look for vigorous discounts.

- *Zero Claims.* Some insurers issue discounts to customers who never file claims. If your claims record is spotless, ask for a break on premiums.

- *Loyalty.* At many companies, longtime customers pay less.

- *Credit Card Payments.* Pay with plastic and pocket the rewards, but *only* if you pay off your cards every month (see Chapter 49).

30.4 Pick a Low–Priced Insurer

After you find the best offers, it's time to investigate insurers.

☐ 30.4.1 Talk With Friends
Ask if they have experience with any of your prospective insurers.

☐ 30.4.2 Research Customer Satisfaction
Some insurance companies pay off claims quicker than others. Review ratings in *Consumer Reports* and at JDPower.com. To view customer complaint records, click on the map of your home state at NAIC.org/state_web_map.htm.

☐ 30.4.3 Research Financial Footings
Buy from solvent insurers only. Check with your state's regulatory agency or with private sources such as A.M. Best and Standard & Poor's.

30.5 Follow Up

☐ 30.5.1 Keep a File
Maintain copies of your policy, endorsements, declarations page, price comparisons, and buying guides.

☐ 30.5.2 Maintain a High Credit Score
At many insurers, those with higher credit scores qualify for lower premiums. Maintain your score by paying bills and loan installments on time. Check with the three major reporting agencies each year to make sure that your credit history is accurate. To request a FREE copy of your report, visit AnnualCreditReport.com.

☐ 30.5.3 Avoid Moving Violations
You pay twice: first you pay a fine and then your premiums jump.

☐ 30.5.4 Don't Drink and Drive
Convictions trigger sky–high premiums (see 14.3).

☐ 30.5.5 Avoid Small Claims
A new claim raises your premium and sometimes makes it difficult to obtain insurance in the future. Self insure for smaller losses and file claims only for major catastrophes.

31

INSURANCE: TERM LIFE INSURANCE

Insurers peddle two types of policies: "cash value" and "term life." The first type builds up value as long as you pay premiums. You can cash out the policy by canceling it at anytime. If you die before you cancel, your beneficiaries collect. For most people, cash value policies represent a bad value, so this checklist covers only term life insurance. Term life provides coverage for a specific length of time— 10, 15, or more years—and pays out only if you expire before the policy does. Term life policies don't build up cash value and under some contracts, premiums increase as you age. Follow these strategies to find the best values.

31.1 Research the Product

Term life policies are complex products, so educate yourself. The National Association of Insurance Commissioners (NAIC) publishes a "Life Insurance Buyer's Guide." Visit NAIC.org. The American Council of Life Insurers (ACLI) publishes "What You Should Know About Buying Life Insurance." Visit ACLI.com.

31.2 Decide Whether You Need Insurance

The purpose of life insurance is to provide your dependents with a replacement income stream in case you die. Depending on your current stage of life, you might be able to skip the expense.

- *No Dependents.* If you lack dependents, you don't need insurance because no one other than you relies upon your income.

- *Empty Nests.* Your kids are independent, so drop the insurance.

- *Ample Assets.* If your nest egg can fund your dependents' expenses for years to come, you can skip this line item altogether.

31.3 Measure Your Needs

If you buy too much coverage, you overpay. To find the right fit, offset your beneficiaries' future expenses against their available assets and income. Several web–based calculators walk you through the process:

- Bankrate.com/calculators/insurance/life-insurance-calculator.aspx

- SmartMoney.com/personal-finance/insurance/how-much-life-insurance-do-you-need-12949/

- Insurance.va.gov/sglisite/calculator/needscalc.htm.

31.4 Shop Around

☐ **31.4.1 Seek Online Quotes**
Popular price comparison sites include Insure.com, AccuQuote.com, Term4Sale.com, and InsWeb.com.

☐ **31.4.2 Visit Insurance Company Websites**
Many insurers sell low–cost plans, but don't list on price comparison sites, including Ameritas and USAA. Visit their websites.

☐ **31.4.3 Call an Independent Agent**
Locate a good deal online and then ask an agent to find you something better. If the agent beats the offer you found, you save.

☐ **31.4.4 Seek Discounts**
Look for these deals whenever you pay a bill or shop around for new life insurance policies.

- *Bundles*. If you now pay multiple insurers for home, life, and auto, consider buying it all from a single company. Run the numbers.

- *Group Discounts*. Look for price breaks if you belong to certain groups—retirees, seniors, veterans, current military, AAA, or AARP.

- *Annual Premium Payments*. Some insurers grant discounts if you pay a year in advance.

- *Loyalty*. At many companies, longtime customers pay less.

- *Good Health Discounts*. Look for lower premiums if you don't smoke and score well on blood pressure, body mass index, or cholesterol counts.

- *Credit Card Payments*. Pay with plastic and pocket the rewards, but *only* if you pay off your cards every month (see Chapter 49).

31.5 Pick a Low–Priced Insurer

After you find the best offers, it's time to investigate insurers.

☐ **31.5.1 Talk With Friends**
Ask if they have experience with any of your prospective insurers.

☐ **31.5.2 Research Customer Satisfaction**
Some insurance companies pay off claims quicker than others. Review ratings in *Consumer Reports* and at JDPower.com. To view customer complaint records, click on the map of your home state at NAIC.org/state_web_map.htm.

☐ **31.5.3 Research Company Finances**
Buy from solvent insurers only. Check with your state's regulatory agency or private sources such as A.M. Best and Standard & Poor's.

31.6 Follow Up

☐ **31.6.1 Keep a File**
Maintain copies of your policy, endorsements, declarations page, price comparisons, and buying guides.

☐ **31.6.2 If Necessary, Use "Free Look" Laws**
Most states provide a "free–look" period during which consumers can cancel policies and get their money back.

☐ **31.6.3 Seek Adjustments**
Call your agent every few years and ask about cheaper premiums or improved benefits. Why? As life expectancies increase, the deals improve. Five years from now you might get better terms.

☐ 31.6.4 Review Your Policy upon Major Life Events

Key life events can change your ideas about who to list as beneficiaries, how much coverage to buy, or whether you need any insurance at all. Revisit your coverage upon births, marriages, divorces, graduations, new jobs, pay raises, large inheritances, financial windfalls, and retirements.

☐ 31.6.5 Avoid Changing Carriers

A switch in life insurance carriers is often costly: run the numbers carefully before you make any moves.

☐ 31.6.6 Pay on Time

This avoids penalties, lapses in coverage, and hits to your credit rating.

31.7 Save With Life Choices

The way you live can affect how much you pay for life insurance.

☐ 31.7.1 Pursue a Healthy Lifestyle

Don't smoke, drink moderately, eat a balanced diet, exercise regularly, and manage stress levels. Track metrics: body mass index (18.5–24.9), blood sugar (80–120), blood pressure (≤120 systolic and 80 diastolic), and cholesterol (≤ 200).

☐ 31.7.2 Favor Jobs With Life Insurance

The more coverage your employer buys, the less coverage you need to carry.

☐ 31.7.3 *Spend Less Now!*

The lower your household's annual expenses, the less coverage you need (see 31.3).

32

HEALTHCARE: HEALTH INSURANCE

In 2010, the Affordable Care Act (ACA) became law. In 2012, the Supreme Court upheld its constitutionality. The ACA doesn't take full effect until 2014, so for now, follow these reliable strategies. In 2014, new alternatives will emerge, including health insurance exchanges. Check for updates at FrugalFringe.com.

32.1 Get Coverage Through Employers or Parents

If you receive health insurance through your job, congratulations. You belong to a dwindling group. In January 2008, 50 percent of Americans received coverage from their employer, but by January 2011, the figure had slumped to 44.6 percent. Part of this downturn stemmed from greater unemployment, but much of it occurred because premiums rose so high that many employers decided they could no longer afford the expense. If your workplace provides health insurance, think hard before leaving. If you're job hunting, favor positions with benefits.

Under the ACA, insurers that cover dependents must offer such coverage until dependents reach the age of 26. If you're young enough to qualify, ask your parents to include you on their policy. This will increase their premiums substantially, so offer to pay your fair share.

32.2 Research Policies

When you shop for health insurance, you swim in deep waters, so educate yourself. Download the "Health Insurance Buyer's Guide" at eHealthInsurance.com.

The biggest point to keep in mind as you research policies is the difference between Health Maintenance Organizations (HMOs) and

Preferred Provider Organizations (PPOs). In both arrangements, insurers contract with medical providers for lower prices and require that you obtain care from those sources. In HMOs, the restrictions on where you get your medical services are more severe. Typically, if you use providers outside the approved network, you have to pay for everything yourself. In PPOs, fewer restrictions are imposed. Typically, if you use providers outside the approved network, you pay some of it yourself, but the insurer still pays a large percentage.

To assist your search for insurance, here's a list of major provisions to consider.

- *Eligibility for Tax Savings.* Find out whether your policy qualifies you to open a Health Savings Account (HSA), which generates welcome tax advantages (see 32.3.3).

- *Premium.* The monthly amount you pay the insurer for coverage.

- *Annual Deductible.* The yearly threshold in out–of–pocket medical expenses at which the insurer begins to pay its share.

- *Coinsurance.* Under this provision, the insurance company pays a percentage of the expense and you—the coinsurer—take care of the rest. An example: if the policy covers maternity services for "20 percent coinsurance after deductible," this means that once total medical expenses exceed the annual deductible, the insurer pays 80 percent and you pay 20 percent.

- *Annual Out–Of–Pocket Limits.* Once your yearly costs for deductibles and coinsurance reach a stated threshold, the insurer pays any other covered expenses for the rest of the year.

- *Lifetime Limits.* The ACA bars insurers from imposing lifetime caps on paid benefits.

- *Office Visits.* Many insurers cover general exams that spot problems early and reduce medical claims.

- *Preventive Care.* Look at how the policy covers diagnostics such as colonoscopies and mammograms.

- *Dentists and Optometrists.* Find out whether these are covered.

- *Special Needs Medicine.* If anyone in your family needs care for maternity, mental health, or substance abuse, ask about this coverage when you shop.

- *Alternative Medicine.* If you visit chiropractors, acupuncturists, or homeopaths, figure out in advance whether you're covered.

- *Drugs.* Some policies cover prescriptions, while others ignore them completely or give you drug discount cards.

- *Pre–Existing Conditions.* Under the ACA, insurers can't deny coverage simply because you suffer from conditions that predate your insurance application.

- *Exclusions.* Some policies specifically exempt certain types of care from coverage, which means that the insurer pays nothing and you pay 100 percent out of your own pocket.

32.3 Shop Around

☐ 32.3.1 Seek Online Quotes
Visit HealthCare.gov or eHealthInsurance.com to compare plans.

☐ 32.3.2 Look at Policies From Associations
For any organizations to which you belong, check whether they offer insurance to members.

☐ 32.3.3 Look for HSA Compatible Health Insurance Plans
HSAs offer three levels of tax savings: (1) deposits are deductible; (2) earnings grow tax–free; and (3) withdrawals avoid taxation when spent on qualified medical expenses (other spending triggers taxes and sometimes penalties).

☐ 32.3.4 Pick the Highest Deductible You Can Afford
As always, the higher your deductible, the lower your premiums.

32.4 Pick a Low–Priced Insurer

After you create a list of the lowest offers, it's time to investigate the insurers that made them.

☐ **32.4.1 Ask Friends**
Ask if they have experience with any of your prospective insurers.

☐ **32.4.2 Research Customer Satisfaction**
Some insurance companies pay off claims faster than others. Review ratings in *Consumer Reports* and at JDPower.com. To view customer complaint records where you live, click on the map of your home state at NAIC.org/state_web_map.htm.

☐ **32.4.3 Research Company Finances**
Buy from fully solvent companies only. Check with your state's regulatory agency or private sources such as A.M. Best and Standard & Poor's.

☐ **32.4.4 Use the Comparison Shopping Checklist**
Keep track of insurance offers with the Comparison Shopping Checklist located at the end of this chapter.

32.5 Follow Up

☐ **32.5.1 Keep a File**
Maintain copies of your policy, endorsements, declarations page, price comparisons, and buying guides.

☐ **32.5.2 Tap Your Health Savings or Flexible Spending Accounts**
Use these accounts to pay for deductibles or exclusions. This saves money because you pay with pre–tax dollars. The precise savings depend upon your top marginal rate.

☐ **32.5.3 Seek a Deduction**
Medical expenses, including health insurance premiums, generally are tax deductible in any year where your out–of–pocket medical costs exceed 10 percent of your adjusted gross income (AGI). Save your receipts and consult a tax advisor. Note: payments from HSAs and FSAs don't qualify for deductions, because you already received a tax benefit when you first funded those accounts.

☐ **32.5.4 Pay With Credit Cards**
Pay with plastic and pocket the rewards, but *only* if you pay off your cards every month (see Chapter 49).

☐ 32.5.5 Make Sure Providers Report Spending to Insurers

The care provider usually reports this information on your behalf, but you need to double–check because giant bureaucracies sometimes make mistakes.

☐ 32.5.6 Pursue a Healthy Lifestyle

Don't smoke, drink moderately, eat a balanced diet, exercise regularly, and keep stress levels low. Track the metrics: body mass index (18.5–24.9), blood sugar (80–120), blood pressure (≤120 systolic and 80 diastolic), and total cholesterol (≤ 200).

COMPARISON SHOPPING CHECKLIST FOR HEALTH INSURANCE

	Policy 1	Policy 2	Policy 3
HMO/PPO/Other			
HSA Eligibility			
Monthly Premium			
Annual Deductible			
Coinsurance			
Annual Out of Pocket Limits			
Office Visits			
Preventive Care			
Dental/Vision Coverage			
Special Needs Medicine			
Alternative Medicine			
Prescription Drugs			
Preexisting Conditions			
Exclusions			

33

HEALTHCARE: PRESCRIPTIONS

When a pharmacy dispenses refills month after month, it's easy for pill takers to coast along for years without evaluating their costs. If anyone in your household takes medications—and almost half of all Americans do—save with these strategies.

33.1 Ask Your Doctor to Help You Save

Never go cheap when your health is at stake. But do ask basic questions that might lead to savings.

☐ **33.1.1 Ask if You Can Get By Without**
Some conditions respond well to changes in diet or exercise.

☐ **33.1.2 Ask for Free Samples**
And also confirm that you can safely switch to cheaper drugs once the freebies run out, because sometimes you can't.

☐ **33.1.3 Ask for Generic Drugs**
Generics sell for a small fraction of their branded counterparts.

☐ **33.1.4 Ask for Cheaper Brands**
If no generic is available, a cheaper brand of medicine might work. Research prices at ConsumerReportsHealth.org/Health/Best-Buy-Drugs, which covers drugs for many ailments, including diabetes, elevated blood pressure, and high cholesterol.

☐ **33.1.5 Ask for Over–the–Counter Drugs**
Some conditions respond every bit as well to OTC drugs.

☐ **33.1.6 Ask for Longer Prescriptions**
Doctors usually prescribe monthly doses. To qualify for volume discounts, ask for 90–day prescriptions.

☐ 33.1.7 Ask About Pill Splitting

A splitter cuts the pills—and your bills—in half. This option won't work with all medications (gel caps and time–release formulas, for example) so consult with your doctor.

33.2 Shop Around

☐ 33.2.1 Before You Shop, Read a Buying Guide

As mentioned above, *Consumer Reports* publishes guides for many drugs. Visit ConsumerReportsHealth.org/Health/Best-Buy-Drugs.

☐ 33.2.2 Buy From Reputable Online Sources

The National Association of Boards of Pharmacy (NABP) has reviewed 7,000 internet drug sellers and concluded that 97 percent of them violate professional standards. Although the NABP may have an ax to grind because it wants consumers to buy from its members, the risks of ineffective or harmful medications seems real enough. For approved sites, visit NABP.net/programs/accredidation/vipps.

☐ 33.2.3 Visit Warehouse Clubs

Many locations feature in–store pharmacies that offer competitive prices. By law, these usually are open to everyone, members and nonmembers alike. Call ahead for prices.

☐ 33.2.4 Visit Discount Stores

Walmart and Target are embroiled in intense price wars on generic drugs. Check out their websites or call ahead for prices.

☐ 33.2.5 Call for Bids

Ask for the same dosage so that you receive comparable offers.

☐ 33.2.6 Seek Bids Online

Register at BidRX.com where local druggists vie for your business.

☐ 33.2.7 Seek Member Discounts

The AAA runs a prescription savings program, as do other groups to which you might belong.

☐ 33.2.8 Search for Coupons

Major drug companies offer coupons, so visit their websites.

☐ 33.2.9 Carry Drug Discount Cards

Visit websites such as PSCard.com, PatientAssistance.com, and RXAssist.org, where you can print out discount cards honored by participating pharmacies.

☐ 33.2.10 Become a Repeat New Customer

Pharmacies often offer discounts to attract new customers. Take advantage. When you see new customer offers, move your business. Or save yourself the hassle of moving. Simply show the competition's ad to your pharmacy and ask whether it can match the offered discount. Do this every year and save.

33.3 Save With Payment Methods

☐ 33.3.1 Investigate Policy Coverage for Drug Purchases

Check whether your health insurer pays prescriptions so you don't have to.

☐ 33.3.2 Tap Your HSA or FSA

With these accounts, you can use pre–tax dollars to buy medicine.

☐ 33.3.3 Take Tax Deductions

Prescription drug costs become deductible once your total out–of–pocket medical expenses exceed 10 percent of your adjusted gross income. Save receipts and consult a tax advisor. Note: payments from HSAs and FSAs don't qualify for deductions, because you already received a tax benefit when you first funded those accounts.

☐ 33.3.4 Seek Credit Card Rewards

If you don't have an HSA or FSA, pay with plastic and at least rack up some rewards. And even if you do have one of these accounts, pay with plastic anyway: when you charge a $1,000 in prescriptions to your three percent cash rewards card and reimburse yourself with a withdrawal from your HSA or FSA, you pocket an extra $30.

☐ 33.3.5 Seek Financial Help

Many programs help those who meet certain income and age requirements. Visit NeedyMeds.org or PPARX.org.

34

HEALTHCARE: MEDICAL SERVICES

In 2011, American households spent an average of $179 on physicians and $129 on hospitals. Obviously, some households were lucky enough to avoid any medical expenses, while others suffered catastrophic costs that dwarfed the national averages. Whenever you need a doctor or hospital, keep your expenses low with these strategies.

34.1 Make Insurers Pay

Once you have insurance, you need to make sure that the insurer doesn't try to stick you with the bill—insurance companies excel at this. Follow these tactics.

☐ **34.1.1 Confirm Coverage in Advance**
For nonemergency procedures, confirm ahead of time that your policy provides coverage.

☐ **34.1.2 Stay Within Your Network**
Whether you join a PPO or HMO (see 32.2), you spend less if you visit doctors and hospitals within your plan's network of providers. Confirm in advance of treatment that health care providers have registered with your insurance company.

☐ **34.1.3 Exploit Wellness Programs**
The more you avoid big medical expenses, the more insurers profit. So they dangle incentives to convince you to stay healthy: subsidized gym memberships, FREE screenings, stress management programs, nurse hotlines, informative websites, and more. Take advantage of all freebies. They deliver more value for your premiums, and they also help improve your health.

☐ **34.1.4 Finesse Deductibles**
As you near the limit of your annual deductible, accelerate any medical care you're planning for next year into the current year so that the insurer picks up part of the bill.

☐ **34.1.5 Challenge Coverage Denials**
Don't be cowed—MOOOOOO!!!—when insurers refuse to pay for treatment. Their denial isn't the final word. Follow the procedures for appeal. If the process gets too complicated, and it easily might, use Appendix 2 to hire a local healthcare advocate.

34.2 Follow Preventive Medicine

☐ **34.2.1 Pursue a Healthy Lifestyle**
Adopt routines that save money and extend lifespans.

- *Smoking.* Tobacco erodes away bodies and nest eggs.

- *Drinking.* No more than two drinks per day for men and one drink per day for women.

- *Diet.* A balanced diet keeps doctors away.

- *Exercise.* Improves circulation and immunity from disease.

- *Mental Health.* Cut your stress by spending less, for example.

☐ **34.2.2 Monitor Metrics**
Pay attention to body mass index (18.5–24.9 is good), blood pressure (120 systolic over 80 diastolic or lower is good), blood sugar (80–120 is good), and total cholesterol (≤ 200 is good).

34.3 Run Background Checks

When vetting doctors and hospitals, follow 8.3 and these tactics.

☐ **34.3.1 Seek Quality**
Your health comes first, so make sure that those responsible for it are well qualified. Don't cut corners by hiring inferior caregivers.

☐ **34.3.2 Check Hospital Safety Records**
Use hospitals that have superior records for patient safety. Visit HospitalSafetyScore.org or LeapFrogGroup.org.

☐ 34.3.3 Ask Around
Whenever you seek referrals, ask for details:

- Bedside manner
- Quality of service
- Quality of communication
- Willingness to haggle.

☐ 34.3.4 Consult the Internet
Visit AngiesList.com, which collects reviews for a wide variety of practice areas and medical facilities. The site charges monthly fees for access. One frugal approach: join for one month, research any services you might need over the next few years, and then cancel.

34.4 Shop Around

☐ 34.4.1 Visit Retail Chain Clinics
More than 1,350 clinics nationwide deliver non–emergency services for colds, flu, infections, and other maladies. Look for them at Walgreens, CVS, Walmart, Kroger, and Target. To find clinics near you, visit HealthCare311.com or CCAClinics.org.

☐ 34.4.2 Seek Volume Discounts
If several household members require services at the same time, it provides an opportunity to negotiate. Another approach: band together with friends who need similar services and seek a group discount.

☐ 34.4.3 Price Major Procedures Online
View the average costs for your zip code at FairHealthConsumer.org or HealthCareBlueBook.com.

☐ 34.4.4 For Major Procedures, Seek Bids
Call around to doctors who scored high on your background checks and see which ones offer the lowest rates.

34.5 Haggle

Whenever you negotiate with doctors and hospitals, select from among these openers.

☐ 34.5.1 *"Do You Charge Insurers Less—Can I Get That Price?"*

☐ 34.5.2 *"Dr. X Bid Lower—Can You Match His Price?"*

☐ 34.5.3 *"Can You Match the Price at FairHealthConsumer.org?"*

☐ 34.5.4 *"I'm a Longtime Patient, Is There a Loyalty Discount?"*

☐ 34.5.5 *"Could I Speak With Your Supervisor, Please."*
General rule: the higher you climb the chain of command, the greater the bargaining authority.

34.6 Ask Your Doctor About Potential Savings

☐ **34.6.1 Ask Whether the Procedure Is Discretionary**
If something is fundamentally wrong, by all means fix it. But for purely discretionary or cosmetic work, do without.

☐ **34.6.2 Ask for Cheaper Options**
If you charm your doctor into talking things over, the conversation might uncover less costly alternatives.

☐ **34.6.3 Seek Second Opinions**
On big ticket procedures, two stethoscopes are better than one. Another physician might figure out a better or cheaper solution.

34.7 Save With Payment Methods

☐ **34.7.1 Offer to Pay *Before* Services Are Provided**
In exchange for a hefty discount, of course.

☐ **34.7.2 Tap HSA and FSA Accounts**
You save because you pay with pre–tax dollars.

☐ **34.7.3 Take Tax Deductions**
Time discretionary medical services for years in which you itemize and your overall medical costs exceed 10 percent of your adjusted gross income. Consult your tax advisor. Note: payments from HSAs and FSAs don't qualify for deductions, because you already received a tax benefit when you first funded those accounts.

☐ **34.7.4 Offer to Pay With Cash**
Look for discounts that exceed the value of your card rewards.

❑ 34.7.5 Seek Credit Card Rewards

If you don't have an HSA or FSA, pay with plastic and at least rack up some rewards. And even if you do have one of these accounts, pay with plastic anyway: when you charge a $5,000 procedure to your three percent cash rewards card and reimburse yourself with a withdrawal from your HSA or FSA, you pocket an extra $150. Buy yourself some flowers.

❑ 34.7.6 Avoid Interest

If you can't immediately pay for the procedure, don't use plastic—you'll only stick yourself with heavy interest costs. Instead, ask for a no–interest payment plan that spreads your payments over several months. Doctors and hospitals make these arrangements often, so don't be shy about asking.

34.8 Follow Up

❑ 34.8.1 Insist on Itemized Bills

If you settle your bill based upon a summary that consists of a few lines only, errors go undetected and you overpay. Insist upon a copy of the line–by–line details.

❑ 34.8.2 Watch for Billing Errors

Medical bills are complicated. Drill down into the minutia, because mistakes are common. Search each entry for duplicate charges, services you never received, and outlandish markups. If any charge seems too high, check it against online cost estimators (see 34.4.3).

❑ 34.8.3 Don't Pay for Medical Mistakes

If a mistake in care caused you to incur additional expenses, refuse to pay. Such costs should be borne by whoever erred, not by you.

❑ 34.8.4 Hire Professional Bill Reviewers

They take a percentage of whatever amount they're able to save you. To find expert bill reviewers near you, visit BillAdvocates.com or Claims.org. Run all hires through Appendix 2.

❑ 34.8.5 Build Relationships

If you like your doctor, refer friends. This might not trigger an immediate discount, but at a minimum, it builds goodwill.

☐ **34.8.6 Retain Paperwork**

Keep a file to document tax deductions or spending from tax–advantaged medical accounts.

CODA: MEDICAL TOURISM

In many foreign countries, treatment costs less than stateside—and also involves fewer delays. On the other hand, if complications occur, patients may lack effective recourse against doctors and hospitals. If despite these risks you're still interested, investigate all specifics thoroughly before you travel. Several books cover this in exhaustive detail, so visit your library.

35

HEALTHCARE:
EYE CARE

About one–half of all Americans wear corrective lenses. If any of them reside in your household, you probably have long–established routines for checkups and prescriptions. Switch off the autopilot. See how much you can save with these strategies.

35.1 Save on Eye Exams

Supplement Appendix 2 with these tactics.

☐ 35.1.1 Visit Shoptometrists
Get your eyes examined at Targets, Walmarts, or warehouse clubs.

☐ 35.1.2 Scope Out Daily–Deal Sites
Groupon and LivingSocial often offer discounts on eye exams.

☐ 35.1.3 Go Less Often
If your eyesight is stable, get checkups every other year.

35.2 Save on Glasses

Follow Appendix 1 and focus on these additional approaches.

☐ 35.2.1 Ask for a Copy of Your Prescription
In most states, eye doctors by law must provide patients with copies of their prescriptions upon request. Be sure to ask because without a current prescription you can't order from other vendors.

☐ 35.2.2 Shop Around
Don't automatically buy eyewear from your optometrist. Compare prices on the internet and at chain stores.

☐ 35.2.3 Consider Internet Dispensers
Online vendors are able to undercut brick–and–mortar stores by

wide margins. If your current frames fit well, use their measurements (in millimeters) when shopping for new ones. The sizes are etched on the inside of temples and nose bridges. Visit EyeglassRetailerReviews.com for the latest information about vendors. Beware: the internet doesn't work well for complicated prescriptions, which often require adjustments. If your prescription is complex, buy from a physical store with generous return policies.

☐ **35.2.4 Consider Costco**
In 2010, *Consumer Reports* surveyed 30,000 readers about their recent vision purchases. Costco Optical garnered the highest score among chain stores for customer satisfaction and low prices.

☐ **35.2.5 Reuse Frames**
Keep the frames, order new lenses.

☐ **35.2.6 Buy Generic Frames**
Designers charge more.

☐ **35.2.7 Buy Frames With Interchangeable Lenses**
Prescription changes are easy to install.

35.3 Save on Contacts

Supplement Appendix 1 with these specific ideas.

☐ **35.3.1 Wear Glasses Exclusively**
If you forgo contact lenses, you save on fitting exams and cleansers.

☐ **35.3.2 Wear Glasses More**
Rely on your glasses for most activities so that you use fewer disposable lenses (and less contact cleanser).

☐ **35.3.3 Buy Monthly Disposables**
If you wear contacts every day, these generally cost less than disposable daily or bi–weekly lenses. Run the numbers.

35.4 Save With Payment Methods

☐ **35.4.1 Tap HSA and FSA Accounts**
Most vision expenses qualify for payments from these accounts. You save because you pay with pre–tax dollars.

☐ 35.4.2 Take Tax Deductions

Vision expenses are deductible if overall medical costs exceed 10 percent of adjusted gross income. Consult your tax advisor. Note: payments from HSAs and FSAs don't qualify for deductions, because you already received a tax benefit when you first funded those accounts.

☐ 35.4.3 Seek Credit Card Rewards

If you don't have an HSA or FSA, at least rack up some rewards by paying with plastic. And even if you do have one of these accounts, pay with plastic anyway: when you charge $1,000 to your three percent cash rewards card and reimburse yourself with a later HSA or FSA withdrawal, you pocket an extra $30.

☐ 35.4.4 Get Financial Help

Many programs help those who meet certain income and age requirements. Visit EyeCareAmerica.org, OptometrysCharity.org, and LionsClubs.org.

CODA: EYE SURGERY AND VISION INSURANCE

I didn't list these as separate strategies because of their cost and doubtful effectiveness. As to eye surgery, I had Lasik performed on both eyes in 1997, but my eyesight has since worsened and I'm back to wearing contacts (but thankfully at lower prescriptions). Investigate carefully before you agree to go under the knife or laser. As to vision insurance, although my survey of such policies is incomplete, the ones I've seen cost more than what you would spend if you simply followed the checklist above. Run the numbers yourself. To price options, visit eHealthInsurance.com.

36

HEALTHCARE: DENTAL CARE

In 2011, the average American household spent $286 on dentists. Obviously, some households that year were lucky enough to avoid any major expenses, while others suffered catastrophic costs that dwarfed the national averages. Before you take the chair of tooth repair, brush up on these strategies.

36.1 Follow Checklists for Products and Prescriptions

Consult Appendix 1 whenever you buy dental products. If your dentist prescribes any drugs, visit Chapter 33.

36.2 Follow Preventive Maintenance

☐ **36.2.1 Practice Daily Maintenance**
Follow a habitual path to hygienic bliss: brush, floss, and use mouthwash or rinses.

☐ **36.2.2 Schedule Regular Checkups and Cleanings**
The National Institute of Health reports that every $1 spent on prevention saves $4 on crowns, implants, and root canals.

☐ **36.2.3 Pursue a Healthy Lifestyle**
Attend to these health issues and save both teeth and money.

- *Smoking.* Tobacco erodes teeth and gums.
- *Sugar.* Limit to keep healthy teeth. Chew sugarless gum.
- *Diet.* A balanced diet promotes healthy gums and bones.
- *Exercise.* Improves circulation and immunity; benefits gums.
- *Mental Health.* Less stress means fewer disorders—dry mouth, Bruxism (grinding teeth), and Temporomandibular Joint Disorder (dysfunction in the mandible and skull joint).

36.3 Run Background Checks

Whenever you vet dentists, follow 8.3 and these additional tactics.

☐ 36.3.1 Seek Quality

Lowball dentists cost you more if you're forced to fix work that wasn't done right in the first place. (Example: a bad job on a filling eventually can lead to a root canal—I've been there and done that!)

☐ 36.3.2 Ask Around

When you ask friends for referrals, ask for details about why they like their current dentist:

- Chair side manner

- Willingness to haggle

- Management of patient pain

- Quality of work

- Communication and explanations of procedures

- Location compared to where you work or live.

☐ 36.3.3 Consult the Internet

Dentist reviews abound. Visit AngiesList.com or DoctorOogle.com. Angie's List charges a monthly fee for access. One frugal approach: join for one month only, research any services you might need for the next few years, and then cancel the subscription.

☐ 36.3.4 Take a Dentist for a Test Drive

Hire for cleanings and checkups first.

36.4 Shop Around

☐ 36.4.1 Scope Out Daily–Deal Sites

Groupon and LivingSocial often feature good bargains on cleaning.

☐ 36.4.2 Price Major Procedures on the Internet

Visit OneDollarDentist.com for ballpark estimates on crowns, bridges, and root canals. If you need greater precision, visit the interactive dental cost estimator at FairHealthConsumer.org.

36.4.3 For Major Work, Seek Bids

Get the precise Current Dental Terminology (CDT) codes from your dentist or from FairHealthConsumer.org. Cite the relevant CDT codes when you call around for bids.

36.4.4 Seek Volume Discounts

If several household members require services at the same time, it provides an opportunity to negotiate. Another approach: band together with friends who need similar services and seek a group discount.

36.4.5 Hire Students

If price matters more to you than quality (see 36.3.1), consider visits to dentistry and hygienist schools that offer FREE or discounted services. For a comprehensive list of programs where you live, visit NIDCR.nih.gov/FindingDentalCare.

36.4.6 Barter or Trade

If you have tartar, consider barter. As always, beware the complex tax morass (see IRS Publication 525 and consult your advisor).

36.5 Haggle

☐ 36.5.1 *"If Insurers Pay Less, Could I Get That Price?"*

☐ 36.5.2 *"Dr. X Gave a Low Bid, Could You Match His Price?"*

☐ 36.5.3 *"Can You Match the Price at FairHealthConsumer.org?"*

☐ 36.5.4 *"Is There a Loyalty Discount?"*

36.6 Ask Your Dentist About Potential Savings

36.6.1 Ask Whether You Need the Service

If something is fundamentally wrong, by all means fix your teeth. But if the work is purely cosmetic, do without.

36.6.2 Ask Whether You Need New X–Rays

Some offices use x–rays to boost cash flows. You get stuck with the bill and extra radiation. According to the FDA, healthy adults at low risk for dental problems need x–rays only once every 24–36 months. If your dentist wants to zap you more than that, seek an explanation.

☐ 36.6.3 Ask for Cheaper Options

Material costs vary. For fillings, metal costs less than resin and usually lasts longer. Crowns come in a wide variety of materials: resins, base metals, noble metals, porcelain, ceramics, and titanium. Perhaps the most expensive option isn't your best choice.

36.7 Save With Payment Methods

☐ 36.7.1 Tap HSA and FSA Accounts

Most dental expenses qualify for payment out of these accounts. You save because you pay with pre–tax dollars.

☐ 36.7.2 Take Tax Deductions

Time discretionary dental work for years in which you itemize and your overall medical costs exceed 10 percent of your adjusted gross income. Consult your tax advisor. Note: payments from HSAs and FSAs don't qualify for deductions, because you already received a tax benefit when you first funded those accounts.

☐ 36.7.3 Seek Credit Card Rewards

If you don't have an HSA or FSA, pay with plastic and at least rack up some rewards. And even if you do have one of these accounts, pay with plastic anyway: when you charge $1,000 to your three percent cash rewards card and reimburse yourself with a later HSA or FSA withdrawal, you pocket an extra $30.

☐ 36.7.4 Get Financial Help

Programs help those who meet income and age requirements. Visit OralHealthAmerica.org or NIDCR.nih.gov/FindingDentalCare.

36.8 Follow Up

☐ 36.8.1 Check the Math

Drill down into the bill's details. Look for overcharges; confirm the accuracy of all CDT codes. Mistakes on dental bills are common. Make sure you haven't been overcharged.

☐ 36.8.2 Build a Relationship

If you like your dentist, refer friends. This may trigger discounts. At a minimum, it builds up goodwill for the next time you chip a tooth.

□ 36.8.3 Retain Paperwork

In order to document spending from medical accounts or tax deductions.

CODA: DENTAL INSURANCE AND DENTAL PLANS

I didn't list these as strategies because of their doubtful usefulness. As to dental insurance, the cheaper policies impose low annual caps on benefits. Because of these limitations, you might decide to skip the insurance and deposit what you save on premiums into a fund that covers general emergencies, including dental expenses. If you still want to shop for coverage, eHealthInsurance.com lists policies sold in your zip code. One tax tip: dental insurance may be deductible if your overall medical costs exceed 10 percent of your adjusted gross income. Read IRS Publication 502 and consult a tax advisor.

Dental *plans* differ from dental *insurance*. In the case of plans, a company negotiates with dentists for lower rates. You pay a fee to the company in return for access to discounting dentists. Again, you probably can save more if you follow the strategies in this checklist. If you still want to shop around for plans, visit DentalPlans.com, which helps you compare prices and benefits from more than 30 companies.

37

GROCERIES

Americans average about 100 grocery store visits per year. The ritual is expensive. According to the 2011 CES, households spend $3,838 on food consumed at home, which represents 8.6 percent of a typical budget (after backing out Social Security and pensions). Follow this step–buy–step system.

37.1 Make Shopping Lists

According to a Food Marketing Institute survey, 44 percent of consumers use lists most of the time when they grocery shop for healthy foods. These shoppers are savvy. Lists streamline shopping trips and help avoid impulse purchases. Build your own lists based upon: (1) your immediate needs; and (2) the available savings opportunities.

YOUR HOUSEHOLD'S NEEDS

☐ **37.1.1 Inventory Fridge, Freezer, and Pantry**
If you're short any items, add them to the list.

☐ **37.1.2 Consider Menu Planning**
Plan in advance and shop only for what you intend to eat over the next few days.

☐ **37.1.3 Seek Requests From Household Members**
This not only keeps the peace, it involves them in the checklists, which increases the odds that they might follow other frugal tactics (they might even turn off the lights once in awhile).

SAVINGS OPPORTUNITIES

☐ **37.1.4 Peruse Weekly Specials**
Most grocers publish weekly flyers of current sales. Find them in newspapers or on the internet. Sign up for promotional emails.

☐ 37.1.5 Find Coupons Online
Visit Coupons.com and SmartSource.com. Type in your grocery list at GroceryServer.com and the site pulls up local deals and coupons.

☐ 37.1.6 Seek Double Coupons
Patronize grocery stores that double your coupons.

☐ 37.1.7 Run Your List Through 37.2 and 37.3
Test each item you listed against frugal food choices and alternate vendor options. Substitute cheaper items.

37.2 Consider Lower Cost Alternatives

Change your habits by replacing the foods you eat with less expensive choices.

☐ 37.2.1 Buy Generic
Experiment with store brands and save.

☐ 37.2.2 Buy Frozen
Fruits and vegetables usually cost less frozen. If fresh happens to be cheaper (as when it's in season), stock your freezer.

☐ 37.2.3 Buy in Bulk
Stock up on sales, look for buy one get one FREE (BOGO) deals, and opt for king sizes. Repackage large quantities into smaller containers.

☐ 37.2.4 Buy Dry
Dry foods cost less and provide backups when you run out of fresh.

Wet Version	Dry Version
☐ Potatoes	Potato flakes
☐ Canned beans	Dry beans
☐ Canned Chicken/Beef Broth	Bouillon cubes
☐ Gravy in jars	Powdered mix
☐ Pudding cups	Boxed mix
☐ Bottled iced tea	Tea bags
☐ Fruit punch	Powdered mix
☐ Dairy case dinner rolls	Powdered mix
☐ Frozen Pizza	Flour and tomato paste

□ 37.2.5 Buy Alternate Foods

A less expensive substitute might meet your requirements every bit as well.

Food Item	Substitute
□ Potato chips	Home popped popcorn
□ Cashews or almonds	Peanuts
□ Dry cereal	Oatmeal
□ Stuffing Mix	Leftover bread
□ Soda pop	Home brewed coffee or tea
□ Chocolate bars	Chocolate chips

□ 37.2.6 Buy DIY Versions

The more processing your food receives, the more you pay. The markups are often outrageous. Perform small labors yourself and reward yourself with big savings.

Processed Item	DIY Method
□ Shredded Cheese	Grate block cheese
□ Washed Lettuce	Use a spinner
□ Pre–Cut Coleslaw	Chop cabbage
□ Salad dressing	Mix oil with vinegar
□ Peeled Carrots	Use a peeler
□ Trail Mix	Mix ingredients yourself
□ Bakery dep't cake	Use a cake mix
□ Frozen waffles	Mix batter and use a waffle iron
□ Breakfast/energy drink	Blend them yourself
□ Bottled water	Use a water filter
□ Frozen Pizza	Make from scratch or buy a mix
□ Snack popcorn	Pop your own
□ TV Dinners	Microwave leftovers
□ Cartons of orange juice	Prepare from frozen concentrate
□ Store bought cookies	Bake cookies from scratch
□ Store–bought bread	Run a bread machine

□ 37.2.7 Buy Organic Strategically

If you buy organic fruits and vegetables, it's probably to avoid chemical residues. Instead of paying extra for everything, limit your organic purchases to those items that tend to retain the most contaminants. Based upon a study of the Environmental Working Group (EWG.org), here's a short list of "do buys" and "don't buys:"

Do Buy Organic:	Don't Buy Organic:
☐ Apples	☐ Asparagus
☐ Bell peppers	☐ Avocadoes
☐ Blueberries (domestic)	☐ Cabbage
☐ Celery	☐ Cantaloupe (domestic)
☐ Grapes (imported)	☐ Corn
☐ Lettuce	☐ Eggplant
☐ Kale/Collard greens	☐ Grapefruit
☐ Nectarines (imported)	☐ Kiwi
☐ Peaches	☐ Mangoes
☐ Potatoes	☐ Mushrooms
☐ Spinach	☐ Onions
☐ Strawberries	☐ Peas
	☐ Pineapples
	☐ Sweet Potatoes
	☐ Watermelon

37.3 Consider Alternatives to Grocery Stores

Other vendors might undercut supermarket prices.

☐ **37.3.1 Join Food Co–Ops**
Co–ops deal directly with suppliers for lower prices. Visit UnitedBuyingClubs.com or CoopDirectory.org.

☐ **37.3.2 Join Membership Warehouse Clubs**
Shop here for foods you consume in bulk. Combine forces with others to buy gargantuan sizes and divvy them up later. (Look for flour, rice, beans, and sugar in twenty–five pound sacks.)

☐ **37.3.3 Shop at Discount Stores**
Target and Walmart set competitive prices. Check online ads.

☐ **37.3.4 Shop at Dollar Stores**
Good for dry foodstuffs and canned goods.

☐ **37.3.5 Support Food Producers**
Buy direct from farms and ranches.

□ **37.3.6 Support Farmers' Markets**
They don't always deliver the lowest prices, but usually they deliver the freshest produce. Experiment and decide for yourself.

□ **37.3.7 Grow Gardens**
Grow a few herbs or plant a full garden.

37.4 Visit the Grocery Store

Now you're ready to shop. Follow these tactics to maximize your in-store savings.

□ **37.4.1 Pack for the Trip**
Equip yourself as follows:

- *Your Shopping List.* Naturally.

- *A Copy of 37.4.* Bring it along until the tactics become habits.

- *Coupons.* You collected these when you prepared your shopping list, didn't you?

- *Loyalty Card.* Most grocers offer them. Sign up for one.

- *Canvas Bags.* Many stores issue small credits for each bag you supply. These can save about $20 per year.

- *The Best Credit Card.* Bring along whichever card offers the highest rewards for grocery purchases. If you spend at the national average, a three percent cash back card saves you about $114 per year.

- *Calculator.* Looks nerdy, but helps you figure per unit prices. Tip: your cell phone has this function installed—pretend you're checking emails.

□ **37.4.2 Stick to Your Shopping List**
It doesn't stop impulse purchases unless you follow it.

□ **37.4.3 Shop on a Full Stomach**
If you visit the grocery store when your stomach is growling, you spend more. Never shop when you have the munchies.

☐ 37.4.4 Shop in the Morning

At many stores, night crews mark down prices so products are priced for sale when the doors open. Visit early in the day.

☐ 37.4.5 Look for In–Store Bargains

For frugal fringers, no grocery trip would be complete without a look at damaged packages and discounted meats. Troll these areas frequently.

☐ 37.4.6 Look Down

Grocers place their most profitable items at eye level. Scout lower shelves for better deals.

☐ 37.4.7 Don't Accept Empty Shelves

If sale items are missing, flag down a clerk and ask whether any linger in the stockroom. If not, seek a rain check.

37.5 Avoid Supermarket Pitfalls

The bad boys of grocery shopping appear below.

☐ 37.5.1 Buy Nonfood Items Elsewhere

Usually, cosmetics, cleansers, and other nonfood items cost less at other stores.

☐ 37.5.2 Buy in Volume Only What You Use in Volume

Bulk purchases save you nothing if most of it sees the landfill.

☐ 37.5.3 Avoid Impulse Items

There's a special on rutabagas so you add them to your cart. Weeks pass. They languish unloved in your vegetable drawer. Impulse purchases are among the most likely food items to get trashed, so stick to your grocery list.

☐ 37.5.4 Think Twice About Specialty Items

Avoid recipes that require unusual sauces or fresh herbs, the bulk of which are predestined to lounge in the fridge—sometimes for years.

☐ 37.5.5 Beware Deceptive Packaging

The container may exaggerate the quantity of product within. Always compare prices on a per unit basis.

37.6 Follow Up: Cut Food Waste

According to government estimates, Americans discard about 25 percent of the food they buy. For the average grocery budget, that works out to $960 in losses per year. These tactics begin at the grocery list stage and end at the rim of your trash can.

☐ 37.6.1 Plan Ahead

As in making a list (see 37.1) and sticking to it. You waste less if you only buy what you actually consume.

☐ 37.6.2 Use What You Have

You inventory the fridge, freezer, and pantry whenever you prepare a shopping list. Use the opportunity to identify anything near the end of its life. Write "EAT ME" on the package and advance it to the front of the shelf. If several items teeter on the edge of doom, plug their names into the recipe finder at Allrecipes.com and cook up something new.

☐ 37.6.3 Shop More Often

If planning menus for the week ahead seems like drudgery, shop for the next few meals only. You'll waste less food because of the shorter time horizon.

☐ 37.6.4 Try Before You Buy

Although impulse purchases often lead to waste, life gets boring if you limit yourself to the same old foodstuffs all the time. Go ahead and try new items, but to cut waste sample them first or buy small amounts only.

☐ 37.6.5 Don't Throw Away, Return

If something you bought was spoiled when purchased, don't be shy, return it to the grocer for a refund. Some supermarkets issue full refunds even when the only reason for your return is that you didn't like the product's taste.

☐ 37.6.6 Look Before You Toss

Check with ShelfLifeAdvice.com about whether you can scramble around and still use those expired eggs. The site works for any food with an expiration date.

☐ 37.6.7 Donate
As pantry items near their "best by" dates, give them to food banks.

☐ 37.6.8 Increase Awareness, Decrease Waste
Food waste is notoriously difficult to measure because study subjects become highly "reactive"—they throw out less because the very process of measuring changes their behaviors. This is human nature, and here are several ways to harness it for your own benefit.

> ☐ *Log Losses.* Consider tracking your tossed food, at least for awhile. If you throw out the same items repeatedly, a log reminds you to buy less. If you constantly toss leftovers, you learn to have more "rerun" meals. If you burn food often, a log prompts you to take a cooking class. Sample entries appear below. Post something similar at your own trashcan.

Date	Item	Volume	Reason	Loss
04/02	Potatoes	8 tubers	Sprouted	$ 2.00
04/03	Pasta	1.5 cups	Spoiled	$ 5.00
04/06	Apples	2 apples	Rotted	$ 1.00
04/08	Cat food	1/2 can	Lost in fridge	$ 1.75
04/08	Toast	2 slices	Burnt	$ .40
04/08	Cheese	1 block	Moldy	$ 6.50
04/09	Lettuce	3 heads	Turned brown	$ 4.25

> ☐ *Compost Biodegradables.* If a log seems like too much work, compost instead. The process will make you more mindful of what you waste.

> ☐ *Switch to Pay–As–You–Throw.* Join a PAYT trash removal program (see Chapter 24). When you pay more for each incremental discard, it persuades you to toss out less.

☐ 37.6.9 If You Waste Something, Buy a Longer–Lasting Version
If you waste fresh vegetables, buy them canned or frozen instead. If potatoes sprout, buy fewer of them and supplement with flakes.

☐ 37.6.10 Try Cryogenics
Don't toss food into the trashcan, toss it into the freezer instead. For the details about any food's freeze–ability, visit StillTasty.com.

☐ **37.6.11 Discover Mini Spoonulas**
These concave silicone spatulas help you scoop the last bit from jars and blenders. Find them on the internet or at gourmet kitchen stores.

☐ **37.6.12 Post a Trash Talking Checklist**
And encourage other household members to join your quest to cut waste (see Appendix 5).

37.7 Pursue Miscellaneous Meat Savers

Meats—including poultry, fish, and eggs—take the single biggest bite out of the average food budget, a total of $832 per year. If you're a carnivore or omnivore, chew over these tactics.

☐ **37.7.1 Substitute Cheaper Proteins**
Occasionally replace meat with protein–rich alternatives:

- Beans [red, kidney, navy, pinto]
- Lentils
- Soy products [tofu, tempeh]
- Protein–rich grains [quinoa, barley, bulgur, brown rice]
- Nuts [pumpkin seeds, almonds, peanuts, walnuts, pecans]
- Peanut butter [also butters of other nuts]
- Protein powders [great for smoothies]
- Eggs
- Cottage cheese.

☐ **37.7.2 Stretch Meats**
Use common stretchers:

- Recipes that use less meat
- Chicken and beef broths
- Stir fries
- Casseroles
- Crackers, breadcrumbs, or grains added to ground beef.

☐ 37.7.3 Choose Cheaper Cuts
With the right preparation, they taste great: tenderize, marinate, slow cook, or grill.

☐ 37.7.4 Buy a Bone
Add flavor by tossing one into the slow cooker with your next soup.

☐ 37.7.5 Invest in a Freezer
If you spend at the national average for meats, a standalone freezer easily pays for itself in two years. (The math: if you average 40 percent off meats with bulk purchases, you save $665.)

☐ 37.7.6 Build a Relationship With a Butcher
This isn't about Sam and Alice of *The Brady Bunch*. A butcher gives good advice and alerts you to the best deals.

☐ 37.7.7 Buy Rotisserie Chickens
Possibly the best food deal in America. At Costco they're $4.99, which is cheaper than the same birds *uncooked*. Feeds two people at least three times.

☐ 37.7.8 *Spend Less Cow*!
Meats don't represent the best of social values—given the wasted water, misallocated food grains, dubious sanitation, and higher cholesterol numbers—but the only values addressed here are those that affect your pocketbook. For the meatiest savings of all, consider the way of the vegetarian. Alternatively, convert yourself into a flexitarian (one who eats meat infrequently). In either case, the interrupting cow will—MOOOOOO!!!—thank you.

38

AUTOS: DEPRECIATION

Depreciation is what any product, including a vehicle, loses in market value over time. This is a hidden expense. You don't write a check for depreciation every month, but it keeps on costing you anyway—and costing you big when it comes to cars. *Consumer Reports* has studied the five–year cost of ownership on more than 300 vehicles and concluded that, on average, depreciation accounts for almost one–half of that total cost—a whopping 48 percent. Contain this monster expense with these strategies.

38.1 Ditch the Car

You don't have to worry about depreciation if you never own a car in the first place (see Chapter 44).

38.2 Drive the Car Until It Dies

If you drive the car into the ground and then sell it for salvage (or donate it), depreciation becomes an academic issue.

38.3 Slow the Rate of Depreciation

☐ **38.3.1 Limit Miles**
The less you drive, the less your car depreciates. For tactics, see 39.4.

☐ **38.3.2 Avoid Accidents**
Whenever your car incurs major bodywork, it loses value.

☐ **38.3.3 Follow Maintenance Schedules**
Your car fetches more on resale if you perform the recommended upkeep (see Chapter 40). Retain all paperwork so that you can prove your diligence to future buyers.

☐ **38.3.4 Keep Up Appearances**
Clean cars fetch more. Wax and vacuum them regularly.

38.4 Rent Even if You Own

For long trips that last a few days only, it's often cheaper to rent. An example: Jane Dough plans to travel 1,800 miles roundtrip in a single weekend for her high school reunion. A rental would cost $129. How much would it cost to drive her own car? Jane owns a 2008 Honda Accord that she bought used with 50,000 miles on it for $15,000, with sales tax. It's reliable and she figures it will last 200,000 miles if she stays accident–free. With this information, she can calculate the car's depreciation from an 1,800 mile road trip. Here's the formula:

Purchase Price with sales tax x (Trip Mileage / (Projected Mileage– Mileage When Purchased Used)) = Depreciation from Trip

To plug in the numbers for the reunion: $15,000 x (1,800 / (200,000 – 50,000) = $180. In this case, then, it's cheaper for Jane to rent. If any doubts had remained, Jane could also have calculated her tire wear ($450 for new tires installed x 1,800 / 50,000 miles tire life expectancy = $16.20) and oil use ($40 for oil change x 1,800 / 5,000 miles between changes = $14.40).

38.5 Consider Depreciation When Buying Vehicles

☐ **38.5.1 Buy Used**
Let someone else pay for most of the depreciation (see Chapter 43).

☐ **38.5.2 If Buying New, Buy Vehicles With High Resale Values**
The *Consumer Reports New Car Buying Guide*, published annually, lists the models that retain their value the longest.

☐ **38.5.3 Buy Cars That Appreciate**
Scoop up "near classics," drive them a few years, and then sell them for a profit once they become "true classics." This requires a keen sense for collector trends.

39

AUTOS:
GASOLINE

The 2011 CES pegs annual fuel costs (including motor oil) at $2,655, which is 5.9 percent of the typical budget (after backing out Social Security and pensions). Each time you buy a new tank, revisit these strategies and add a few new habits to your gas savings repertoire.

39.1 Ditch the Car

You don't have to worry about gasoline prices if you never own a car in the first place (see Chapter 44).

39.2 Buy Gas Efficient Vehicles

This way, you save whenever you get behind the wheel. Consider hybrids.

39.3 Perform Maintenance That Maximizes Mileage

□ **39.3.1 Keep Tires Inflated**
Buy a quality gauge and check tires monthly. Find the recommended pressure on the driver's side doorjamb or in the owner's manual.

□ **39.3.2 Align Wheels**
Misaligned wheels hinder gas mileage.

□ **39.3.3 Keep Oil Filled and Changed**
Low oil causes low mileage, so check it regularly.

□ **39.3.4 Use the Proper Grade of Oil**
According to the Department of Energy (DOE), a failure to follow manufacturer recommendations cuts mileage by 1–2 percent.

□ **39.3.5 Tune Engines**
The DOE reports that this improves mileage by 4 percent on average.

☐ **39.3.6 Replace Air Filters**

On older cars with carburetors, replace clogged filters to improve their mileage. On newer cars with computerized engines, replacing the filter won't improve mileage, but it will improve acceleration.

39.4 Limit Miles

Curb your transportation costs. When you drive less, you save on both gas and depreciation.

GET THERE SOME OTHER WAY

☐ **39.4.1 Walk**

Exercise this option and save on gas *and* doctor bills.

☐ **39.4.2 Use Alternative Vehicles**

Motorcycles, scooters, bikes, and skateboards—to name a few.

☐ **39.4.3 Carpool or Rideshare**

Many websites match drivers with riders. Visit eRideShare.com, ZimRide.com, GoLoCo.org, Ridester.com, or search for "rideshares."

☐ **39.4.4 Use Public Transportation**

A great choice for foul weather.

STAY WHERE YOU ARE

☐ **39.4.5 Embrace Telecommutes**

One less trip to work each week saves 20 percent on commuting costs. Discuss it with your employer.

☐ **39.4.6 Use Virtual Travel for Meetings**

Visit FreeConferenceCall.com or GoToMeeting.com.

☐ **39.4.7 Use the Mail**

Mail carriers pick up from your front door. Visit Stamps.com to print out the precise postage.

☐ **39.4.8 Make Grocers Come to You**

Order online and take delivery. You pay extra, but it might cost less than driving. Run the numbers.

☐ 39.4.9 Shop Less at Malls and Box Stores
Shop online or by telephone instead.

☐ 39.4.10 Never Drive to Health Clubs
Outfit a home gym or walk to nearby parks. For more ideas, see 10.1.

☐ 39.4.11 Cut Down on Library Trips
Visit bookmobiles. Download e–books from your library's website.

☐ 39.4.12 Use Recreation Car Pools
Hitch rides with friends. Keep drivers happy by chipping in for gas.

☐ 39.4.13 Move Movies In–House
Watch DVDs at home.

☐ 39.4.14 Dine Locally
Try neighborhood eateries or visit diners on the way home from work. Reduce restaurant visits (see 13.1).

☐ 39.4.15 Keep Kids' Activities Close
Favor lessons, programs, and sports nearer to home.

☐ 39.4.16 Vacation Locally
Within 150 miles are many special places you've never visited. Check with your AAA office or read travel guides. Contact your state's tourism office.

39.5 Plan Ahead

☐ 39.5.1 Avoid Short Trips
Frequent cold starts suck petrol. Combine errands so that your engine remains warm and energy efficient.

☐ 39.5.2 Remove Items not in Use
An extra 100 pounds of junk in the trunk cuts gas mileage by as much as two percent. Don't haul around heavy items—golf clubs, tools, doggie crates—unless they're in use on your current trip.

☐ 39.5.3 Remove Idle Recreational Racks
These add weight and inhibit aerodynamics.

☐ **39.5.4 Use GPS or Maps**
If these keep you from getting lost, you save both time and gas.

☐ **39.5.5 If You Own Two Vehicles, Strategize**
Use the fuel–efficient car more often. Plan ahead for the eventual replacement of your gas guzzler.

39.6 Adopt Gas Friendly Driving Techniques

☐ **39.6.1 Avoid Speeding**
According to the DOE, every five miles per hour over the speed of 60 costs you 27 cents more per gallon.

☐ **39.6.2 Avoid Fast Acceleration**
Jackrabbit starts are costly.

☐ **39.6.3 Avoid Hard or Frequent Braking**
Whenever you brake, your car's inertia is disrupted. Follow at a safe distance and let up on the accelerator to slow your car.

☐ **39.6.4 Avoid Crawls**
You waste gas whenever you troll for parking spaces, inch forward at drive–thrus, or crawl along in traffic jams. Park your car at outlying spaces, avoid fast food, and drive off–peak.

☐ **39.6.5 Turn Off the Engine at Long Lights**
According to studies, whenever the wait exceeds 10 seconds, you're better off shutting down the engine. Note: in many states it's illegal to cut the engine if you're in street traffic, apparently because of concerns about rear–end accidents. Check your local laws.

☐ **39.6.6 Limit Air Conditioning**
The AC sucks gas, so below 45 MPH roll down windows. At speeds above 45 MPH, open windows interfere with aerodynamics, so close them and run the fan.

☐ **39.6.7 Install a "Fuel Economy Monitor"**
These give real time feedback and change driving habits fast.

☐ **39.6.8 Limit the Use of Four–Wheel Drive**
This drains gas, so use it only when conditions warrant.

☐ **39.6.9 Use Cruise Control**
A big gas saver in light highway traffic.

☐ **39.6.10 Use the Overdrive Gear**
If your manual transmission includes this feature, use it and save both on gas and engine wear.

39.7 Shop Around

☐ **39.7.1 Know the Lower Priced Stations**
Watch for gas station prices as you cruise frequent routes.

☐ **39.7.2 Buy Warehouse Club Gas**
Plan visits for when your tank is low.

☐ **39.7.3 Patronize Loyalty Discount Programs**
Does your grocer issue gas discounts whenever you reach monthly benchmarks? If so, buy there.

☐ **39.7.4 Buy Discounted Gas Cards**
Look for gas station gift cards discounted by as much as five percent at GiftCardGranny.com, PlasticJungle.com, or GiftCardRescue.com.

☐ **39.7.5 Locate Low Prices Online**
Many sites report the latest prices in your neighborhood, including GasBuddy.com, GasPriceWatch.com, and GasPrices.MapQuest.com.

39.8 Save at the Pump

Keep a copy of Appendix 6 in your car and look it over whenever you stop for gas (and keep using it until the listed tactics become ingrained habits).

40

AUTOS: MAINTENANCE

As much as it hurts, fringers sometimes spend money in order to save money. Maintenance is a prime example of this. Whenever your vehicle requires routine attention, choose from among these tightfisted strategies.

40.1 Ditch the Car

You don't have to worry about maintenance if you never own a car in the first place (see Chapter 44).

40.2 Follow the Owner's Manual

The manual lists maintenance you should perform at stated mileage levels or months of operation. By following these schedules, you keep warranties alive, forestall repairs, and extend your vehicle's lifespan.

40.3 DIY

For these easy jobs, don't pay a mechanic who charges $60 per hour and marks up parts by 20 percent.

☐ **40.3.1 Replace Fluids**
These include brake fluid, coolant, transmission fluid, and wiper juice. An oil change shop might refill these for FREE, but if it charges, do it yourself.

☐ **40.3.2 Change Windshield Wipers, Air Filters, and Lights**
Follow Appendix 1 for these purchases and install them yourself.

☐ **40.3.3 Switch Out Batteries**
Dispose of old ones responsibly.

☐ 40.3.4 Perform Your Own Oil Changes

Well, maybe. You need heavy–duty ramps to raise your vehicle while you work underneath. You also need a plan to dispose of used oil and filters (which some national car part chain stores accept). If this all seems like too much trouble, proceed to 40.4.

40.4 Save on Oil Changes

Stacking works great here. You can use your credit card (2 percent reward) to buy a discounted gift card (8 percent off) to a national lube chain that issues online coupons (33 percent off). With three tiers of savings, after your next visit the only thing left squeaking will be your wallet.

☐ 40.4.1 Avoid Dealers, Except for Special Offers

Dealers usually don't cut deals. In contrast, competition among oil change shops is heated.

☐ 40.4.2 Ignore the Big Lie of Every Three Months or 3,000 Miles

Manufacturers now design most engines to run 5,000 miles or more between oil changes. Follow the schedules in your owner's manual and ignore what oil change shops say.

☐ 40.4.3 Use Synthetic Oils

These cost more, but you save because you change oil only half as often. Check the manufacturer's latest guidelines about which synthetics work best for your model.

☐ 40.4.4 Buy Discounted Gift Cards to Oil Change Shops

Visit GiftCardGranny.com, PlasticJungle.com, or GiftCardRescue.com.

☐ 40.4.5 Seek Discounts

Search online for coupons. Or join your favorite shop's mailing list and the coupons will show up just in time for your next oil change.

☐ 40.4.6 Decline Upsells

Stick to entry level services. Extras usually trigger hefty markups.

☐ 40.4.7 Decline Fluid Flushes and Other Extras

Follow the schedules in your owner's manual.

☐ **40.4.8 Procure the Oil Yourself**
Recently, I saved $8 by supplying the synthetic oil myself (the garage hadn't stocked the right grade, so I shopped around). Confirm with the shop ahead of time whether it will accept this arrangement.

40.5 Save on Windshields

☐ **40.5.1 Hire Windshield Repair Services**
Act fast, and a repair shop can fill a chip with resin before it grows into a large crack. Check your policy; many insurers cover this.

☐ **40.5.2 Buy Windshield Repair Kits**
Apply the resin yourself. Amazon sells several products.

☐ **40.5.3 Purchase Glass Insurance**
If your car runs through windshields, consider buying coverage.

40.6 Save on Tires

According to the CES, the largest single cost of car maintenance is the purchase, replacement, and mounting of tires. No wonder. New tires for a small sedan now run about $450, and more for larger vehicles. To manage costs, follow Appendix 1 and these additional tactics that save you money where the rubber meets the road.

☐ **40.6.1 Find the Best Tires for Your Vehicle**
Visit these sources when you shop.

- *Consumer Reports.* The annual *Used Car Buying Guide* lists the best–rated tires, including winter tires.

- *Chat Rooms.* Visit to find the best–liked tires for your model.

- *The Best Online Resource for Tires.* Go to TireRack.com and enter your vehicle's year, manufacturer, model, and trim line. Up pops a long list of tires that fit your car, which you can sort to find the bestsellers. Customer reviews abound. Even if you buy elsewhere, TireRack provides a goldmine of information.

☐ **40.6.2 Shop the Internet**
The prices at TireRack.com, TireMonkey.com, and Tires-Easy.com often undercut warehouse clubs, which usually offer the lowest

prices among physical stores. If you buy online, don't forget to factor in the costs for shipping and mounting tires.

☐ 40.6.3 Seek Rebates and Coupons
Special offers are common for tires. Look for them before you buy.

☐ 40.6.4 Haggle
Use prices from websites to dicker with local shops. For additional approaches, revisit Chapter 5.

☐ 40.6.5 Avoid Bells and Whistles
When you buy tires, don't pay extra for road hazard protection. If you run over a nail, the repair only costs about $12.

☐ 40.6.6 Don't Buy Used Tires . . . Unless
Usually, this line item is no place to save with a secondhand purchase. Tires salvaged from wrecks might have serious problems that are undetectable to the naked eye. One exception: when you buy from someone you trust who can vouch for the tires' history.

40.7 Follow Up on Tire Purchases

Prolong the life of your tires with these steps.

☐ 40.7.1 Drive Fewer Miles
Limit mileage to save on gas and tire wear. For tactics, see 39.4.

☐ 40.7.2 Drive Easy
The basics: avoid peel outs, sudden stops, heavy loads, and hard cornering (see 39.6).

☐ 40.7.3 Keep Tires Inflated
Reduces wear and improves gas mileage. Buy a good tire gauge.

☐ 40.7.4 Rotate, Balance
Good care prevents bad wear.

☐ 40.7.5 Maintain Shocks and Suspension
If your car drives choppy or your tires wear unevenly, have the shocks and suspension checked.

41

AUTOS:
CAR REPAIRS

Despite faithful maintenance, cars break down eventually. When it's your turn to seek repairs, follow these strategies.

41.1 Ditch the Car

You don't have to worry about repairs if you never own a car in the first place (see Chapter 44).

41.2 Perform Preventative Maintenance

Usually the cheapest way to limit repair costs (see Chapter 40).

41.3 Check for Warranties

Some warranties extend deep into a car's life, including those for emission systems, power train components, and hybrid batteries. Don't schedule repairs without first checking your car's paperwork—you still might have coverage.

41.4 Avoid Dealers

Dealerships are pricey. Avoid them except in narrow situations:

- *Warranties.* Warranty work is FREE, so schedule it with a dealership. Beware: having the work performed away from the dealer might render the warranty void.

- *Recalls.* Recall work is also FREE. Schedule it with the dealership.

- *Specialized Repairs.* Some repairs require complicated techniques that dealers can handle, but most shops can't. One solution: contact a shop that specializes in your make of vehicle. It might have the know–how.

- *Special Offers.* If a dealer issues coupons that undercut your local shop, by all means, hire the dealer. Just don't hold your breath for this to happen.

41.5 Find a Good Repair Shop

Locate someone honest and competent *before* your car needs work.

☐ 41.5.1 Ask Around
The best source of recommendations: those you know.

☐ 41.5.2 Ask the Oracle
Read online recommendations at Angie's List, CarTalk.com, or AAA.com (over 7,700 AAA approved shops nationwide).

☐ 41.5.3 Ask the BBB
The Better Business Bureau steers you clear of shops with high complaint volumes. Visit BBB.org.

☐ 41.5.4 Look for ASE Certification
The National Institute for Automotive Service Excellence (ASE) certifies technicians, not shops, so the sign outside doesn't mean that the person who does the work is ASE certified. When you schedule repairs, ask for someone certified to do the specific work you need (e.g., brakes, A/C, or engine overhauls). For a list of shops with ASE technicians near you, visit ASE.com.

☐ 41.5.5 Seek Warranties on Parts and Services
Mechanics should stand behind their work. AAA shops provide a 12 month/12,000 mile limited warranty on parts and labor.

☐ 41.5.6 Test Drive a Mechanic
For starters, try basics like oil changes and tire rotations.

☐ 41.5.7 Consider Specialty Chains
They often offer discounts that undercut generalist shops.

41.6 Participate in the Diagnosis

If you help diagnose your car's troubles, you cut the risks of anyone taking advantage of you.

☐ 41.6.1 Use Online Diagnostics

Several sites help interpret strange noises and shudders. Visit AutoMD.com or Car-Trouble.com.

☐ 41.6.2 Ask an Online Mechanic

Experts answer questions for FREE. Visit JustAnswer.com/car/, FreeAutoMechanic.com, 2CarPros.com, and DriverSide.com.

☐ 41.6.3 Visit Your Car's Chat Room

Someone who owns your model probably has written about your problem, or, if you post a question, will respond in detail.

☐ 41.6.4 Decode Engine Lights for FREE

Many chain stores—including AutoZone and Pep Boys—lend handheld units that decode "check engine" lights.

☐ 41.6.5 Always Ask About Repair Options

Maybe there's a way to fix your vehicle for less. It never hurts to ask and a short conversation often uncovers better choices.

41.7 Compare Before You Repair

Once you know what needs fixing, seek quotes.

☐ 41.7.1 For Small Repairs, Check Online Cost Estimators

Find guidance about repair costs at RepairPal.com, DriverSide.com, AutoMD.com, RepairTrust.com, InstantEstimator.com (body work). Price parts at RockAuto.com.

☐ 41.7.2 For Big Repairs, Get *Written* Estimates

Ask for hourly rates, estimated times for each stage of the repair, part charges, and extras such as environmental disposal fees.

☐ 41.7.3 Know When to Replace Your Car

If the repairs cost more than your car is worth, it might be time to shop for a replacement. To assess your vehicle's value, visit Kelly Blue Book (KBB.com) or Edmunds.com.

41.8 Use a Haggle Script

☐ 41.8.1 *"Can You Match These Online Estimates?"*

Listed in 41.7.1, estimators make good negotiating tools.

☐ **41.8.2** *"Can You Beat These Other Bids?"*
Create some competition among shops and lower your repair bill.

☐ **41.8.3** *"Can you Throw in a Tire Rotation and Oil Change?"*
When you schedule major repairs, the shop might perform some minor maintenance for FREE.

☐ **41.8.4** *"My Car Isn't Worth That Much. Can You Go Lower?"*
If you own a clunker, a shop might give you a deal because you're likely to need help again soon.

41.9 Consider Ultra Low Cost Strategies

If you can't afford to hire a local repair shop, try a cheaper option.

☐ **41.9.1 Contact Your Local Community College or Vo Tech**
You need repairs. Students need experience. Instructors supervise.

☐ **41.9.2 Procure Your Own Parts**
With Appendix 1, you might be able to buy reliable name brand parts for less than your mechanic can. Ask upfront whether this approach is acceptable. To price parts on the internet, go to RockAuto.com. To price salvage parts, visit eBay Motors or Car-Part.com. One drawback with DIY procuring: mechanics don't warrant parts they don't supply.

☐ **41.9.3 Barter or Trade Services**
If you have a pickup equipped with a plow and the guy down the road runs a garage, ask whether you can work out a snow removal for rotor replacement deal. As always, beware the tax complications. See IRS Publication 525.

☐ **41.9.4 DIY**
If you like to tinker, it pays dividends on car repairs. Then you become the one who exchanges rotor work for snow removal.

41.10 Avoid Pitfalls

The best way to avoid rip-offs is to find a shop with an established reputation for honesty and fair dealing. If you're still paranoid about scams, consider these common rip-offs and the tactics to avoid them.

☐ 41.10.1 Make Sure Parts Are Replaced

The scam: you're charged for parts that are never installed. The fix: before the repair, place an inconspicuous scratch or mark on the items that face replacement. When you pick the car up, ask to see the removed parts and look for your mark.

☐ 41.10.2 Make Sure Work Gets Performed

The scam: you're charged for work, but it's never performed. The fix: stay at the shop and watch over the repairs.

☐ 41.10.3 Prevent Unnecessary Work

The scam: you're told some expensive work is necessary, which in fact isn't true. The fix: (1) participate actively in the diagnostics (see 41.6); (2) get a second opinion from another shop; or (3) take your car to a diagnostic–only shop that doesn't do repairs, and thus has no incentive to deceive.

☐ 41.10.4 Avoid Overcharges

The scam: you're told the brake job costs $500, which is twice the going rate. The fix: before work begins (1) check internet repair cost databases (RepairPal.com, InstantEstimator.com, RepairTrust.com); and (2) obtain estimates from other shops.

☐ 41.10.5 Sidestep Oversells and Upsells

This is more about aggressive salesmanship than an outright scam: you go in for an oil change, and the shop recommends an "upscale" oil or new air filter. The fix: politely decline the upgrade and stick to the schedules in your owner's manual. If the shop suggests repairs that weren't discussed upfront, seek a second opinion.

☐ 41.10.6 Decline Cheap Parts

This isn't a scam either, but neither is it a good idea. For most repairs, the biggest cost component is labor. So don't skimp on parts. Instead, insist on brand names, especially when it comes to brakes, where a knockoff's failure to perform can be catastrophic.

☐ 41.10.7 Prevent Theft

The scam: outright theft of personal items. The fix: remove all valuables before you drop off the car.

41.11 Follow Up

☐ 41.11.1 Keep All Repair Records
This paperwork helps if you resell the car, if a friend faces a similar repair, or if any disputes arise.

☐ 41.11.2 Agree to Form of Payment
Discuss whether discounts are available for payments in cash. If not, pay with plastic and reap the rewards (but *only* if you pay the cards off every month).

☐ 41.11.3 In Case of Disputes, Contact the AAA
If you're an AAA member and have any disagreement with an AAA–approved shop, ask the local office to serve as a referee.

42

AUTOS: LOANS

According to *Consumer Reports*, loan interest represents 11 percent of the five–year cost of owning a new vehicle (based on a five–year loan with 15 percent down and interest at 6 percent). You only sign a few of these loans in the course of your lifetime. You need a solid game plan because lenders have completed far more of these transactions than you have. Here are strategies that level the playing field.

42.1 Ditch the Car

You don't have to worry about auto loans if you never own a car in the first place (see Chapter 44).

42.2 Don't Borrow

☐ **42.2.1 Pay Cash**
On a four–year loan for $15,000 at eight percent, you pay $2,577 in interest plus applicable fees. To run the numbers for any loan you're considering, visit these auto loan calculators:

- BankRate.com/calculators/auto/auto-loan-calculator.aspx
- Edmunds.com/calculators/
- Money-Zine.com/Category/Auto-Loan-Calculators

☐ **42.2.2 Go Car Free Temporarily**
A medium sized sedan costs about $9,000 per year to own and operate. Go without a car for eighteen months (see Chapter 44), and you save enough to buy your next vehicle outright.

42.3 Read a Reliable Guide

Car loans are complex beasts. Educate yourself with one or more of these guides:

- BankRate.com/finance/auto/auto-loans-101.aspx
- Edmunds.com/car-loan
- FTC.gov/bcp/edu/pubs/consumer/autos/aut04.pdf

42.4 Favor Small Loans

If borrow you must, try these methods to minimize loan costs.

☐ 42.4.1 Buy a Used Car

And slash your finance costs (see Chapter 43).

☐ 42.4.2 Buy a Cheaper Car

Usually, small cars cost less than larger ones.

☐ 42.4.3 Get More Money for Your Trade–In

To limit the amount you borrow, get as much as possible for your current vehicle. Sales to private parties yield the highest returns, but they also take the most time and effort.

☐ 42.4.4 Increase the Down Payment

The more you pay upfront, the less you pay in interest.

☐ 42.4.5 Shorten the Loan's Term

This increases the size of your monthly payments, but the sooner you repay, the lower your interest rate.

☐ 42.4.6 Maintain a High Credit Score

Those with higher scores qualify for lower interest rates, so pay all bills and loan installments on time. Also, make sure your credit report is accurate. For a FREE copy, visit AnnualCreditReport.com.

42.5 Use House Money

When you borrow on your home to finance a vehicle, you save twice. First, unlike interest on car loans, mortgage interest is deductible. Second, interest rates for home mortgages undercut car loan rates.

But you won't receive any savings unless you first convince a lender to increase the size of your home's mortgage. If you have ample equity and a high credit rating, your chances for approval are good. These tactics guide you through the process.

☐ 42.5.1 Weigh the Risks

If real estate values drop, you could go "underwater" (own a house worth less than its mortgage).

☐ 42.5.2 Use a Car Loan vs. Home Equity Calculator

Access online tools to figure how much you can save.

- Money–Zine.com/Calculators/Auto-Loan-Calculators/Auto-or-Home-Equity-Loan-Calculator

- Chase.com/home-equity/home-equity-calculator

- Autos.aol.com/calculators/

☐ 42.5.3 Refinance Your Home

One way to tap your home's equity is to refinance for an amount that pays off the old mortgage and leaves enough left over to pay for a car. If you take this path, you embark upon one of the most complicated transactions of your life. This is one instance where you have to educate yourself to avoid disaster. The Federal Reserve Board publishes "A Consumer's Guide to Mortgage Refinancing," available at FederalReserve.gov/pubs/refinancings/refinancing.pdf.

☐ 42.5.4 Apply for a HELOC

Home Equity Lines of Credit work well for car financing because: (1) your borrowing minimum is low (about $5,000); and (2) you can tap a HELOC without the bank's renewed permission. HELOCs are complicated, so read "What You Should Know About Home Equity Lines of Credit," available at ConsumerFinance.gov/.

CODA: AVOID SECOND MORTGAGES

Generally, these have long terms (10 or 20 years) and you have to borrow large amounts (usually, at least $40,000). Such requirements make this a poor choice for auto financing.

42.6 Shop Around

Sources of auto loans include local banks, online banks, credit unions, and car dealerships. Follow these steps to find the best deals.

☐ 42.6.1 Line Up Financing First

Secure a loan before you shop. If the dealer pitches a loan to you, say you've already arranged one, but would entertain better offers. Never let the dealer mix price negotiations with loan discussions, as in "if you finance with us, I'll drop $600 off the car's price." This increases the risk that you overpay for the car, for the loan, or for both.

☐ 42.6.2 Price Interest Rates at Internet Comparison Sites

When shopping, the main consideration is the annual percentage rate (APR), which varies daily depending upon market conditions. The lower the APR, the better. On a four–year car loan of $15,000, a rate of five percent instead of eight percent saves about $1,000. Review the latest offers at these sites:

- BankRate.com
- eLoan.com
- LendingTree.com

☐ 42.6.3 Visit Your Local Consumer Credit Union

They often offer the best deals on car loans.

☐ 42.6.4 Use a Comparison Shopping Checklist for Auto Loans

Under the Truth in Lending Act, lenders must disclose such key terms as the APR, monthly payment amounts, total finance charges, and late payment fees. As you shop, use the Comparison Shopping Checklist below to keep all the offers straight.

42.7 Avoid Pitfalls

☐ 42.7.1 Avoid Bells and Whistles

The lender may try to sell you coverage that pays off the balance owed if your car is destroyed or stolen (guaranteed auto protection), if you die or become disabled (credit insurance), or if you lose your job (unemployment insurance). Decline all extras.

☐ 42.7.2 Retain the Right to Pay Off Early Without Penalty

Make sure that the repayment schedule spreads interest out evenly over the life of the loan. This is called "simple interest," and that precise phrase should appear somewhere in the documents. If it's missing, then interest is likely front–loaded, which means that if you repay early, the payoff amount will be higher because the first payments were allocated to pay interest instead of principal.

☐ 42.7.3 Don't Refinance Auto Loans

You may see ads about refinancing auto loans. You probably can do better if you pay off your loan early with a home loan (see 42.4) or your savings (and these pile up fast with *SL☑N!*).

☐ 42.7.4 Avoid Leases

Leases save on interest costs, but you save more if you buy a used car instead. Run the numbers yourself with these online calculators.

- SmartMoney.com/spending/autos/to-buy-or-to–lease-7868

- Bankrate.com/calculators/auto/buy-or-lease-calculator.aspx

- Edmunds.com/calculators

☐ 42.7.5 Avoid Long Term Loans

Don't sign loans that last more than 72 months. These look attractive because of their low monthly payments. But they also carry rates that are one or two points higher than loans for shorter terms, and you pay hundreds more in interest over the loan's life.

☐ 42.7.6 Read Before You Sign

Before you sign final papers, read them carefully and confirm that their language matches each of the key terms outlined in the Comparison Shopping Checklist below.

COMPARISON SHOPPING CHECKLIST FOR AUTO LOANS

	Lender 1	Lender 2	Lender 3
Total amount financed			
Annual Percentage Rate (APR)			
Is the interest rate variable? (This is rare for auto loans.) If so:			
(a) When do rates change?			
(b) How often can they change?			
(c) How much can they change?			
Fees, including credit check fee, loan origination fees, application fee, etc.			
Total finance charges			
Monthly payments			
Length of contract in months			
Total payments in dollars			
Penalty for late payments?			
Any penalty for paying loan off early?			
"Simple interest" or front–loaded interest?			
Does loan include extras like credit insurance, guaranteed auto protection, or extended service contracts?			

43

AUTOS:
USED CARS

Buying secondhand saves massive amounts over the course of your driving years. Not only do you pay less upfront, as each year passes you spend less for insurance, ownership taxes, and interest (if you borrow). Follow these strategies whenever you shop for pre–owned cars.

43.1 Ditch the Car

You don't have to worry about shopping if you don't need a vehicle (see Chapter 44).

43.2 Consult Buyer's Guides

Each year, reputable sources rank the best used models in each vehicle class. These guides save you hours of research and boost your chances of making a good purchase.

- *Consumer Search.* Aggregates opinions from reliable sources and lists the "best reviewed" cars. Visit ConsumerSearch.com.

- *Edmunds.* Lists the "best bets" in used vehicles. Visit Edmunds.com/car–reviews/best-used-cars.html.

- *Consumer Reports.* The leader in guides, but unless you visit the library, you have to pay for the information. Read the annual *Used Car Buying Guide.*

43.3 Look for Models That Retain their Value

Depreciation is biggest single cost of car ownership (see Chapter 38). If you plan to someday resell the car you're buying, favor used models that depreciate slowly. Buying guides list which models hold their value the longest (43.2).

43.4 Look for Models With Low Fuel Costs

□ **43.4.1 Favor Vehicles With High Fuel Economy Ratings**
If gas averages $3.50 per gallon and you drive 15,000 miles a year, a
25 MPG improvement in mileage saves you $1,050 annually, or
$5,500 over five years. For MPG data on hundreds of vehicles, visit
FuelEconomy.gov.

□ **43.4.2 Favor Vehicles That Use Regular Gas**
Avoid vehicles that require premium gas and save $50–$75 per year.

□ **43.4.3 Favor Manual Transmissions**
Make a clutch decision: these cost less to buy and repair. They also
improve a vehicle's gas mileage.

□ **43.4.4 Consider Hybrids or Electrics**
You're no greenie, but a Toyota Prius will make you look like one.

□ **43.4.5 Consider Diesel Fuel Vehicles**
The upside: diesels cost less to operate, fetch higher prices on resale,
and last longer. The downside: diesel vehicles cost more and so can
the fuel. If you're torn between a diesel (such as the VW Jetta) and a
gas engine competitor (such as the Toyota Yaris), compare their
overall costs of ownership at the Department of Energy's Alternative
Fuels Data Center. Visit AFDC.energy.gov/calc/.

□ **43.4.6 Consider Flexible Fuel Vehicles (FFVs)**
These run on a mixture of gasoline and 85 percent ethanol or
methanol, also known as E85, the price for which usually runs 10–15
percent less than regular gas. But because E85 contains less energy
than gas, the car's MPG will drop. Whether the price break
outweighs the lost efficiency depends upon current gas prices and
the car's performance. For a current list of gas stations that sell E85,
visit E85Vehicles.com.

43.5 Look for Models That Cost Less to Insure

□ **43.5.1 Avoid Vehicles With High Theft Rates**
Some vehicles attract thieves because of poor alarms or a strong
demand for replacement parts. Search online for the latest data about
which cars get stolen most often.

□ **43.5.2 Avoid Oversized Engines**

Many insurers charge higher premiums for larger engines. (My RAV4 has a peppy V6 engine and because of that I pay an extra $120 per year. I think the pep is worth it.)

□ **43.5.3 Check Insurance Costs Before You Buy**

Visit Edmunds.com to gauge the costs to insure different vehicles. Once you focus on a specific model, call your insurance agent and ask for the estimated premium. Also, get a list of safety features that trigger discounts and look for used cars with those features.

43.6 Consider Reliability

□ **43.6.1 Read** *Consumer Reports*

Each year, the editors survey more than a million vehicle owners about seventeen different trouble spots. Results appear in the annual *Used Car Buying Guide*.

□ **43.6.2 Search for Recalls**

The model you like may have been the subject of one or more recalls. Visit SaferCar.gov.

43.7 Consider Safety Ratings

□ **43.7.1 Review NHTSA Ratings**

The National Highway Traffic Safety Administration uses a five star safety rating system that covers front crashes, side crashes, and rollover resistance. Visit SaferCar.gov.

□ **43.7.2 Review IIHS Ratings**

The Insurance Institute for Highway Safety (IIHS) tests for frontal offset crashes, side impact crashes, roof strength, and rear crash protection/head restraint. Visit IIHS.org.

□ **43.7.3 Read** *Consumer Reports*

The annual *Used Car Buying Guide* republishes crash data from the NHTSA and IIHS, so you only have to consult a single source.

43.8 Choose Where to Shop

When you shop for used cars, you typically have two choices.

◻ **43.8.1 Consider Dealers (More Expensive)**

Dealers have big overheads, and their prices reflect those expenses. On the other hand, they're convenient and often provide limited warranties (read the provisions carefully before you buy).

◻ **43.8.2 Consider Private Sellers (Less Expensive)**

Private parties don't have the overhead dealers do, so they can sell for less. Review current listings at AutoTrader.com, eBay Motors, Cars.com, and Craigslist.

CODA: GOVERNMENT FLEET SALES

The General Services Administration (GSA) leases vehicles to federal agencies. When leases expire, typically after three to five years, the GSA holds public auctions. All vehicles are sold "as is" and all sales are final. Bidders can't test drive the cars or take them to mechanics, but they can start engines and inspect interiors. Despite the obvious risks, you might be able to score a low price that leaves room to cover all but the most costly repairs. The GSA auctions off 40,000 cars and trucks per year. For details, visit AutoAuctions.gsa.gov.

43.9 Prearrange a Loan

At this point, you know your model and whether you're buying from a dealer or private party, so you know the likely price range. Unless you have enough money saved up, it's time to pick a lender (see Chapter 42).

43.10 Inspect Vehicles

You've done the research and, if you're borrowing, the loan is prearranged. Welcome to the dance. It's time shop for cars in all their metallic—and plastic—glory.

◻ **43.10.1 Test Drive the Car With an Inspection Checklist**

A short spin tells much if you know what to look for, so use a checklist.

- ConsumerReports.org/content/news/wheeling/worksheets/test_drive_checklist.html

- Autos.msn.com/advice/articles/testdrivechecklist.aspx

- Anytime.CUNA.org/10897/used_car/pages/Used_Car_Test_Drive_Chklist.htm

☐ 43.10.2 Review Records
Complete paperwork suggests the car was treated well. Ask for a copy and study the details.

☐ 43.10.3 Order a Vehicle History Report
If the car checks out based on the test drive and maintenance records, use its VIN to order a report that details the ownership history, title problems, and, in many cases, service and repair records. The report may also list accidents, but only if those mishaps made it into the system (beware: the lack of a listed accident isn't absolute proof that none occurred). If the report shows problems, you can shift your search to another vehicle before you pay for an inspection. Order vehicle histories at CarFax.com, AutoCheck.com, or VehicleHistory.gov.

☐ 43.10.4 Schedule a Mechanical Inspection
Unless you're a confirmed motor head who can inspect all aspects of the car yourself, take this indispensible step before you commit to buy. Plan to spend $100–$150. Obvious point: don't let the buyer pick the mechanic. If you don't know any mechanics, contact your local AAA office or run through the tactics for picking repair shops in Chapter 41. Anyone who regularly inspects vehicles should follow a standard checklist. Ask to see it in advance.

☐ 43.10.5 For Cars With Body Work, Visit a Body Shop
If the car's been in an accident, and if despite that misfortune you're still interested, have the vehicle checked by a reputable body shop.

☐ 43.10.6 Check for a Warranty
If the seller offers the car "as is," there's no warranty and you bear the risk of any problems. If a warranty exists, read it carefully before you buy (including the inevitable exceptions and exclusions).

43.11 Haggle

☐ 43.11.1 *"Can You Match the Online Price Listings?"*
Most guides list separate prices for dealers and private party sales.

The leaders are Consumer Reports New & Used Car Price Service, Edmunds.com Pricing Reports, Kelly Blue Book, and NADA. Bring along printouts for some show and tell.

☐ 43.11.2 *"Can You Match the Recent Local Sales Prices?"*

If a 2003 Honda Accord with similar mileage sold last week in your state for $9,500, you can use that to convince your seller to drop the $12,000 asking price. Where to find sales data? Try the advanced product search at eBay.com. Enter your make, model, year, and check the box for "completed listings."

☐ 43.11.3 *"Problems Exist. Can You Drop the Price?"*

If the inspection uncovered some issues, but they weren't enough to scare you away from the car, use that information to argue for a lower price. Go to websites that estimate repair costs (see 41.7.1), and argue that the sales price should drop by at least that amount. Show the seller all the relevant paperwork.

☐ 43.11.4 *"Here's My Offer."*

The seller is at $12,000. You'd like to pay $11,000, but haven't made a counter–offer yet. Consider making a $10,000 counter that signals your acceptable price and steers discussions into the "let's split the difference" territory.

44

AUTOS:
THE CARLESS LIFESTYLE

According to the AAA, driving 15,000 miles per year in a mid–sized car costs $8,946. If you spend at the national average ($44,600) and ditch the sedan, you save 20 percent on your annual expenses, and do it in one fell swoop. Few other single decisions can cut your expenses by so much and do it so fast. Consider these strategies.

44.1 Live Where Cars Are Optional

The way most cities are laid out, few can enjoy the advantages of forswearing their cars. Here's how to make it work for you.

☐ **44.1.1 Telecommute or Live Near Work**
If you work at home or live within walking distance of your workplace, you remove the biggest reason for car ownership: the daily commute.

☐ **44.1.2 Live Near Public Transit**
Another way to skin the cat of commuting is to locate your home close to public transportation—bus, train, light rail, subway—that whisks you away to work and other destinations. An added bonus: many employers subsidize travel expenses.

☐ **44.1.3 Live Near Bicycle Paths**
Housing near public transit usually costs more, but you might not pay extra for easy access to a bike trail system.

☐ **44.1.4 Live Near Taxis or Car Services**
Which costs less: $9,000 spent per year to own a car, or $1,500 spent per year on occasional cab fares? If taxis are scarce, visit Uber.com, an on–demand car service app that lets you request rides from nearby drivers who have spare seats available (now in seventeen US cities).

☐ 44.1.5 Live in Compact Communities

Live in a neighborhood within easy walking distance of groceries, shopping, and entertainment. How do you find such pedestrian nirvanas? Enter prospective addresses at WalkScore.com, which rates locations for their walkability. Scores of 90 or more qualify as "walker's paradises" where most daily errands don't require cars.

☐ 44.1.6 Live Near Car Shares and Rentals

Trips out of your walkable neighborhood might require temporary access to a vehicle. If you live near a parked car share (ZipCar.com), reaching an auto is easy. Even if you live far away from car shares, many rental agencies deliver vehicles to your front door.

☐ 44.1.7 Live Near Peer–to–Peer Car Shares

Similar to ZipCar, except a central agency doesn't supply the cars; instead, individuals make their own vehicles available to others. A clearinghouse provides insurance, screens driving records, and provides secure keyless entry boxes. This business model is relatively new. Visit RelayRides.com, GetAround.com, JustShareIt.com, and Wheelz.com.

☐ 44.1.8 Live Near Peers

Contact family and friends with this proposition: if they lend you their cars occasionally, you'll pay them the same rate as a peer–to–peer lending site. It's a win–win for both sides. You avoid the cost of ownership; they receive extra cash to defray vehicle expenses. Everyone deals with people they know and trust instead of strangers. Before you take the wheel, check with each owner's insurer to find out what happens if you're involved in an accident. You might need to buy non–owners liability insurance or an umbrella policy to protect yourself and those from whom you borrow, but that protection costs much less than a car does.

44.2 Limit Your Need for a Car

Stay closer to home and use alternatives to car travel (see 39.4).

44.3 Go Car Free Lite

Test drive the carless life without going cold turkey on ownership.

☐ 44.3.1 Take the Car Free Life for a Test Drive

Dock your car in the garage for a few weeks. Debrief yourself.

☐ 44.3.2 Cut Back on Vehicles

Apply the above tactics to pare down to a single car.

☐ 44.3.3 Cut Back Temporarily

You don't have to go carless forever. Rent a place in the city for starters and earmark the savings to fund a move to suburbia. You might even decide that you prefer living downtown.

45

HOUSING:
HOUSING COSTS

For almost everyone, this by far is the biggest expense. The 2011 CES reports that housing expenses average $16,803 and represent about 38 percent of the annual household budget (not counting Social Security and pensions). To reduce your own outlays on this massive line item, try these strategies, most of which work for owners and renters alike. They're arranged according to how much they disrupt your life, with the easiest changes appearing first.

45.1 Spend Less on Household Operations

Cut housing–related costs with these checklists:

Line Item	Chapter
Real Estate Taxes	20
Home Energy	22
Water	23
Trash Collection	24
Homeowners' Insurance	29
House Repairs and Remodels	46

45.2 Do More at Home

Your house provides the room you need to save on many expenses.

☐ **45.2.1 Host Weddings and Reunions**
Why rent a hall or meeting space? Host events at home.

☐ **45.2.2 Avoid Auto Expenses**
Telecommute and shop online. It saves gasoline and reduces your vehicle's wear and tear.

☐ **45.2.3 Dine In**
Use the kitchen to save on restaurants.

☐ **45.2.4 Reduce Your Bar Tabs**
Stock a home bar and drink in the friendliest of confines.

☐ **45.2.5 Favor Entertainment at Home**
Instead of visits to movie theaters, stay at home and watch DVDs. Host potlucks and family game nights.

☐ **45.2.6 Skip Health Clubs**
A home gym furnished with used equipment pays for itself fast.

45.3 Capture Tax Benefits

Important: consult your tax guru before you pursue these tactics.

☐ **45.3.1 Take Deductions**
If you itemize, deduct home–related expenses such as loan origination fees, mortgage interest, and property taxes.

☐ **45.3.2 Operate Home Offices and Businesses**
If you use certain areas exclusively for business purposes, consider whether you can deduct their costs on a square–footage basis. For details, read IRS Publication 587.

☐ **45.3.3 Pursue Tax Incentives**
Look for deductions and tax credits on home improvements that save energy.

45.4 Reduce Cramping

Regardless of whether you own or rent, whenever you feel crowded, pursue these tactics to live well in less space. They all cost less than a move to a bigger home.

INCREASE YOUR LIVING SPACE

☐ **45.4.1 Create Multi–Use Rooms**
Relieve space–cramping with rooms that serve several functions. Try these classic approaches.

- Den/Guest Bedroom
- Media Room/Home Gym
- Laundry Room/Mud Room
- Dining Room/Hobby Area
- Kitchen /Dining Space
- Garage/Work Bench Area

☐ 45.4.2 Share

When you share bedrooms, bathrooms, and desks, you don't need nearly as much space.

☐ 45.4.3 Avoid Space Eaters

Large items eat away at your living space.

- *Pool Tables.* Nothing consumes square footage like these behemoths. Visit friends with tables instead.

- *Beds.* If spare beds see sporadic use only, buy sofa sleepers, bunk beds, Murphy beds, and convertible futons. To save even more room, store your guest beds in closets: air mattresses, fold up cots, and sleeping bags.

- *Oversized Vehicles.* To gain extra garage space, switch to a smaller SUV.

- *Multiple Vehicles.* Drop a car or two. Use freed–up garage bays for extra workspace and storage.

- *Furniture.* Favor the moveable, foldable, collapsible, and stackable. Mount heavy items on sliders or casters so that you can push them aside whenever you need more room.

- *Desks and Office Chairs.* A laptop or tablet lets you work at the dining room table.

- *Washers and Dryers.* If your household is small, consider a stackable unit.

☐ 45.4.4 Expand Outdoors

Increase your square footage with outside living spaces. The cost is miniscule when compared to interior build–outs. Consider these projects.

- Gazebos and pagodas
- Adirondack chairs
- Tree houses
- Play houses
- Yurts and outbuildings
- Hammocks
- Patios
- Porches
- Decks
- BBQ pits

☐ 45.4.5 Expand Indoors
Finish basements and attics, close in porches, and repurpose garages.

INCREASE YOUR STORAGE SPACE

Excess stuff cramps your living space. You have two options. First, you can sell, donate, or throw it out. Second, you can boost your storage space with these expansive—and inexpensive—solutions.

☐ 45.4.6 Digitize
Convert your media into bytes.

- Books → e–books
- Photos → JPEGs
- Records/CDs → MP3s
- DVDs → internet streaming
- Paper files → .pdfs
- Magazines → websites
- Guidebooks → websites

☐ 45.4.7 Use Walls
Bare walls present storage opportunities.

- Wall mounts for TVs
- Bookcases
- Shelves
- Racks
- Hooks
- Brackets

☐ 45.4.8 Use Ceilings
Suspended splendor awaits: hang pots and pans above kitchen islands, bikes in garages, and plants in the sunlight.

☐ 45.4.9 Pick Furniture That Supplies Storage
A long chest doubles as a coffee table and as storage for blankets.

☐ 45.4.10 Store Underneath Beds, Bureaus, and Other Furniture
Increase the available space with the use of sturdy risers.

☐ 45.4.11 Attach Racks to Door Backs
Good for lightweight items.

☐ 45.4.12 Go Vertical
Buy stackable plastic boxes; translucent ones show what's inside. In closets, use "space saving hangers" (many types exist, search online).

45.4.13 Fill Empty Suitcases
Use them to store spare linens or other rarely used items.

45.4.14 Go Offsite
Borrow storage space from accommodating friends.

45.5 Cut Mortgage Costs

45.5.1 Get Educated
Mortgages are complicated beasts. Don't make any changes without educating yourself first. Visit these sources:

- *HSH Associates.* A comprehensive site. Visit HSH.com.
- *Mortgage Professor.* Not as slick as HSH, but offers good guidance. Visit MtgProfessor.com.
- *Mortgage101.* This source is more commercial, but still offers great information. Visit Mortgage101.com.

45.5.2 Increase Your Down Payment
Whether you buy or refinance, the larger your down payment, the less you pay in interest over the life of the loan.

45.5.3 Cancel Private Mortgage Insurance
Ask your lender whether you now pay for private mortgage insurance (PMI). If you do and the current principal balance on your loan is 80 percent or less of your home's value, you can drop the coverage. According to the Federal Trade Commission (FTC), on a $100,000 loan with 10 percent down, ditching the PMI saves $480 annually. For details, read the FTC Consumer Alert "Cancellation of Private Mortgage Insurance: Federal Law May Save You Hundreds of Dollars Each Year."

45.5.4 Refinance
At this writing, mortgage interest rates hover near historic lows. If you refinance, you can save thousands in interest expenses. For a detailed guide to this complicated process, visit HSH.com and work through the "Mortgage Refinancing Starter Kit."

45.5.5 Cut the Mortgage's Length
Consider a mortgage that lasts fifteen instead of thirty years. To

calculate the savings, visit Bankrate.com/calculators/mortgages/15-year-30-year-mortgage-calculator.aspx.

☐ **45.5.6 Pay Off the Mortgage Early**
If you can do it, this saves thousands. I paid mine off in 2003. Over the next decade, I saved $131,066.40 in pretax dollars (not that I was counting). To see what you might save, use a payoff calculator.

- Bankrate.com/calculators/mortgages/mortgage-loan-payoff-calculator.aspx
- Mtgprofessor.com/CalculatorArticles/Mortgage%20Payoff%20Calculators.html
- AARP.org/money/credit-loans-debt/mortgage_payoff_calculator/

45.6 Hire Out Your House (or Part of it)

☐ **45.6.1 Vacate and Rent**
Whenever your town hosts special events, rent your house and skedaddle elsewhere. Visit VRBO.com.

☐ **45.6.2 Rent Excess Space**
If you have acreage or outbuildings to spare, rent them to others.

☐ **45.6.3 Trade Vacations**
Swap a week's stay in your home for a week's stay in someone else's. Visit HomeExchange.com or HomeLink.org.

☐ **45.6.4 Seek Short Term Roommates**
Rent couches or spare rooms for overnight stays. Sign up at AirBNB.com, Roomorama.com, or similar sites.

☐ **45.6.5 Seek Long Term Roommates**
Roomies add rental income and reduce utility costs.

45.7 Relocate

☐ **45.7.1 Downsize**
If you no longer need as much space, move somewhere smaller.

☐ **45.7.2 Live in an Income Producer**
Buy a duplex or home with a rentable apartment.

☐ 45.7.3 Relocate to Lands of Lower Living Costs—Domestic

In some parts of the country—many of them scenic—beautiful homes sell for less than luxury sedans. Financial magazines and their websites list the latest low–cost havens.

☐ 45.7.4 Relocate to Lands of Lower Living Costs—Foreign

Join expatriates who live cheaper on distant shores. For popular destinations, look at financial magazines and their websites.

☐ 45.7.5 Bypass the Broker

Borrow "for sale by owner" books at the library or visit these sites: ForSaleByOwner.com or FrontDoor.com.

45.8 Consider Alternatives to Ownership

☐ 45.8.1 Rent

If you rent, the costs of ownership become someone else's headache. But in the process, you also lose many benefits—including tax deductions, the freedom to remodel, and the accumulation of equity. For a calculator that weighs the merits of rentals versus home ownership, take a look at NYTimes.com/interactive/business/buy-rent-calculator.html.

☐ 45.8.2 Flip

The current housing market makes this difficult, but if you're a good carpenter, you can live for much less than the typical mortgage slave.

☐ 45.8.3 Seek Jobs With Housing or Housing Subsidies

Look for employment with lodgings attached. Become a part–time caretaker or apartment super.

☐ 45.8.4 Live Nomadically

You might live cheaper if you sell the house and replace it with a used RV or boat. Adventures await, but run the numbers first.

☐ 45.8.5 Move Back Home

As Robert Frost wrote, "home is the place where, when you have to go there, they have to take you in." If you're of younger years, moving into your parents' basement may be an option. But that doesn't mean it's anyone's idea of permanent housing solution.

45.9 When Buying, Find the Right Size

Although the real estate bubble has burst, it's still possible to buy excess housing. Mortgage rates have dipped to all–time lows. Apparent bargains exist on larger homes. But a McMansion socks you right away with higher brokerage commissions, points, and closing fees. This only begins the pain. As each month passes, you pay more for: (1) mortgage interest; (2) property taxes; (3) homeowners insurance; (4) utilities (bigger houses cost more to heat and cool); (5) furniture (more rooms means more beds, chairs, and lava–lamps); (6) decorations (more paint, pictures, and knick–knacks); (7) maintenance and repairs (the more the house, the more that breaks); and (8) cleaning expenses (3.5 baths means a lot of Tidy–Bowl, my friend). You can save yourself acres of headaches if you match the square footage of the house to the size of your true needs.

CODA: MICRO HOUSING

Hard times produce bold measures. Some pioneers have resized the American dream with moves into constricted spaces that deliver big savings (and low carbon footprints). I didn't list this as a strategy because I believe few will be interested, but I'd be glad to be proven wrong when it comes to you. To learn more about micro houses, visit TheTinyLife.com or TinyHomeBuilders.com. To "roominate" over downtown apartments as small as 220 square feet, search the web for "micro apartments" and read the latest stories.

46

HOUSING:
REPAIRS AND REMODELS

Repairs and remodels are rare, but the costs can be breathtaking. You need a plan to control expenses, because those you hire have incentives to squeeze as much money from the project as they can. The next time you face a fix–up, follow these strategies and tactics.

46.1 Rent Instead of Own

By renting, you sidestep all repairs—and they become your landlord's problem. For a great calculator that weighs the merits, visit NYTimes.com/interactive/business/buy-rent-calculator.html.

46.2 Consider Lower Cost Alternatives

☐ **46.2.1 Avoid Major Repairs and Remodels**

☐ *Tread Lightly.* When you take it easy on your home, things last longer and you incur fewer repairs. Good luck convincing kids of this.

☐ *Perform Maintenance.* Avoid costly repairs through regular inspections. The National Center for Healthy Housing publishes a "Healthy Homes Maintenance Checklist." Visit HUD.gov.

☐ *Investigate.* Check out any suspicious creaks, weird noises, odd smells, or water stains. Address problems early and save yourself from huge repair bills later.

☐ **46.2.2 Procrastinate on Big Projects**
You don't have to immediately begin an expensive kitchen, basement, or bath remodel. Stall before you install.

☐ *Adopt Temporary Fixes.* These buy time to find long term fixes.

☐ *Wait Until Off–Peak Times.* Repair furnaces in the summer and air conditioners in winter. Tackle remodels while school's still in session.

☐ *Wait Until the Next Downturn.* Labor costs will plummet and qualified craftsmen will anxiously take on your small project.

☐ 46.2.3 Plan Ahead

☐ *Track Your Infrastructure.* Research home systems that are due for replacement or repair before they fail. This buys time to make better decisions.

☐ *Anticipate Emergency Repairs.* Prepare as suggested in 8.4.7.

☐ *Hire Advisors.* Many contractors and architects provide advice for lower fees. Since they're experts, you're almost guaranteed to learn helpful information.

☐ *Procure Early.* If you procure your own materials, get them early, especially if you order from internet–based suppliers. Delivery problems are common. Avoid costly delays by having all supplies onsite when work begins.

☐ 46.2.4 DIY

☐ *DIY Diagnosis.* The more you know about the repair or remodel, the more low–cost solutions you can find. Immerse yourself in details. Quiz bidders about how to get the job done for less without sacrificing quality.

☐ *DIY Entire Projects.* The modern DIYer enjoys access to more educational resources than ever. Even if the project exceeds your current competence, that doesn't mean you can't get up to speed with DVDs, manuals, and expert advisors. To learn more about how to frame new spaces, tile bathrooms, and add dry wall, volunteer at Habitat for Humanity.

☐ *DIY In Part.* Do the easy parts yourself and pay only for what requires expertise. If you have the time, volunteer to move materials, run to hardware stores, or load dumpsters. You can also demolish, clean up, sand, and paint as well as any contractor—and do it for much less.

☐ 46.2.5 Save on Materials

☐ *Procure Supplies Yourself.* Ask service providers for lists of necessary materials and estimated costs. Run them through Appendix 1 and see whether you, the incentivized owner, can get them for less. If the basement remodel calls for two–by–fours and particleboard, buy them at stores that sell reused building materials (visit Habitat.org/restores).

☐ *Reuse What's There.* Cannibalize what you can. Reuse mirrors and cabinet hardware. Save bathtubs and toilets.

☐ *Look for Stock Sizes and Solutions.* You can pay someone to make a vanity cabinet from scratch, or you can buy a prefabricated model for less at a box store.

☐ *Sell or Donate Old Stuff.* Cut your project's net cost. Sell old fixtures, doors, and cabinets on Craigslist or donate them to a local reuse store (and receive a deduction if you itemize).

☐ 46.2.6 Avoid Discretionary Remodels

Determine whether your decision to remodel is based upon a real need (water leaks, structural problems, mold, failed systems) or merely a desire to update to the latest decor. If it's the latter, consider a postponement. Ancient pink bathrooms are popular again (visit SaveThePinkBathrooms.com) and your own color scheme might be due for a comeback.

☐ 46.2.7 Limit the Scope of Work

A few early decisions can cut your costs significantly.

☐ *Keep Plumbing in Place.* Retain all water lines and drains for sinks, showers, bathtubs, and toilets. Moving them adds thousands to your remodel.

☐ *Keep the same Electrical Scheme.* Contain electrician costs. Keep lights, appliances, and outlets in their current positions.

☐ *Love the Walls You're With.* If they stay where they're at, you avoid big expenses.

☐ *Reface Instead of Replace.* Bathroom tiles, bathtubs, and shower stalls can be re–glazed with fresh colors. Instead of installing new floors, have the current ones sanded and refinished. Replace cabinet facades and doors, but retain the frameworks.

☐ *Install Light Tubes.* Get your natural light for less with flexible reflective tubes.

☐ *Spend More on What You Use Most Often.* Allocate remodel dollars so they deliver the most bang for your buck. If you shower instead of bathe, pick a cheaper bathtub. If you fire up the oven on holidays only, you don't need to buy the top of the line.

☐ *Decline Upsells.* When we remodeled our master bath, the contractor suggested a heated floor (price tag: $1,500). We opted instead for a $50 solution: a small radiant heater on a timer that warms the room automatically on cold mornings.

☐ **46.2.8 Trade or Barter**
As always, beware the tax complications of bartering for services (see IRS Publication 525).

46.3 Run Background Checks

Unless you've used the service before, spend ample time on this step to avoid problems later.

☐ **46.3.1 Review Qualifications**
Choose from among the same tactics for miscellaneous services. For details, reread 8.3.4.

☐ *Consider the Time in Business.*

☐ *Look for Trade Memberships, Certifications, and Licenses.*

☐ *Know the Level of Specialization Required.*

☐ *Know the Level of Experience Required.*

☐ 46.3.2 Review Customer Feedback

Again, the same ideas apply here as on the miscellaneous service checklist. For details, reread 8.3.1.

☐ *Consider Your Own Experience.*

☐ *Seek Recommendations.*

☐ *Read Internet Reviews.*

☐ *Visit the Better Business Bureau.*

☐ *Check Out the Service's References.*

☐ 46.3.3 Review Samples of Work

For more expensive projects, ask to see samples of workmanship.

☐ *View Finished Jobs.* Many services maintain portfolios of past projects on DVDs or websites.

☐ *View Work in Progress.* Ask to visit a current worksite. If it's a sloppy mess, maybe you should hire elsewhere.

☐ *Try Before You Buy.* If you can, hire prospects for smaller tasks and see how things go.

☐ 46.3.4 Learn the Prospect's Policies

- *Bonds.* Ask whether the service is "bonded." A bond is a promise by a third party—someone other than the service itself—to make good on the contract's performance. Bonds vary in language and scope, but they often cover such matters as payment of subcontractors and material suppliers, fulfillment of deadlines, and reimbursement for employee thefts. Ask to see the paperwork.

- *Worker's Compensation.* If a worker on your property gets hurt, he can file a claim for compensation, but only if his employer has coverage. Without a policy, the worker most likely will come after you, and your homeowners coverage might be inadequate. Before you hire anyone for work that involves risk to limb or life, ask to see a declarations page that proves the existence of coverage. You pay more for companies that carry insurance, but at least you don't bear the risks of a mishap. And if a company skimps on insuring its own employees, how else does it skimp?

- *Property Damage and Liability Insurance.* Any contractor you hire should carry property damage and liability coverage. If you suffer losses, this funds a recovery. Ask for a copy of the policy's declarations page.

- *Rates and Fees.* Ask what they charge on the specific tasks your project entails.

- *Subcontractors.* If any subcontractors are involved, find out their abilities, experience, and qualifications.

46.4 Find the Best Rates

☐ 46.4.1 Use Online Cost Estimators/Calculators

Online estimators give a ballpark idea of what your project will cost. Choose sites that don't require you to enter any contact information—you need estimates, not solicitations from eager contractors. Search the web for "[enter name of project here] cost estimator calculator." CostEstimator.com provides estimates for a wide array of home improvement projects, including kitchens, baths, roofs, painting, decks, patios, flooring, floor refinishing, furnaces, and air conditioners.

☐ 46.4.2 Seek Multiple Written Bids

For expensive projects, obtain multiple bids in writing.

- ☐ *Only Seek Bids From Acceptable Sources.* Don't request bids from those you're unlikely to hire, you only waste their time and yours.

- ☐ *Prepare Your Own Scope of Work.* Break the project down into small parts and provide the list to bidders. For example, on a bath remodel, state the work you want done for each separate area: shower, toilet, vanity cabinet, tub, floor, wall, electrical, etc. This makes it easier to compare bids and forces you to define the scope of your project at an early stage.

☐ *Seek Detailed Bids.* Ask for the anticipated hours and materials needed for each step of the project. These details help in later negotiations if you're able to do some of the work yourself.

☐ *Ask Questions When Bidders Visit the Site.* Complex projects require back–and–forth discussions. Favor contractors who are good communicators.

☐ 46.4.3 Haggle

Remember that nice guys finish first. Show respect and kindness. The potential dialogues are endless, but consider these possibilities.

☐ *"Can you match your competitor's bid?"*

☐ *"Why is your bid higher than this internet estimate?"*

☐ *"If I did some parts of the job myself, could you drop your bid?"*

☐ *"If I supplied materials myself, could you drop your bid?"*

☐ *"Would you add one small project at no extra charge?"*

☐ *"Would you trade or barter services?"*

☐ 46.4.4 Review the Form of Contract

Any projects that cost more than a few hundred dollars should involve written contracts. Ask to see the contractor's typical forms and look for these terms.

- *Payments.* Any schedule should allow you the leeway to withhold the last payment until you give your final approval of the work performed.

- *Building Permits and Inspections.* Who notifies the building inspector or pays for inspection fees? If these are your responsibilities, add them to the cost of the project.

- *Warranties and Guarantees.* What promises does the contractor make to back up its work? If they're inadequate, they could cost you money down the road.

46.5 Avoid Common Consumer Traps

The best way to avoid problems is to hire someone with an established reputation for honesty and fair dealing. If you're still worried, revisit the common pitfalls (see 8.5).

46.6 Monitor Work

As work progresses, follow these steps to control costs.

☐ 46.6.1 Keep Communicating
Talk is cheap. Additional labor from misunderstandings isn't.

☐ 46.6.2 Review Work Daily
Visit the worksite each evening. Discuss the latest with your contractor in person or by phone.

☐ 46.6.3 Use Change Orders
Obtain written descriptions of any proposed alterations along with a detailed statement of what they will cost.

46.7 Follow Up

The miscellaneous services checklist covers this in detail (see 8.6).

PART III

TOOLBOX

PART III OVERVIEW

Parts I and II presented checklists that helped you spend less on products, services, and monthly expenses. Part III presents several tools that make those checklists work better yet. Revisit these chapters often to turbocharge your *SL⊠N!* savings.

47

CHECKLIST
MOTIVATORS

SL☑N! provides an *easier* passage to frugality, not an *effortless* one. For the checklists to work their magic, they require active use.

Let's say the decidedly unfrugal Jane Dough consults the products buying checklist for twenty purchases in a row, but buys at retail only. Clearly, Jane doesn't *use* the checklist, she simply *reads* it. Having fallen into this abyss of passivity, she should ask herself a key question: how do I dump my everyday habits so that I can enjoy real savings? The answer comes down to personal motivation, and this chapter lists various tactics that inspire just that. Naturally, they take the form of a handy checklist.

PRELUDE: TRUST THE PROGRAM

SL☑N! motivates automatically because the checklists appear right as—MOOOOOO!!!—you're in the midst of spending. That's the best time to review frugal strategies, because that's when you're most incentivized to follow them. If you ever need a reminder about the checklists' many advantages, revisit the Introduction.

MOTIVATE WITH NUMERICS

Not everyone is a numbers person, but real time data delivers huge motivation even to those who dislike math. The designers of my Prius know this. The dashboard gives me precise figures on fuel efficiency in crystal clear graphics. When I pounce on the gas, I see my mileage plummet; when I release the pedal, I see it soar. The instant feedback motivates me to conserve. If you're interested, you can get similar data about your progress with this program, and you can get it without crunching too many numbers. Design your *SL☑N!* dashboard to include these helpful metrics.

☐ *Keep a Checklist Savings Log.* One of the best motivators is simply to track your progress. The sample log below shows some of my recent savings on products. (For my "savings annuities" on line items, see the chart in How to Use this Book).

Moose's Savings on Products

	Description	Tactic Used	Cost Before	Actual Cost	Savings
1	20 hardbacks	Buy used	$ 500	$ 40	$ 460
2	Sleeper sofa	Floor model	$ 2,499	$ 1,899	$ 600
3	Sand wedge	Buy used	$ 60	$ 7	$ 53
4	BBQ cover	Repair	$ 55	$ 1	$ 54
5	Red Sox DVDs	Buy later	$ 80	$ 40	$ 40
6	Batteries	Generic	$ 54	$ 12	$ 42
7	Dry cereal	Eat oatmeal	$ 112	$ 41	$ 71
8	Laundry soap	Generic	$ 36	$ 18	$ 18
9	Toyota RAV4	Buy used	$23,000	$13,900	$ 9,100
10	RAV4 owner tax	Buy used	$ 455	$ 168	$ 287
11	Movies on web	FREE	$ 7	$ 0	$ 7
12	Bird food	Homemade	$ 8	$ 0.10	$ 8
					$ 10,740

A couple of cautions about these logs. First, don't buy more stuff simply to boost your reported savings. If this happens, you give yourself false assurances of economizing. Second, keep it real. You can say that you skipped a trip to Monaco this year, but if that was never in the cards anyway, don't log it in as savings. Compare your actual cost to what you would have paid *but for* the checklists' intervention.

☐ *Track Your Earnings Per Hour.* The Introduction compared Jane Dough's post–tax wages from her job ($780) to her checklist stockpile ($8,920!). The huge gap provides motivation aplenty, so perform the same calculation for yourself. Divide your total logged savings by the hours you've spent with the checklists. Compare the result to your hourly post–tax wages at work (these are *incremental* hours, so apply your uppermost marginal rate).

☐ *Track Your Net Worth.* *SL☒N!* seeks to grow your "nest egg," which in accounting terms is known as your "net worth." Your net worth reveals much about your spending habits. If you consistently spend *less* than you make, your net worth tends to rise over time. If you consistently spend *more* than you make, it tends to fall. Net worth is easier to track than your household expenses. The reason? You have far fewer assets and liabilities (a mere handful) than expenditures (hundreds per year). Apply this formula:

TOTAL ASSETS – TOTAL LIABILITIES = NET WORTH.

Assets consist of everything you own that has value—things you can either cash out (as when you liquidate a bank account or cash value life insurance policy) or sell (stamp collections, farmland, jewelry, etc.). Liabilities consist of the amounts you owe to others. Here's a breakdown:

Assets:		Liabilities:	
Checking accounts	$ _____	Mortgages	$ _____
Savings accounts	$ _____	Car loans	$ _____
Home market value	$ _____	Credit card debts	$ _____
Other real estate value	$ _____	Student loans	$ _____
Brokerage accounts	$ _____	Medical bills	$ _____
Retirement accounts	$ _____	Other IOUs	$ _____
Medical savings accounts	$ _____		
Outstanding loans to others	$ _____		
Cash on hand	$ _____		
Value of life insurance	$ _____		
Certificates of deposit	$ _____		
Other assets (cars, jewelry)	$ _____		
Total:	$ _____	Total:	$ _____

If you want, use the above chart to track your net worth on a monthly basis. Alternatively, you can measure net worth with one of these online calculators:

- AARP.org/money/investing/net_worth_calculator

- Bankrate.com/calculators/smart-spending/personal-net-worth-calculator.aspx

- CGI.money.cnn.com/tools/networth/networth.html.

☐ *Compete Against the National Averages.* Compare your expenses on major line items to that of typical households in your income bracket (visit BLS.gov/cex). If you're in the 75th percentile of household income, but spend like you're in the 40th percentile, you save at an impressive rate.

☐ *Track Your Income and Expenses.* Robert Frost once wrote "nobody was ever meant, to remember or invent, what he did with every cent." Frost was right, but he lived before the internet. Nowadays, you can track your expenses automatically—and you don't have to invent much of anything (Al Gore's already done it for you). For details, read Chapter 50.

MOTIVATE WITH HOMERICS

If at heart you're a poet and numbers make you break out in a rash, don't worry. These tactics boost your motivation without the mess of mathematics.

☐ *Buddy Up.* Any program of change delivers better results when you team up with others. For mutual support, join forces with friends, with fellow fringers at FrugalFringe.com, or with both.

☐ *Experiment.* If you've never visited a junkyard, flea market, or thrift shop—at least not recently—go explore a few. Audition restaurants, generic products, and online services. Test drive gasoline savers (Chapter 39)—not forever, but temporarily. As long as experiments bust up your routines at least some of the time, you nudge yourself to save.

☐ *Mix and Match.* If you suffer from unfrugal habits but can't give them up completely, you can still save if you blend in some frugal options. For instance, if you don't want to quit your health club cold turkey, quit it gradually by buying occasional day passes as you transition to home workouts (see 10.1). If you don't want to give up hotels entirely, give them up partially by staying a few nights of your next vacation at less costly alternatives (see 16.1).

☐ *Debrief Yourself.* If hindsight truly is 20–20, gain some clarity with a detailed review of your latest checklist–assisted transactions. Ask yourself hardnosed questions like these:

☐ Did I use the checklist actively or did I only read it?

☐ What are the pros and cons of my final decision?

☐ If this was mostly a bad decision, how can I fix it?

☐ If this was mostly a good decision, how can I do better?

☐ *Leave Feedback.* After you debrief, share your opinions with others. Tell friends. Post online reviews of products and services. This hones your spending savvy for future transactions.

☐ *Customize the Checklists.* Another great tactic that follows from debriefings: revise the checklists to include your own ideas. Or build DIY checklists for any line item that your household incurs, but these pages don't cover (see Chapter 48).

☐ *Try a Pay–Cation Stay–Cation.* Jumpstart your *SL☑N!* experience with a vacation at home (see 15.1.2). Use it to reprogram your spending habits on whichever expenses concern you the most. As you save on airfares, you'll also begin to save on a wide variety of other line items.

☐ *Set Goals.* Some can motivate themselves with long range goals— pay off all debt in ten years, switch to part time work by age 40, retire fully by age 55—but most do better when they aim for shorter time horizons. Some sample objectives:

☐ Cut this year's total expenses by at least 20 percent

☐ Save $8,000 by year's end

☐ Spend $60 less next month on utilities

☐ Go without paid TV for six months.

Bottom line: set goals if that motivates you, but otherwise, don't worry about it. *SL☒N!* doesn't require precise objectives in order to produce major benefits. Instead, it reflects the reality that spending less is a brick–by–brick process—and you're the mason of a solid financial future.

48

THE DIY
CHECKLIST GENERATOR

Based upon 2011 CES data, *SL⊠N!*'s checklists cover about 95 percent of the average household's expenses (not counting payments to social security and pensions). Yet no one is typical. You may have line items that *SL⊠N!* doesn't address, but which still involve biggish dollars. What to do with such pricey orphans? You could languish in abject despair, but a far better approach is to seize upon *SL⊠N!*'s recurring themes, tailor them to fit your line item, and prepare your own checklist. Do this, and you'll test your uncommon expense against frugality's bedrock principles.

PRELUDE: DON'T REINVENT THE WHEEL

Whatever line item you now confront, others have dealt with it already. Don't duplicate someone else's work; instead, head over to FrugalFringe.com, where your fellow fringers are invited to post their own checklists for less common line items. The one you need might already be there waiting for you. At the home page, click the tab for "Supplemental Checklists."

BUILD A CHECKLIST IN THREE EASY STEPS

1. Pick a Structure

If you've worked with the checklists awhile, you already know their basic frameworks. Begin with the structure that best fits your line item. You have several choices.

☐ *Products.* If you're about to buy a new furnace, Appendix 1 provides a great guide. But furnaces are expensive, so you might decide that such a big purchase warrants more specialized guidance. If so, use Appendix 1 as your starting framework and build it up from there.

☐ *Services.* If you need a lawyer to defend you in a dog bite case and your insurance doesn't cover it, the best starting points are the checklists for services. Build upon the frameworks in Chapters 8, 41, and 46.

☐ *PAYG vs. Flat Fee.* A number of checklists address this frequent choice: general recreation (Strategy No. 9.5), health clubs (Chapter 10), trash collection (Chapter 24), cell phones, (Chapter 27), and internet (Chapter 28).

☐ *Everything Else.* If your expense doesn't easily fit into the above structures, locate the most comparable line item from Part II. For chiropractors, look at the checklists for doctors, optometrists, and dentists (Chapters 34–36). For ocean cruises, draw from the checklists for airfare and lodging (Chapters 15–16). For renter's insurance, start out with the checklist for homeowners insurance (Chapter 29).

2. Insert Strategies and Tactics

Once you've picked your basic structure, the next step is to populate it with strategies and tactics. To begin with, add any relevant content from the structure you chose. Next, pick from among the strategies and tactics listed in the appendixes. Finally, extend your search to include the line item checklists that most resemble your current expense (see Part II). The tactics that you collect from these several sources might need modifications, so be prepared to draw creative analogies. A case study that illustrates this process appears later in this chapter.

3. Cross–Check Against Outside Sources

SL☑N! isn't the only place to find helpful savings tactics. Drink deep from these founts of wisdom.

☐ *Ask Frugal Friends.* Find like–minded souls with answers to your quandaries about expenses. Visit FrugalFringe.com.

☐ *Ask the Internet.* Find blogs and articles about your line item with these searches:

- "How to save money on [enter line item here]."
- "[Enter line item here] buying guide."
- "How to buy a [enter line item here]."
- "[Enter line item here] chat room, discussion board, or forum."

☐ *Ask Online Experts.* Post questions at JustAnswer.com or any specialty sites that address your particular expense.

☐ *Ask the Government.* Some of your tax dollars fund the publication of consumer guides, one of which might address your concern. For the latest titles, visit Publications.USA.gov, and click the link for the "Consumer Information Catalog."

☐ *Ask a Periodical.* A magazine article might discuss your line item. Search recent issues of *Consumer Reports, Kiplinger's, Bottom Line Confidential,* and *Money.*

A CHECKLIST BUILDING CASE STUDY:
MONTHLY PARKING

The increasingly frugal Jane Dough works in a downtown office located 12 miles from her home. She pays $200 a month to rent a parking space in a covered garage (her winters are cold). She's already tackled several line items and now wants to work on her $2,400 per year parking habit. Let's watch her build a checklist.

1. Jane Picks a Checklist Structure

Parking at work presents a classic choice between PAYG and flat rates. So as suggested above, Jane looks over the checklists for recreation, health clubs, cell phones, internet, and trash collection. She sees three basic strategies that might apply to a "monthly parking" checklist: (1) choose PAYG; (2) reduce the need for monthly parking and choose PAYG; and (3) pay a flat rate for monthly parking, but find ways to spend less. Right away, Jane rejects the first option, because she knows that a month's worth of daily rates at her garage costs much more than $200. So she limits herself to the last two options. Now she needs to find some detailed tactics to list under these broad strategies.

2. Jane Picks Several Tactics

Jane scans the PAYG checklists. The health club checklist (Chapter 10) suggests various alternatives to monthly gym memberships—home gyms, rec centers, parks, and trails. She decides to make a similar list of less expensive alternatives to monthly parking—street parking, surface lots, and more. The trash removal checklist (Chapter 24) suggests group negotiations with trash haulers—and Jane reasons that she might join with coworkers to seek bids from nearby garages. Lastly, the internet checklist (Chapter 28) mentions discounts in exchange for annual payments in advance—some garages might agree to the same deal.

Next, Jane searches for additional tactics in Appendixes 1–2. Their condensed format makes this quick work. As she skims Appendix 1, she sees the tactic about credit card rewards—to her chagrin, she realizes that she's paid for parking with checks. She also sees the pitfall about buying too cheap—and makes a note to consider only those garages that provide good security. She comes up empty when she skims Appendix 2, but her checklist is growing fast so she's not worried.

Lastly, Jane looks in Part II for checklists that might generate more ideas about parking. She turns to the automotive checklists. She sees Chapter 44, which states the obvious: if she ditched the car, she'd ditch her parking expense as well (but she decides to keep the car anyway). More helpfully, she sees the "alternatives to car travel" in 39.4. That strategy presents a goldmine of substitutes for her commute, including public transit, car pools, and telecommutes. Another option doesn't appear on any SL☐N! checklist. Jane's company has a suburban satellite office with FREE onsite parking. She figures her boss might let her spend one day per week there.

3. Jane Cross–Checks Against Other Sources

Jane runs several internet searches and comes up with nothing new—a good sign that her list is comprehensive. When she talks with her officemates, several say they're interested in joining forces to seek bids from nearby garages. This increases her confidence that group negotiations might be her ticket to lower rates.

Jane's finished checklist appears below. She starts each strategy with a clearly stated goal, which is one of the motivational tools she saw in Chapter 47 (Jane has become quite a goal–setter). I've referenced in brackets the sources that inspired each of Jane's listed tactics.

MONTHLY PARKING CHECKLIST

Strategy No. 1:
Cut My Need for Monthly Parking and Switch to PAYG

My goal: cut commutes downtown at least in half (from 20 per month to 10 per month), so that daily parking becomes cheaper than my $200 monthly rate.

☐ Consider Alternatives to the Downtown Commute.

  ☐ Ditch the car [Chapter 44]. *No can do since I live in the suburbs. I'm not moving downtown.*

  ☐ Use public transit [39.4]. *Bus passes cost less than parking.*

  ☐ Telecommute [39.4]. *Unlikely my boss agrees, but I'll ask.*

  ☐ Bike/motorcycle/scooter [39.4]. *For me, no way.*

  ☐ Join a carpool [39.4]. *Find five people, and I drive only once per week. I'll visit websites that connect commuters. I'll also talk to some cotenants who work downtown like me.*

  ☐ Work some days at suburban office. *My boss might prefer this to telecommuting.*

☐ Consider Cheaper Alternatives to a Parking Garage [10.1].

  ☐ Use metered parking. *But I'd have to move my car every four hours!*

  ☐ Pay daily fees at surface lots.

  ☐ Park early. *I get early bird rates if I park before 8:00 a.m.*

  ☐ Use outer lots. *Only if the weather's nice.*

☐ Borrow Garage Passes From Travelling Coworkers (if passes are transferable).

☐ Avoid Pitfalls—Don't Buy too Cheap [Chapter 6]. *As in parking somewhere with lax security.*

Strategy No. 2:
Keep My Monthly Space, but Pay Less for it

My goal: cut this line item by 20 percent or more and save at least $480 per year.

☐ Haggle as a Group [24.2.3]. *Combine forces with others and seek bids from several garages.*

☐ Ask for Price Matches [10.2.9]. *My current garage is across the street. Get bids from other nearby garages and ask my garage to match the lowest one. This approach also works in group negotiations.*

☐ Haggle as a Group with Employer.

   ☐ As first position, ask it to pick up our monthly parking [10.2.5].

   ☐ As second position, ask for payroll changes so that we use our pre–tax dollars to pay for parking [20.2.8].

   ☐ As last position, ask it to arrange employee discounts with nearby garages [10.2.6].

☐ Sublet my Space When I Travel [24.2.3]. *If coworkers pay, this offsets my costs. (Issue: is my pass transferable?)*

☐ Mix and Match [Chapter 47]. *Pay monthly rates for the covered garage in winter, then switch to surface parking when it's warmer.*

☐ Payment Methods—

   ☐ Pay a full year in advance [28.3.7].

   ☐ Pay with plastic and reap rewards [Chapter 4].

With this checklist, Jane gives herself many ways to slash parking costs—"lots" of them, in fact. She likes her work, so she posts it on FrugalFringe.com. Now others can benefit from her ideas. If you want to download a copy for yourself, it waits for you now.

49

THE POWER
OF PLASTIC

People fall in love with their little slabs of polyvinyl chloride acetate (PVCA)—and they often fall into debt with them as well. Many are reconsidering the relationship. According to the Federal Reserve, in 2010, 68 percent of consumers held credit cards, which was down five percent from those who held them in 2007. The Great Recession? Anyway, it's easy to get along with your cards, provided you know the one big secret about living with them in perfect harmony:

> *pay credit cards off completely, without fail, each and every month, and never, ever carry a balance.*

Many know this secret and act on it—roughly 45 percent of cardholders, according to the Federal Reserve Board. If you can join these savvy plastic users, you can access the many benefits that make credit cards the best payment vehicle around: better than cash, checks, debit cards, money orders, travelers checks, prepaid cards, online payments, and auto–payments (and of course, you can charge the last five of these to your credit cards).

This chapter has two parts. The first part lists the principal reasons why credit cards are such wonderful tools for spending. My purpose here is to convince you to carry some PVCA in your wallet. The second part lists tactics that maximize your credit card rewards. My purpose here is to convince you to use your PVCA strategically and as often as possible.

PLASTIC IS GOOD

Many financial experts advise consumers to cut up their cards and pay with cash only. They argue this extreme remedy is necessary because plastic makes spending too convenient, which in turn leads to excessive debt and sky–high interest rates. But this argument doesn't apply to devoted checklisters. *SL☒N!* offsets plastic's convenience by injecting into each transaction a large dose of frugal scrutiny. And once you settle into the habit of paying off your credit cards each month, you don't have to worry about debt and interest. Instead, you can exploit the many benefits that credit cards provide. Here's a list.

□ *Earn Rewards.* Imagine that each year the US Treasury thanked you for using greenbacks and presented you with a substantial gift—in cash, naturally. Wouldn't you pay with currency whenever possible? This is pure fantasy, of course, but with reward cards, it all comes true. In 2010, as I paid most of my expenses with plastic, I earned rewards worth $411.87. And here's the kicker: the IRS doesn't treat any of this as taxable income!

□ *Access Cardholder Benefits.* Most cards include many bells and whistles at no extra charge. Study the fine print, and make use of the enhancements:

- Roadside assistance
- Car rental insurance
- Purchase assurance (lost or stolen items)
- Extended warranties
- Lost luggage protection
- Trip cancellation insurance
- Travel life insurance
- Travel assistance (lost luggage, passports)
- Post-purchase price guaranty

□ *Bean Count Automatically.* Credit card issuers make accounting easier because they track your expenses for you.

□ *Qualify for Legal Protection.* By law, you bear no liability for unauthorized use of your credit card provided that you report it as lost or stolen before any fraudulent charges hit the account. Even if you don't report in time, your maximum liability is capped at $50, a fee which most card issuers will waive upon request. No other payment method affords you as much security.

□ *Manage Vendor Disputes.* If you pay with plastic and the merchant does something wrong, you can dispute the charge with the credit card's issuer. In contrast, if you pay cash, your only recourse is to file a complaint in small claims court or with the Better Business Bureau (and then only if you've locked horns with a BBB member).

☐ *Ride the Float.* For each transaction, you receive an interest–free loan that lasts at least twenty days and usually longer.

☐ *Make Foreign Travel Easier.* That London pub rejects US dollars, but allows draws on Visa. Sure, you pay an additional fee for this convenience, but it's well worth it. You can even access the local currency by swiping your card at a nearby ATM.

☐ *Increase Your Convenience.* The major cards—MasterCard, Visa, and American Express—are accepted almost everywhere and take far less room in your wallet than a wad of cash.

CODA: SURCHARGES FOR USING CREDIT CARDS

As of January, 2013, retailers in 40 states gained the legal right to pass along card processing fees to their customers. At this early date, there's no way to tell how many vendors will actually impose these charges—hopefully, most of them won't for fear of losing customers. As the marketplace sorts this all out, watch out for surcharges and avoid any retailers that charge them.

MAXIMIZE YOUR PLASTIC'S VALUE

☐ *Seek the Highest Rewards.* Find the best reward cards at CardHub.com or run this internet search: "best reward credit cards [enter current year here]."

☐ *Maximize Rewards.* Use the PVCA to pay for as many transactions as possible. (Reminder: don't use credit cards at all unless you pay them off in full every month.)

☐ *Schedule Auto–Pays.* If your service providers permit, schedule automatic payments on your card instead of your checking account.

☐ *Plasticize Small Transactions.* Don't pay cash because something costs less than $5: tiny charges add up fast and yield big rewards.

☐ *Volunteer for Reimbursable Charges.* Whenever I'm out for a group dinner, I offer to pay by credit card and take up a cash collection. The reason: it boosts my rewards (and it also cuts down my trips to the ATM). Other examples of reimbursable charges include work travel and club expenses.

☐ *Pick Plastic for PayPal.* PayPal gives you a choice between paying with a credit card or check. Choose the card.

☐ *Strategize Which Cards Work Best.* According to a 2009 survey, the average adopter of credit cards holds 3.7 of them. Carrying several cards gives you options. If one card awards three percent cash back on gas purchases, and another awards only one percent, using the three percent card gains you an extra $53 each year (assuming that you spend at the national average).

☐ *Avoid Annual Fees.* Some cards deliver greater rewards, but charge annual fees. If you're sure your expenses will be large enough to justify this added expense—for instance, if you anticipate big reimbursable expenses at work—go ahead and pay. Otherwise, pick a card with less impressive rewards that's FREE. Note: many premium cards waive the annual fee for the first year, and some issuers waive annual fees after that upon request.

☐ *Use Plastic to Receive Cash Discounts.* Flash the PVCA and offer to pay cash in exchange for a markdown.

☐ *Ask for Fee Waivers.* On rare occasions, I've missed credit card payments and been hit with late fees. I've always been able to have them waived. Why? I don't think it has much to do with my payment record—it's good, but not perfect. I think it has more to do with the cost to recruit new cardholders. Card issuers spend $50–$150 to attract each new account, so it saves them money if they can retain their current customers. You have as good a chance at fetching waivers as anyone. But you have to call.

50

AUTOMATED
BEAN COUNTING

So far, you've attacked unfrugal habits with checklists instead of ledgers and spreadsheets. As a result, you've dodged the many headaches of data entry. But checklists don't show whether you live in the "magic zone" where your income constantly exceeds your expenses. For that level of assurance, you need to enter the realm of bean counting—in other words, you need to track what you make and what you spend. Income is easy to figure. Simply consult your pay stubs, W–2 forms, or tax returns. When it comes to expenses, however, the hassles increase. In any given year, members of your household perpetrate hundreds of transactions. Fortunately, new services help you track it all without turning yourself into a full–time accountant.

MINT.COM

Since 1997, I've entered each expenditure onto a spreadsheet that shows my monthly expenses down to the penny. In 2011, this required over 600 manual entries, and stole about 30 hours that I might have spent on my Nordic Track machine (purchased in 1993; still works great). Although these spreadsheets show that I live well below my means—which gives me great peace of mind—they also require a massive amount of time, effort, and obsessing.

As I've typed away like it's 1999, a revolution has raged at automated budgeting sites such as Mint.com. (Competitors exist, but I focus on Mint because it's garnered the most traffic.) Mint allows users to download their online accounts—credit cards, checking, debit cards—onto a single interface that tracks expenditures and generates detailed reports. I've worked with Mint for more than a year and I'm a convert. The site saves me hours of grunt work and, best of all, it's FREE. I even spend more time on my Nordic Track.

MINT SECURITY

Like most other budgeting sites, Mint asks you to provide the user names and passwords for all the accounts you use to pay expenses. This is highly sensitive information that hackers potentially might use to steal your money. Before you decide whether to use Mint, it's prudent to assess your risk of loss.

Mint utilizes multiple systems to protect your funds. It bars money transfers, so if hackers steal your Mint password, they can look at your account holdings, but they can't make withdrawals. Mint notifies you of any unusual transactions, which lets you take quick action in the event of nefarious activity. Mint encrypts all your data so that it's unreadable without the use of multiple decoding keys, which Mint divides among several "key" executives. So far, these many security measures have worked. Since it began in 2007, Mint has never reported a breach. If you still remain skittish, you can protect yourself in several ways.

☐ *Use a Complicated Password.* The more complex your password, the less likely hackers will ever access your Mint account. Use random numbers, lowercase letters in combination with uppercase letters, and the same symbols that cartoon characters curse with: "!#*&$."

☐ *Don't Link Accounts With Major Assets.* Don't tell Mint about your savings or brokerage accounts. The advantage to you: hackers can never view these holdings if you never list them in the first place. And if you ever draw down on these accounts, you always can record the transactions in Mint with manual entries.

☐ *Buy Software Instead.* If Mint ever gets infiltrated, any user's ultimate backstop against loss will be the federal law that limits personal liability on credit card fraud to $50 per card (see Chapter 49). The problem, however, is that this law has never been tested in courts as applied to budgeting websites. Card issuers will argue that customers lose federal protections when they disclose to budgeting websites their user names and access codes. If the matter ever comes to a head, who will prevail: consumers or the big credit card companies? There's no way to tell in advance. If you're queasy about this legal uncertainty, consider software that retrieves your expense data from the internet and maintains it on your computer's hard drive. The leading product, Quicken, costs about $40 and is offered by the same company that owns Mint. Of course, you're still exposed to loss if anyone steals your account passwords or hacks your computer.

☐ *Try Another Budgeting Site.* At BudgetPulse.com, you don't supply any user names or passwords for your accounts. This provides terrific security, but in return you have to make a truckload of manual entries.

MINT SHORTCUTS

More than ten million users have opted for Mint despite the possible security risks. If you make the same decision, these hints will make tracking your expenses a breeze (and a Minty fresh one at that).

☐ *Push More Spending to Credit Cards.* The more you pay with plastic, the fewer manual entries you need to make. Follow the tactics in Chapter 49 to increase your percentage of plastic transactions. (Reminder: don't ever use cards unless you pay them off in full every month.)

☐ *Teach Mint How to Allocate Expenses.* Let's say that whenever you visit a 7–11 store, you only buy gas. You know this, but Mint doesn't. With a one–time manual entry, you can instruct Mint to categorize all future 7–11 charges as gasoline purchases (highlight any 7–11 entry, click "Edit Details," click "Manage your rules," and follow the onscreen instructions from there).

☐ *Purify Your Spending.* Mint automatically allocates all supermarket receipts to groceries, but if you also buy cleansers and paper towels there, it overstates your food spending. If you limit your supermarket purchases to food only and buy non–food items elsewhere, you improve Mint's accuracy. Other places to purify: at gas stations buy gasoline (no snacks or drinks), at drug stores buy OTC remedies and cosmetics (no food or clothing), and at office supply stores, limit yourself to office staples (no DVDs or foodstuffs).

☐ *Allocate Single Transactions Among Several Line Items.* At some stores, any given receipt can implicate several different expense categories. A stroll down Target's aisles can fill your cart with OTC drugs, house wares, food items, bed linens, books, and more. If you're willing to make manual entries, Mint lets you click on any given transaction and distribute it among several line items (highlight the transaction, click "Edit Details," click "SPLIT," and divvy up as necessary).

☐ *Create Catchall Categories.* Another solution for transactions that inescapably involve multiple line items: assign them to a catchall category. To capture your visits to Target and Walmart, for example, you can create a new "Discount Stores" category. If at any point this line item gets too large—say over two percent of total spending—you can examine individual receipts and allocate them to more specific line items (see above).

☐ *Enter Reimbursements Manually.* Several times a year, you receive money back that Mint can't possibly know about: you charge your credit card $89 for a group dinner and receive $65 cash from others, you pay $199 for contact lenses and a $20 rebate arrives six weeks later, or your insurer refunds you $175 for overpaid premiums. Do nothing, and Mint overstates your spending. If you enter the reimbursements manually, however, Mint's accuracy improves (on the top right hand corner of the Transactions Screen, click "+ Add a Transaction" and follow the on-screen instructions from there).

☐ *Account for Cash Spending.* Mint picks up all of your ATM withdrawals, but it can't report where you spent the cash. One solution is to create another catchall category by telling Mint to treat any ATM withdrawals as "miscellaneous expenses." If this catchall grows too large—again, more than two percent of your overall spending—you can review your receipts and reallocate them to more specific expense categories (click the "+ Add a Transaction" button).

CONCLUSION

SL☑N! has covered household spending in pointillistic detail (with checkboxes instead of brushstrokes). But it hasn't lingered much on the big picture. Here, then, is one last checklist. Short enough to post at your desk, it gives a final overview of the frugal landscape. May you find it useful as you practice the habit of living well below your means by spending less.

A FRUGAL FRINGER'S LIFELONG CHECKLIST

☐ *Live in a Smaller Home.* And your costs of living will be smaller as well.

☐ *Buy Used.* Most secondhand items perform every bit as well as their shiny new counterparts. The only real difference is the price you pay.

☐ *Avoid Debt.* Never borrow except to buy houses, educations, and only if you must, cars.

☐ *Learn to Cook.* And save what others blow at restaurants.

☐ *Recreate Affordably.* Play an instrument, read, hike. Favor activities that involve less travel and equipment.

☐ *Practice Group Buynamics.* Socialize as you save. Join food co–ops, share tools, combine forces with others to buy in volume.

☐ *If You Can Get Away With it, Marry Once.* This means no alimony, less acrimony (hopefully), and fewer resources devoted to separate residences. Nothing kills nest eggs like breaking up nests.

☐ *Defend Your Health.* Your stress level improves if you don't work 70 hours a week for a lifestyle the mainstream culture claims you need and deserve. Exercise, sleep well, and eat right. This costs next to nothing and sidesteps many medical bills.

☐ *Practice Generosity.* Easy to do when your expenses are so low. Feels good too.

☐ *Know This: More Stuff ≠More Happiness.* No way, no how, and no matter what many around you seem to think.

☐ *Keep Using the Checklists.* MOOOOOO!!!

APPENDIXES

APPENDIX 1:
PRODUCTS BUYING CHECKLIST

STRATEGY NO. 1:
DON'T BUY ANYTHING

- ☐ **avoid the purchase** [address my need without buying]
- ☐ **wait until later** [season's end, next sale, new models]
- ☐ **use what I already own** [repair, fix, upgrade, closet shop]
- ☐ **make it myself** [filtered water, cleaners, work lunches]
- ☐ **get it FREE** [Freecycle, C–Span, ManyBooks.net]
- ☐ **borrow** [library, friends, neighbors]
- ☐ **trade or barter** [media, toys, duds]
- ☐ **rent** [tools, sports gear, tuxedos]
- ☐ **flip** [buy, use awhile, sell at profit]
- ☐ **try Group Buynamics** [buy with friends]

STRATEGY NO. 2:
BUY SOMETHING ELSE

- ☐ **buy used** [eBay, Goodwill, yard sales]
- ☐ **buy the flawed** [seconds, dents, demos, returns]
- ☐ **buy other technologies** [shovels for snow blowers]
- ☐ **buy other models** [fewer features, gen3 not gen4]
- ☐ **buy a part instead of a whole** [upgrades, disk drives]
- ☐ **buy generic** [bleach, batteries, frozen veggies]
- ☐ **buy multipurpose merchandise** [heater/fans, 2–way vacs]
- ☐ **stack tactics to save more** [combine two or more of the above]

STRATEGY NO. 3:
RESEARCH THE PRODUCT

- ☐ **read buying guides and product reviews—**
  - ☐ for big ticket items, read buying guides [search web]
  - ☐ ConsumerSearch.com, *Consumer Reports*
  - ☐ Amazon reviews and bestseller lists
  - ☐ CNET, for electronics
  - ☐ YouTube [video demos]
  - ☐ web reviews [search for name, model no., "reviews"]
  - ☐ sources unique to this product [magazines, clubs, blogs]
- ☐ **ask around** [friends' opinions, chat rooms]
- ☐ **try before I buy** [loaners, rentals, demos, samples]
- ☐ **consider hidden ownership costs—**
  - ☐ install/set–up
  - ☐ disposal [old TVs, tires]
  - ☐ storage
  - ☐ service and upkeep
  - ☐ accessories [cases, rechargers]
  - ☐ frequently replaced components [filters, toner]
  - ☐ energy use
  - ☐ insurance
  - ☐ fees, subscriptions, licenses
  - ☐ tax impacts [ownership taxes, deductions, credits]
- ☐ **consider repeating Strategy Nos. 1–2**

STRATEGY NO. 4: FIND LOW PRICES

- ☐ **shop around—**
  - ☐ search price comparison sites
  - ☐ visit web stores not listed on comparison sites
  - ☐ search for low prices offline [call stores, read ads]
- ☐ **delay buying until sales arrive** [search web: "best time to buy xx"]
- ☐ **look for "special offers" on prices–**
  - ☐ coupons and codes
  - ☐ group discounts [consult lists of discounting sellers for each of my groups]
  - ☐ rebates
  - ☐ volume discounts
  - ☐ discounts for preferred form of payment
  - ☐ deal–a–day websites [Groupon, LivingSocial]
- ☐ **seek out "deal sweeteners"** [terms other than price]–
  - ☐ freebies [delivery, accessories]
  - ☐ store loyalty programs [rewards, gift cards]
  - ☐ credit card benefits [rewards, extended warranties, price protection]
  - ☐ zero percent financing
- ☐ **look for "stacking"** [sales+special offers+deal sweeteners]
- ☐ **weigh transaction costs** [sales taxes, shipping, my own time]

STRATEGY NO. 5: PICK A LOW PRICE SELLER

- ☐ **run background checks** [past dealings, friends' experience, customer feedback, time in business]
- ☐ **review the seller's policies—**
  - ☐ extended warranties
  - ☐ price matching before *and* after the sale
  - ☐ rain checks and back orders
  - ☐ surcharges for credit card purchases
  - ☐ returns/exchanges
- ☐ **research product support** [repair sites, parts availability, updates]
- ☐ **research customer service** [JP Power, *Consumer Reports*, theacsi.org]
- ☐ **once I pick a seller, look for discounted gift cards** [*e.g.*, PlasticJungle.com]
- ☐ **once I pick a seller, consider haggling** [on prices, deal sweeteners, shipping costs]

STRATEGY NO. 6:
AVOID PITFALLS

☐ **refuse to pay interest on products** [revisit strategy nos. 1-2]

☐ **buy the right size** [measure twice, buy once]

☐ **avoid stuff that owns me** [spas, RVs, ATVs]

☐ **sweep away dust gatherers** [pasta makers]

☐ **never pay extra for prestige**

☐ **beware of buying too cheap** [seek values, not lowest prices]

☐ **decline to be an "early adopter"** [newest iWhatevers]

☐ **reject fads** [pet rocks, eight-tracks]

☐ **read contracts before signing them**

☐ **say no to middlemen who add no value**

☐ **plan ahead for big ticket items**

☐ **beware of deals "too good to be true"**

☐ **sidestep the "bait and switch"**

☐ **forgo bells and whistles**

STRATEGY NO. 7:
FOLLOW UP

☐ **confirm terms of sale** [check receipt, shipping manifest]

☐ **inspect for imperfections** [dings, defects, malfunctions]

☐ **register with manufacturer** [for recalls, upgrades, news]

☐ **retain receipts, packaging, manuals** [returns, resale, taxes]

☐ **monitor price drops** [seller or credit card might match]

☐ **visit chat rooms** [vehicles, appliances, software]

☐ **buy duplicates** [if item discontinued]

☐ **make the item last** [know rules for operation, upkeep]

☐ **keep a "checklist savings log"** [see Chapter 47]

APPENDIX 2:
MISCELLANEOUS SERVICES CHECKLIST

STRATEGY NO. 1: AVOID THE SERVICE COMPLETELY

☐ **skip discretionary services** [personal trainers, masseuses, caterers, auto detailers]

☐ **delay and hire later** [patch it, live without service for now, seek second opinions, shop around for lowest rates]

☐ **replace high–cost services with low–cost products** [hair clippers for barbers, mousetraps for exterminators, software for tax preparers, slipcovers for upholsterers]

☐ **rid myself of products with high service costs** [rent, borrow, or flip instead]

☐ **perform lower skilled services myself** [house cleaning, mowing, painting, pressure washing, leaf removal]

☐ **study higher skilled services and do them myself** [using books, web videos, or software, learn how to rewire light switches, repair leaking toilets, tune bicycles, plan weddings]

STRATEGY NO. 2: AVOID THE SERVICE IN PART

☐ **hire, but do some of the work myself** [grunt work, demo, site preparation, mop–up]

☐ **hire, but procure materials myself** [lumber, paint, parts, supplies]

☐ **hire advisors only, and do the actual work myself** [tax preparation, landscaping design, redecorating, small lawsuits]

☐ **hire less often** [barbers, masseuses, chiropractors, air duct cleaners]

☐ **hire basic services only** [haircuts but no shampoos, car washes but no detailing, lawn mowing but no edging, upholstery cleaning but no protective coatings]

☐ **practice preventative maintenance** [follow owner's manual, web–based advice]

STRATEGY NO. 3:
RUN BACKGROUND CHECKS

☐ **look for customer feedback—**

    ☐ my own past experience

    ☐ recommendations

    ☐ internet reviews [Angie's List]

    ☐ BBB.org

    ☐ service's own references

☐ **hold tryouts** [especially for less costly services]

☐ **review samples of service's work** [portfolios]

☐ **review qualifications—**

    ☐ time in business

    ☐ trade memberships, certifications, licenses

    ☐ specialization level [match job to it]

    ☐ experience level [match job to it]

☐ **learn the service's policies—**

    ☐ contract terms? [warranties, guarantees]

    ☐ who performs the actual work? [owner or helpers]

    ☐ any unusual fees?

☐ **weigh my own time costs** [don't overdo research for inexpensive services]

STRATEGY NO. 4:
FIND LOW RATES

☐ **shop around—**

    ☐ compare rates on my short list of prospective services

    ☐ ask friends what they pay

    ☐ seek special offers [intro rates, coupons, discounts]

    ☐ seek deal sweeteners [freebies, fee waivers]

    ☐ avoid high overhead operations [new truck fleets, fancy offices, etc.]

☐ **haggle—**

    ☐ *"Can you match your competitor's rates?"*

    ☐ *"If I hired you more often, would you charge less?"*

    ☐ *"I know you pay overhead, but can you get closer to the online rate?"*

☐ **if warranted, seek written bids** [only for most expensive services]

☐ **consider online services** [life coaches, computer help, tutors]

☐ **consider trainees, students, or responsible teens** [schools, vo–techs]

☐ **share services with others** [babysitters, golf lessons, personal trainers]

☐ **anticipate emergency hires** [furnace, plumbing, electrical]

☐ **trade or barter services** [beware tax consequences]

☐ **insure** [weigh costs vs. risks]

STRATEGY NO. 5:
AVOID PITFALLS

☐ require a physical address

☐ never hire anyone who contacts me first
[door to door solicitations]

☐ avoid quick hiring decisions
[plan ahead, follow checklist]

☐ hire the right level of specialization
[if too much, I overpay; if too little, the quality suffers]

☐ hire the right level of experience
[see above]

☐ avoid unnecessary hires

☐ never pay for work that isn't performed

☐ decline oversells and upsells

☐ read contracts before signing them

☐ never use debt to fund discretionary services

☐ research all recommendations
[kickbacks are common]

☐ beware of deals "too good to be true"

STRATEGY NO. 6:
FOLLOW UP

☐ inspect work

☐ oversee touchups

☐ check for math errors

☐ monitor sales taxes

☐ agree to form of payment [cash discounts?]

☐ don't pay until I'm satisfied

☐ build a long–term relationship

☐ make the work last
[seek service's advice, use common sense]

☐ retain paperwork

☐ consider possible tax impacts
[deductions, tax credits]

☐ keep a "checklist savings log"
[see Chapter 47]

APPENDIX 3:
RESTAURANTS CHECKLIST

STRATEGY NO. 1: CUT VISITS [GIVEN REASONS FOR DINING OUT]	STRATEGY NO. 2: CUT VISITS [GIVEN ALTERNATIVES]	STRATEGY NO. 3: SPEND LESS AT RESTAURANTS

STRATEGY NO. 1:
CUT VISITS
[GIVEN REASONS
FOR DINING OUT]

☐ socializing [try dinner parties, pot lucks, pizza delivery, take out, happy hours, coffee shops, brownbag]

☐ convenience [try bulk cooking, grilling, slow cooker, brown–bagging, grocery, deli]

☐ hunger [try stashing food caches in desk at work or in car]

☐ specialized cuisines [cook it yourself, try pre–packaged versions]

☐ atmosphere [visit bar instead]

☐ pampering [trade off meals, cook in bulk]

☐ habit [try internet recipe nights]

☐ novelty [eat in different rooms, in backyard]

STRATEGY NO. 2:
CUT VISITS
[GIVEN
ALTERNATIVES]

☐ deliveries

☐ take out [try grocer's delis, rotisserie chicken]

☐ food caches [stock desk drawers, cars, purses]

☐ bulk cooking [cook big on weekends for next week's meals]

☐ grilling

☐ slow cooker meals [load up in a.m., ready when you return home]

☐ coffee shops [socialize here, not at bars and eateries]

☐ picnics [make lunch dates for parks]

☐ happy hours [Happy–Hour.com]

☐ bar hopping

☐ dinner parties

☐ pot lucks

☐ progressive dinners

☐ brownbag lunches

☐ home cooking

STRATEGY NO. 3:
SPEND LESS AT
RESTAURANTS

☐ match venues to occasions [cut upscale dining]

☐ choose value alternatives

☐ get free kids meals [MyKidsEatFree.com]

☐ visit diners without waiters

☐ eat off–peak

☐ seek diner discounts

☐ buy discounted gift certificates [Costco, Restaurant.com]

☐ visit daily–deal sites

☐ use entertainment books

☐ use group discounts

☐ skip items [drinks, salads, sides, desserts]

☐ eat bread to save bread

☐ share items

☐ eat appetizers only

☐ eat at the bar

☐ use doggie bags

☐ know my plastic rewards

☐ limit sales taxes

☐ tip fair [15–20%]

APPENDIX 4:
APPLIANCES CHECKLIST

CLOTHES WASHER

□ **disfavor whites**
[white textiles use hot water]

□ **wear clothes more than once** [cuts laundry loads; ups garment lives]

□ **wash full loads only**
[fewer loads = lower bills]

□ **wash in cold water**
[use hot water for whites or heavily soiled; still use cold for rinses]

□ **use shorter wash cycles**
[lightly soiled fabrics need only 6 minutes; pre–treat or presoak dirty items]

□ **cut back on extra rinses**

□ **wash off peak**
[if utility charges less at certain times]

□ **follow owner's manual**

List additional savings ideas here:

CLOTHES DRYER

□ **favor fast–drying clothes**
[lightweight fabrics dry fast]

□ **use clothes lines**
[put outside or in shower]

□ **use drying racks**

□ **use plastic hangers**
[for extra drying capacity]

□ **use dryer's moisture sensor**
[reduces wasteful over–drying]

□ **dry off peak**
[if it costs less at certain times]

□ **tumble press**
[if clothes stiffen when air dried, run them in dryer 5 minutes]

□ **dry several loads in a row**
[dryer won't have to reheat]

□ **clean lint traps and vents**
[increases dryer efficiency]

□ **follow owner's manual**

List additional savings ideas here:

DISHWASHER

☐ **avoid hand washing dishes**
[most studies conclude machines do the job for less]

☐ **avoid pre–rinsing**
[try soaking dishes in cold water instead]

☐ **run full loads only**
[fewer loads = lower bills]

☐ **wash off–peak**
[if it costs less at certain times]

☐ **use energy saving modes**
[all newer models have them]

☐ **air dry**
[heating elements consume energy; air doesn't]

☐ **check filters and drains**
[assures peak efficiency]

☐ **follow owner's manual**

List additional savings ideas here:

REFRIGERATOR FREEZER

☐ **use energy saving modes**

☐ **set fridge to 37°–40°F**
[test temps with thermometer in glass of water]

☐ **set freezers to 5°F**
[test temps with thermometer]

☐ **turn off the ice maker**
[if there's enough ice]

☐ **stock them full**
[they consume less energy]

☐ **keep doors closed**
[remove items promptly]

☐ **keep hot foods out**
[let leftovers cool to room temp]

☐ **keep foods covered**
[uncovered foods release moisture, humid air costs more to cool]

☐ **vacuum coils regularly**
[dust bunnies suck energy]

☐ **maintain gaskets**
[leaking seals cut efficiency]

☐ **follow owner's manual**

List additional savings ideas here:

STOVETOP	OVEN
☐ **boil water elsewhere** [electric kettles, microwaves use less energy, boil there then transfer to stovetop]	☐ **use alternatives** [slow cookers, toaster ovens, microwaves, pressure cookers use less energy]
☐ **run the microwave** [uses less energy than stovetop]	☐ **preheat sparingly** [prepare first, then preheat]
☐ **use hot plates for small jobs** [ditto]	☐ **bake double batches** [cheaper than running oven twice]
☐ **use smaller cookware** [big pots take more energy]	☐ **keep the door closed** [meat thermometer near oven window shows temperature without letting heat escape]
☐ **cook with flat bottoms only** [warped bases cost more to heat]	☐ **leave the door open** [in winter, leave oven door open after cooking to help heat kitchen]
☐ **use the right sized burner** [oversized burners waste energy]	**List additional savings ideas here:**
☐ **use vent fans sparingly** [crack windows open]	
☐ **turn burners off early** [use residual heat to finish cooking]	
List additional savings ideas here:	

APPENDIX 5:
GARBAGE CAN CHECKLIST

**DON'T TOSS ME UNTIL YOU
ANSWER THESE QUESTIONS:**

CAN YOU OR CAN YOU NOT—

☐ **eat me?**
[test "best by" and expiration dates at
ShelfLifeAdvice.com]

☐ **freeze me?**
[for freeze-ability advice about any food item, visit
StillTasty.com]

☐ **compost me?**
[for neighbor's garden or your own]

☐ **recycle me?**
[paper, solid plastics, plastic bags, glass, metals,
electronics]

☐ **donate me?**
[food banks, Goodwill]

☐ **repair me?**
[fix and give away]

☐ **reuse me?**
[paper towels, plastic bags, peanut butter jars]

☐ **stop buying me?**
[avoid wasted foods, excessive packaging, disposable
products]

☐ **buy a smaller version of me?**
[so there's less of me to toss]

☐ **squash me?**
[less bulk means lower PAYT costs]

List additional savings ideas here:

APPENDIX 6:
SAVE AT THE PUMP CHECKLIST

SAVE AT THE PUMP

☐ **refuel early**
[before light goes on to reduce fuel system wear]

☐ **shop around**
[GasBuddy.com, etc.]

☐ **use credit card with highest rewards for gas**

☐ **or visit stations with best cash discounts**

☐ **use loyalty discounts**
[grocery stores, etc.]

☐ **stack gas deals**
[loyalty + card reward or cash discount]

☐ **buy the right octane**
[follow owner's manual]

☐ **don't overfill**
[spilt gas costs $$$]

☐ **print a receipt**
[to calculate MPG]

☐ **skip drinks and snacks**
[bad value, complicates accounting]

☐ **monitor MPGs**
[drops suggest low oil, low tire pressure]

☐ **drive sensibly**
[follow tips in 39.6]

List additional savings ideas here:

ACKNOWLEDGEMENTS

I'm indebted to several authors who long ago convinced me of frugality's power: Thomas J. Stanley and William D. Danko, *The Millionaire Next Door*; Andrew Tobias, *The Only Investment Guide You'll Ever Need*; and Joe Dominguez and Vicki Robin, *Your Money or Your Life*. If you're still straddling the rail about frugality, don't give up the ship (or rowboat). Add these books to your reading list.

SL⊠N! benefited greatly from a close and sympathetic review by Ally E. Machate, a smart and talented editor. If you're working on your own book, I recommend her services highly.

Several generous friends critiqued early drafts of *SL⊠N!*: Brian E., Jennifer F., Henry G., Dick H., Sam H., Ed K., Todd L., Kent L., Cathy M., Ellis P., and Paul P. I'm deeply grateful for their advice and encouragement (and I hope I also saved them some cash).

Last of all, I thank Cathy M., my partner in marriage and life and also the sage rejecter of many bad puns that didn't make the final text (you'll probably see them later at FrugalFringe.com).

NOTES

Unless otherwise indicated, the italicized text appears in the opening paragraphs of the referenced chapter.

PREFACE

68 percent of those surveyed: Jim Forsyth, "More than Two-Thirds in U.S. Paycheck to Paycheck—Survey," Reuters, September 19, 2012, http://www.reuters.com/article/2012/09/19/usa-survey-paycheck-idUSL1E8KJAZV20120919.

55.1 percent of card holders: Jesse Bricker, Arthur B. Kennickell, Kevin B. Moore, and John Sabelhaus, "Changes in U.S. Family Finances from 2007 to 2010," *Federal Reserve Bulletin* 98 (June, 2012): 67, http://www.federalreserve.gov/Pubs/Bulletin/2012/articles/scf/scf.htm.

46.6 square feet of retail space: "Frequently Asked Questions," International Council of Shopping Centers, accessed November 4, 2012, http://www.icsc.org/srch/faq_category.php?cat_type=research&cat_id=3.

INTRODUCTION

HOW MUCH WILL *SL⊠N!* SAVE YOU?

about 20 percent each year: Joe Dominguez and Vicki Robin, *Your Money or Your Life* (New York: Penguin, 1992), 154.

$50,000 annually . . . the national average: "Consumer Expenditure Survey, 2006-2011," US Bureau of Labor Statistics, accessed November 1, 2012, http://www.bls.gov/cex/2011/standard/multiyr.pdf.

Social Security Withholding . . . 6.2%: "Compliance Update," American Payroll Association, accessed November 2, 2012, http://info.americanpayroll.org/pdfs/fpi/12k15-ComplianceUpdateAPA.pdf.

Medicare Withholding . . . 1.45%: Ibid.

Federal Tax Withholding . . . 25%: "2011 Tax Table," Internal Revenue Service, accessed November 2, 2012, http://www.irs.gov/pub/irs-pdf/i1040tt.pdf.

State Tax Withholding . . . 5.04% average rate: "TAXSIM Calculated Net State Rate after Federal Deduction," National Bureau of Economic Research, accessed February 8, 2012, http://www.nber.org/~taxsim/state-marginal/state-fix.html (2010 average).

about $44,600: "Consumer Expenditure Survey, 2006-2011," US Bureau of Labor Statistics, accessed November 1, 2012, http://www.bls.gov/cex/2011/standard/ multiyr.pdf (reports average annual expenditures of $49,705, and subtracting average Social Security and pension expenses of $5,106, yields $44,599).

AND NOW, THE *REALLY* NOT SO HUMBLE CHECKLIST

habits involve three basic steps: Charles Duhigg, *The Power of Habit* (New York: Random House, 2012), 19.

1

Avoid the Purchase Altogether

A Kindle holds 3,500: "Kindle DX, Free 3G, 9.7" E Ink Display, 3G Works Globally," Amazon, accessed November 1, 2012, http://www.amazon. com/Kindle-DX-Wireless-Reader-3G-Global/dp/B002GYWHSQ.

you save $1,200: "Billy," IKEA, accessed November 1, 2012, http://www.ikea.com/ us/en/catalog/products/83688210/#/83688210.

Wait Until Later

delay . . . about four months: Lauren A.E. Schuker and Ethan Smith, "Hollywood Eyes Shortcut to TV," *Wall Street Journal*, May 22, 2010, http://online.wsj.com/ article/SB10001424052748704167704575258761968531140.html.

2

Buy Other Technologies

You could spend $300: "Bose® QuietComfort® 15 Acoustic Noise Cancelling® Headphones," Amazon, accessed November 1, 2012, http://www.amazon.com/ Bose%C2%AE-QuietComfort%C2%AE-Acoustic-Cancelling%C2%AE-Headphones/.

Buy Generic

account for 22.3 percent: Todd Hale, "U.S. Store Brands have Room to Grow," Nielsen News, July 20, 2011, http://blog.nielsen.com/ nielsenwire/consumer/u-s-store-brands-have-room-to-grow/.

3

more than 23,000 results: Author's search for "coffee makers" at Amazon.com on November 1, 2012.

Read Buying Guides and Product Reviews

Time *magazine named Consumer Search*: Adam Fisher, "50 Best Websites of 2009— ConsumerSearch," *Time*, August 24, 2009, http://www.time.com/time/specials/ packages/article/0,28804,1918031_1918016_1917951,00.html.

5

Review the Seller's Policies

Retailers in 40 states: Joyce Rosenberg, "Small retailers say no to passing along credit card fees to patrons," *Denver Post*, February 1, 2013, http://www. denverpost.com/business/ci_22494382/.

8

most spending on services goes for auto repairs and home remodels: "Consumer Expenditure Survey, 2006-2011," US Bureau of Labor Statistics, accessed November 1, 2012, http://www.bls.gov/cex/2011/standard/multiyr.pdf.

9

average household spends $2,572: Ibid.

10

10.1 *costs about $500 per year*: Kelli B. Grant, "Six Ways to Cut the Cost of a Gym Membership," *Wall Street Journal*, January 6, 2010, http://online.wsj.com/article/ SB10001424052748703436504574640651941267992.html.

11

11.4.4 *skip this coverage*: Consumer Reports, "Spend Less on Everything," Yahoo Finance, accessed December 15, 2011, http://finance.yahoo.com/news/ spend-less-on-everything.html.

12

$115 per year: "Consumer Expenditure Survey, 2006-2011," US Bureau of Labor Statistics, accessed November 1, 2012, http://www.bls.gov/cex/2011/standard/ multiyr.pdf.

12.1.3 *Books published before 1923 reside in the public domain*: "Copyright Term and the Public Domain in the United States," Cornell University, accessed November 1, 2012, http://copyright.cornell.edu/resources/publicdomain.cfm.

12.3.2 *More than 8,000 magazines host websites*: "Magazine Handbook— Engagement to Action, a Comprehensive Guide and Factbook 2010/11," Magazine.org, downloaded on or about November 1, 2011, www.magazine.org.

13

household paid $2,620: "Consumer Expenditure Survey, 2006-2011," US Bureau of Labor Statistics, accessed November 1, 2012, http://www.bls.gov/cex/2011/ standard/multiyr.pdf.

14

14.3.6 *yielded 174 results*: Author's search for "alcohol breath analyzers" at Amazon.com on November 1, 2012.

15

15.1.4 *currently average $19*: Josh Sanburn, "Reinventing the Wheels: A Fresh Look Coaxes Riders Back on the Bus," *Time*, November 15, 2012, http://business.time.com/2012/11/15/reinventing-the-wheels-megabus-and-boltbus/.

15.3.2 *lowest point on Tuesday afternoons*: Scott McCartney, "Whatever You Do, Don't Buy an Airline Ticket On . . .," *Wall Street Journal*, January 27, 2011, http://online.wsj.com/article/SB10001424052748704062604576105953506930800.html.

15.3.4 *great tip from FareCompare.com*: Rick Seaney, "Airline Tickets—Shop One Passenger First and Save on Trips of Two or More, Fare Compare, last modified November 21, 2010, http://www.farecompare.com/news/airline-tickets-shop-one-passenger-first/.

16

16.1.8 *2,600 locations nationwide, but only 130 of them still sport living quarters*: George W. Rhodes, "At Home at the YMCA," *The Sun Chronicle*, March 9, 2011, http://www.thesunchronicle.com/articles/2010/07/11/news/7663311.prt.

19

19.1 *$1,721 in 2011*: "Consumer Expenditure Survey, 2006-2011," US Bureau of Labor Statistics, accessed November 1, 2012, http://www.bls.gov/cex/2011/standard/multiyr.pdf.

19.1.9 *no more than 25 percent*: "Top 10 Best Practices of Savvy Donors," Charity Navigator, accessed November 2, 2012, http://www.charitynavigator.org/index.cfm?bay=content.view&cpid=419.

20

29.2 percent of the nation's gross income: William McBride, "Special Report Tax Freedom Day 2012," April 2012, http://taxfoundation.org/article/special-report-no-198-tax-freedom-day-2012.

20.1 *6.85 percent or higher*: "State Sales Tax Rates along with Average COMBINED City and County Rates," The Sales Tax Clearinghouse, accessed November 2, 2012, http://thestc.com/strates.stm.

CODA: BYPASS SALES TAXES ALTOGETHER

must pay something called a "use tax": Laura Saunders, "The Sales Tax that Comes Back to Bite," *Wall Street Journal*, March 27, 2010, http://online.wsj.com/article/SB10001424052748704211704575139833572294198.html.

22

typical home energy uses: "Your Home's Energy Use," US DOE, accessed January 17, 2011, http://www.energysavers.gov/tips/home_energy.cfm.

22.1.1 *save about 5-15 percent*: "Thermostats and Control Systems," US DOE, June 24, 2012, http://energy.gov/energysaver/articles/thermostats-and-control-systems.

22.5.6 *consumes 446 kilowatt hours*: Elisabeth Rosenthal, "Cable Boxes Guzzle Energy," *New York Times*, June 25, 2011, http://www.nytimes.com/2011/06/26/us/26cable.html.

22.6.20 *about $40 per year*: "Dishwasher vs. Handwashing Dishes," Energy Star, accessed November 2, 2012, http://www.energystar.gov/index.cfm?c=dishwash.pr_handwash_dishwash.

25

$86 per month: "Pay-TV bills continue to increase by 6 percent, year-over-year, as consumer-spending power remains flat," NPD Group, April 10, 2012, https://npd.com/wps/portal/npd/us/news/pressreleases/pr_120410.

26

now costs about $500 per year: Centris Marketing, "Science Research Note," January 17, 2012, accessed via Google November 2, 2012, www.centris.com/docs/.../Monthly%20spending%201.12.pdf.

26.1 *14 percent . . . used cell phones only . . . wireless-only households had jumped to 34 percent*: Stephen J. Blumberg and Julian V. Luke, "Wireless Substitution: Early Release of Estimates from the National Health Interview Survey, July-December 2011," Centers for Disease Control and Prevention, June, 2012, http://www.cdc.gov/nchs/data/nhis/earlyrelease/wireless201206.pdf.

26.2 *deliver the fastest internet*: "ISP Reliability and Costs," ConsumerSearch, last modified October, 2011, http://www.consumersearch.com/isp/review.

27

321 million cell phone subscriptions: CITA The Wireless Association, "Wireless Quick Facts," accessed November 2, 2012, http://www.ctia.org/consumer_info/index.cfm/AID/10323.

average cell phone user pays $78: "J.D. Power and Associates Reports: Average Length of Time Wireless Customers Keep their Mobile Phones Increases Notably," JD Power, September 23, 2010, http://businesscenter.jdpower.com/news/pressrelease.aspx?ID=2010185.

cost jumps to $1,500: "2012 U.S. Wireless Network Quality Performance Study Volume 2 Results," JD Power, August 27, 2012, http://www.jdpower.com/content/study/Vf9wjMm/2012-u-s-wireless-network-quality-performance-study-volume-2-results.htm.

28

average household pays $552: Centris Marketing, "Science Research Note," January 17, 2012, accessed via Google November 2, 2012, www.centris.com/docs/.../Monthly%20spending%201.12.pdf.

29

premiums now average $917: "Home Insurance Rate Report," HomeInsurance.com, accessed February 20, 2012, http://homeinsurance.com/rates-in-your-state/.

30

policy costs about $1,200: "Auto Insurance Rate Report," HomeInsurance.com, accessed November 2, 2012, http://homeinsurance.com/auto-insurance/auto-rates-per-state/.

32

32.1 *50 percent of Americans . . . slumped to 44.6 percent*: Elizabeth Mendes, "Fewer Americans Have Employer-Based Health Insurance," Gallup, February 14, 2012, http://www.gallup.com/poll/152621/fewer-americans-employer-based-health-insurance.aspx.

33

almost half of all Americans: Quiping Gu, Charles F. Dillon, and Vicki L. Burt, "Prescription Drug Use Continues to Increase: U.S. Prescription Drug Data for 2007-2008," Centers for Disease Control and Prevention, September, 2010, http://www.cdc.gov/nchs/data/databriefs/db42.htm.

33.2.2 *97 percent of them violate professional standards*: "Buying Medicine Online: Internet Pharmacies and You," National Association of Boards of Pharmacy, accessed March 25, 2011, http:// www.nabp.net/programs/consumer-protection/buying-medicine-online/.

34

$179 on physicians and $129 on hospitals: Based on unpublished estimates from the integrated 2011 CES set forth in BLS e-mail message to the author, November 1, 2012.

34.4.1 *1,350 clinics nationwide*: Pamela Lewis Dolan, "CVS Retail Chain Clinics Expand while Walgreens Operation Stalls," American Medical Ass'n, January 23, 2012, http://www.ama-assn.org/amednews/2012/01/23/bis0123.htm.

35

one-half of all Americans wear corrective lenses: Prevent Blindness America and the National Eye Institute, "Vision Problems in the U.S.: Prevalence of Adult Vision Impairment and Age-Related Eye Disease in America," Prevent Blindness America, last modified April, 2011, http://www.preventblindness.net/site/DocServer/VPUS_2008_update.pdf.

35.2.4 *surveyed 30,000 readers*: "Costco Tops List of Eyeglass Retailers," Consumers Union, November 1, 2010, http://pressroom.consumerreports.org/pressroom/2010/11/costco-tops-list-of-eyeglass-retailers.html.

36

spent $286 on dentists: Based on unpublished estimates from the integrated 2011 CES contained in BLS e-mail message to the author, November 1, 2012.

36.2.2 *every $1 spent on prevention saves $4*: "Policy and Advocacy," National Center for Oral Health Access, accessed November 2, 2012, http://www.nnoha.org/advocacy.html.

36.6.2 *x-rays only once every 24-36 months*: American Dental Association and U.S. Department of Health and Human Services, "The Selection of Patients for Dental Radiographic Examinations," US Food and Drug Administration, 2004, http://www.fda.gov/Radiation-EmittingProducts/RadiationEmittingProductsandProcedures/MedicalImaging/MedicalX-Rays/ucm116504.htm.

37

about 100 grocery store visits: "Supermarket Facts: Industry Overview 2010," Food Marketing Institute, accessed November 2, 2012, http://www.fmi.org/research-resources/supermarket-facts.

household spends $3,838: "Consumer Expenditure Survey, 2006-2011," US Bureau of Labor Statistics, accessed November 1, 2012, http://www.bls.gov/cex/2011/standard/multiyr.pdf.

37.1 *44 percent of consumers use lists*: "And Reveal 19th Annual 'Shopping for Health' Survey Results," Food Marketing Institute, accessed November 2, 2012, http://fmi.org/news-room/news-archive/view/2011/07/21/.

37.6 *discard about 25 percent*: Dana Gunders, Wasted: How America Is Losing Up to 40 Percent of Its Food from Farm to Fork to Landfill, National Resources Defense Council, August, 2012, http://www.nrdc.org/food/files/wasted-food-IP.pdf.

37.6 *that works out to $960 in losses per year*: "Consumer Expenditure Survey, 2006-2011," US Bureau of Labor Statistics, accessed November 1, 2012, http://www.bls.gov/cex/2011/standard/multiyr.pdf.

37.7 *$832 a year*: Ibid.

38

a whopping 48 percent: "What that Car Really Costs to Own," *Consumer Reports*, last modified August, 2012, http://www.consumerreports.org/cro/2012/06/what-that-car-really-costs-to-own/index.htm#.

39

fuel costs . . . at $2,655: "Consumer Expenditure Survey, 2006-2011," US Bureau of Labor Statistics, accessed November 1, 2012, http://www.bls.gov/cex/2011/standard/multiyr.pdf.

39.3.4 *cuts mileage by 1-2 percent*: "Energy Savers Booklet: Tips on Saving Energy & Money at Home," US DOE, accessed November 2, 2012, http://www1.eere.energy.gov/consumer/tips/pdfs/energy_savers.pdf.

39.3.5 *4 percent on average*: "Keeping Your Car in Shape," US DOE, last modified November 2, 2012, http://www.fueleconomy.gov/feg/maintain.shtml.

39.3.6 *replacing the filter won't improve mileage*: Ibid.

39.5.2 *cuts gas mileage by as much as two percent*: "Energy Savers Booklet: Tips on Saving Energy & Money at Home," US DOE, accessed November 2, 2012, http://www1.eere.energy.gov/consumer/tips/pdfs/energy_savers.pdf.

39.6.1 *27 cents more per gallon*: "Driving More Efficiently," US DOE, last modified November 2, 2012, http://www.fueleconomy.gov/feg/driveHabits.shtml.

39.6.5 *whenever the wait exceeds 10 seconds*: Brendan Koerner, "Is an Idle Car the Devil's Workshop," *Slate*, May 27, 2008, http://www.slate.com/articles/health_and_science/the_green_lantern/2008/05/is_an_idle_car_the_devils_workshop.html.

40

40.6 *largest single cost of car maintenance . . . tires*: Based on unpublished estimates from the integrated 2011 CES contained in BLS e-mail message to the author, November 1, 2012.

42

loan interest represents 11 percent: "What that Car Really Costs to Own," *Consumer Reports*, last modified August, 2012, http://www.consumerreports.org/cro/2012/06/what-that-car-really-costs-to-own/index.htm#.

42.2.2 *costs about $9,000*: "Cost of Owning and Operating Vehicle in U.S. Increased 1.9 Percent According to AAA's 2012 'Your Driving Costs Study," American Automobile Association, April 27, 2012, http://newsroom.aaa.com/2012/04/cost-of-owning-and-operating-vehicle-in-u-s-increased-1-9-percent-according-to-aaa%E2%80%99s-2012-%E2%80%98your-driving-costs%E2%80%99-study/.

43

43.4.6 *car's MPG will drop*: Steve Raabe, "E85 is cheaper for Denver-area motorists, but you have to do the math on mileage," *Denver Post*, May 1, 2011, http://www.denverpost.com/business/ci_17963665.

44

15,000 miles per year in a mid-sized car costs $8,946: "Cost of Owning and Operating Vehicle in U.S. Increased 1.9 Percent According to AAA's 2012 'Your Driving Costs Study,'" American Automobile Association, April 27, 2012, http://newsroom.aaa.com/2012/04/cost-of-owning-and-operating-vehicle-in-u-s-increased-1-9-percent-according-to-aaa%E2%80%99s-2012-%E2%80%98your-driving-costs%E2%80%99-study/.

national average ($44,600): "Consumer Expenditure Survey, 2006-2011," US Bureau of Labor Statistics, accessed November 1, 2012, http://www.bls.gov/cex/2011/standard/multiyr.pdf (reports average annual expenditures of $49,705, and after subtracting average Social Security and pension expenses of $5,106, this amounts to $44,599).

45

housing expenses average $16,803: Ibid.

45.5.3 *ditching the PMI saves $480*: "Cancellation of Private Mortgage Insurance: Federal Law May Save You Hundreds of Dollars Each Year," US Federal Trade Commission, July, 2000, http://www.ftc.gov/bcp/edu/pubs/consumer/alerts/alt072.pdf.

45.8.5 *"home is the place where . . ."*: Robert Frost, The Poetry of Robert Frost (New York: Holt, Rinehart and Winston, 1969), 38.

47

MOTIVATE WITH METRICS

"nobody was ever meant . . . :" Ibid. at 309.

48

about 95 percent of the average household's expenses: Author's calculation based upon a comparison of 2011 CES figures and the checklists contained in this book.

49

68 percent of consumers held credit cards: Jesse Bricker, Arthur B. Kennickell, Kevin B. Moore, and John Sabelhaus, "Changes in U.S. Family Finances from 2007 to 2010," *Federal Reserve Bulletin* 98 (June, 2012): 67, http://www.federalreserve.gov/Pubs/Bulletin/2012/articles/scf/scf.htm.

roughly 45 percent of cardholders: Ibid.

Earn Rewards. *the IRS doesn't treat any of this as taxable income*: Connie Prater, "Reward Point Gifts are Taxable, Says the IRS," CreditCards.com, January 31, 2012, http://www.creditcards.com/credit-card-news/irs-taxable-income-credit-card-rewards-points-gift-1277.php.

Qualify for Legal Protection. *no liability for unauthorized use*: 15 U.S.C. § 1643.

CODA: SURCHARGES FOR USING CREDIT CARDS

retailers in 40 states: Joyce Rosenberg, "Small retailers say no to passing along credit card fees to patrons," *Denver Post*, February 1, 2013, http://www.denverpost.com/business/ci_22494382/.

Strategize which Cards Work Best. *holds 3.7 of them*: Kevin Foster, Erik Meijer, Scott Schuh, and Michael A. Zabek, "The Survey of Consumer Payment Choice," Federal Reserve Bank of Boston, last modified April, 2011, http://www.bos.frb.org/economic/ppdp/2011/ppdp1101.pdf.

Ask for Fee Waivers. *Card issuers spend $50-$150*: Dayana Yochim, "The Hidden Perks of Plastic," The Motley Fool, accessed February 2, 2012, http://www.fool.com/ccc/manage/manage02.htm.

50

MINT SECURITY

Mint has never reported a breach: Stacy Rapacon, "Best Online Money-Management Tools," *Kiplinger*, October, 2012, http://www.kiplinger.com/magazine/archives/best-online-money-management-tools.html.